D1228212

MAN STANDS ALONE

MAN STANDS ALONE

By

JULIAN HUXLEY

Essay Index Reprint Series

 BOOKS FOR LIBRARIES PRESS
FREEPORT, NEW YORK

Copyright © 1941 by Julian S. Huxley

All rights reserved

Reprinted 1970 by arrangement with
Harper & Row, Publishers, Inc.

QH 311
H92

INTERNATIONAL STANDARD BOOK NUMBER:
0-8369-1961-0

LIBRARY OF CONGRESS CATALOG CARD NUMBER:
72-128265

PRINTED IN THE UNITED STATES OF AMERICA

TO MY WIFE,

TO WHOM ALSO MY FIRST VOLUME OF ESSAYS
WAS INSCRIBED, THESE MATURER FRUITS OF
A SHARED LIFE ARE GRATEFULLY DEDICATED

161328

PREFACE

I WRITE these lines in the London Zoo's basement shelter, to the sound of A.A. guns outside, and inside the Holst Quartet playing Sibelius' beautiful *Voces Intimae* on the wireless. It is as good an epitome as any other of that uniqueness of man which I have taken as the title of this book.

It also prompts me to try to pull together some of the threads of thought that, in a book consisting of occasional articles, inevitably lie somewhat scattered. The fifteen essays here reprinted were written at various times between 1927 and 1939, and for very diverse audiences. But they all have this in common, that they were written during that strange restless indecisive period during which an age was dying but most of us were refusing to face the imminence of its dissolution. Yet anyone who troubled to think knew that a radical change was overdue; and the large majority of these articles are efforts towards some new formulation of our basic beliefs and attitudes, or at least attempts to state some of the bases on which the new formulation will have to build.

But now the war is tying up the threads. First came the eight quiet months, when thinking was unhurried, general, and on the whole abstract; and then the last six months, when history has forced the pace of thought and hammered out its own conclusions in men's minds. Now I begin to see where my earlier attempts were leading. If civilization is to recreate itself after the war, it can only do so on the basis of what, for want of a better word, we must call a social outlook. The essentially economic and mechanistic ideals of the great era of *laisser-faire* no longer either satisfy or convince. Indeed, it is man's despair at their complete failure to honour their rosy promises which has produced the fantastic and evil system against which we are now fighting for our lives and for the survival of anything that can be called civilization. They were founded in freedom and promised prosperity and equality. But in place of freedom, men have found themselves enslaved to the impersonal machinery of the market; their purely political equality has been accompanied by gross economic and social inequality; and the promise of prosperity has been replaced by mass insecurity and frustration.

The Nazi system is a negation of any civilized order. It is a form of black magic designed to exorcize the despair of men caught in the death-struggles of the *laisser-faire* world; but it is negative, nihilistic, and can only advance by destroying. If the Nazis win the war, the western world is headed for a period of regimentation which yet will be unable to hold violence in check, a period in which destruction will proceed within a portentous framework of empty organization.

But if we win, civilization is not necessarily safe. It will only be saved if it can transform itself so as to overcome insecurity, frustration and despair. And it can only transform itself if it finds a new basis, a new substance for its belief in itself. The new belief must be a social one, based on the concept of society as an organic whole, in which rights and duties are balanced deliberately, as they are automatically balanced in the tissues of the animal body. Economic values must lose their primacy, and become subordinated to social values.

Force of circumstances has pushed the nations some way along this road. Subsidized housing, free milk, social security legislation, health insurance, free education, *Kraft durch Freude* in Germany, the C.C.C. in America—these are all symptoms of the change. But they have all been conceived *ad hoc*, to meet some particular need, and are still, in the democratic countries, somewhat apologetic interlopers into a world ruled by economic ideals. The war is an interlude—appallingly urgent, but yet an interlude. The most vital task of the present age is to formulate a social basis for civilization, to dethrone economic ideals and replace them by human ones.

A foreword is not the place to discuss such a formidable project, even if I were competent to do so. But it is within my competence to point out that biology has some relevance to the task. The task is not merely an empirical one. It cannot be accomplished on a basis of pure logic and rationality, or on one of preconceived abstract ideas. It requires a new world-picture as its basis, a new framework of ideas. And biology is needed to give that picture its proper background. Man as an organism, but a unique and very strange organism, human evolution as an integral part of life's evolution, but operating through novel and peculiar mechanisms—without this background our world-picture will be falsified, and our attempts at transforming our civilization will wholly or partly fail.

That is where the biologist, provided he is willing to face the unfamiliar problems of human biology and not take the easy course of excluding his own species from his subject, can make his contribution—not an immediately practical nor a very large one, but yet one that is essential.

To the biologist who is not afraid of being a humanist as well, the essence of human life is seen in social relationships. Out of those relations of men in society spring the values which we must excavate from their matrix of custom and organization, and clarify as the conscious basis of the new order.

I do not pretend that this formulation was present in my mind when I wrote any of the essays here collected. But in one way or another it is implicit in most of them, and it is in its light that I hope they may be read.

The separate articles appeared as follows:—'Religion as an Objective Problem' in *Discovery*; 'Eugenics and Society' in the *Eugenics Review*; 'The Intelligence of Birds' in the *Strand Magazine*; 'Life Can Be Worth Living' in *The Nation* and *John o' London's Weekly*; 'Climate and Human History' and 'The Size of Living Things' in the *Atlantic Monthly*; 'The Courtship of Animals' in *The Forum*; 'The Concept of Race in the Light of Modern Genetics' and 'Mice and Men' in *Harper's Magazine* (the latter also in the *Cornhill*); 'The Analysis of Fame' in the *Saturday Review of Literature*; 'Science, Natural and Social' ('The Science of Society') and 'The Origins of Species' in the *Scientific Monthly* and the *Virginia Quarterly Review*; 'Scientific Humanism' ('Human Power and Its Control') and 'The Uniqueness of Man' in the *Yale Review*; 'The Way of the Dodo' in *The Times*. To the editors and proprietors of these journals I offer my thanks for their kind permission to reprint.

London,
October 29th, 1940.

CONTENTS

PREFACE   *page* vii

    I. MAN STANDS ALONE   I

   II. EUGENICS AND SOCIETY   34

  III. CLIMATE AND HUMAN HISTORY   85

  IV. THE CONCEPT OF RACE   106

   V. THE SIZE OF LIVING THINGS   127

  VI. THE ORIGINS OF SPECIES   152

 VII. MICE AND MEN   164

VIII. THE WAY OF THE DODO   183

  IX. THE COURTSHIP OF ANIMALS   190

   X. THE INTELLIGENCE OF BIRDS   207

  XI. SCIENCE, NATURAL AND SOCIAL   222

 XII. THE ANALYSIS OF FAME   252

XIII. SCIENTIFIC HUMANISM   260

XIV. RELIGION AS AN OBJECTIVE PROBLEM   277

 XV. LIFE CAN BE WORTH LIVING   291

xi

FIGURES IN TEXT

A diagram of relative sizes. In each major
    division (A, B, C, D, E) of the diagram,
    all the creatures are drawn to the same
    scale. The smallest of each division is
    enlarged to make the largest of the divi-
    sion following   *pages* 128-129

MAN STANDS ALONE

Man's opinion of his own position in relation to the rest of the animals has swung pendulum-wise between too great or too little a conceit of himself, fixing now too large a gap between himself and the animals, now too small. The gap, of course, can be diminished or increased at either the animal or the human end. One can, like Descartes, make animals too mechanical, or, like most unsophisticated people, humanize them too much. Or one can work at the human end of the gap, and then either dehumanize one's own kind into an animal species like any other, or superhumanize it into beings a little lower than the angels.

Primitive and savage man, the world over, not only accepts his obvious kinship with the animals but also projects into them many of his own attributes. So far as we can judge, he has very little pride in his own humanity. With the advent of settled civilization, economic stratification, and the development of an elaborate religion as the ideological mortar of a now class-ridden society, the pendulum began slowly to swing in the other direction. Animal divinities and various physiological functions such as fertility gradually lost their sacred importance. Gods became anthropomorphic and human psychological qualities pre-eminent. Man saw himself as a being set apart, with the rest of the animal kingdom created to serve his needs and pleasure, with no share in salvation, no position

A   I

in eternity.   In western civilization this swing of the
pendulum reached its limit in developed Christian theology and in the philosophy of Descartes: both alike in-
serted a qualitative and unbridgeable barrier between all
men and any animals.

With Darwin, the reverse swing was started.   Man
was once again regarded as an animal, but now in the light
of science rather than of unsophisticated sensibility.   At
the outset, the consequences of the changed outlook were
not fully explored.   The unconscious prejudices and attitudes of an earlier age survived, disguising many of the
moral and philosophical implications of the new outlook.
But gradually the pendulum reached the furthest point of
its swing.   What seemed the logical consequences of the
Darwinian postulates were faced: man is an animal like
any other; accordingly, his views as to the special meaning of human life and human ideals need merit no more
consideration in the light of eternity (or of evolution) than
those of a bacillus or a tapeworm.   Survival is the only
criterion of evolutionary success: therefore, all existing
organisms are of equal value.   The idea of progress is a
mere anthropomorphism.   Man happens to be the dominant type at the moment, but he might be replaced by the
ant or the rat.   And so on.

The gap between man and animal was here reduced not
by exaggerating the human qualities of animals, but by
minimizing the human qualities of men.   Of late years,
however, a new tendency has become apparent.   It may be
that this is due mainly to the mere increase of knowledge
and the extension of scientific analysis.   It may be that it
has been determined by social and psychological causes.
Disillusionment with *laisser-faire* in the human economic

2

sphere may well have spread to the planetary system of *laisser-faire* that we call natural selection. With the crash of old religious, ethical, and political systems, man's desperate need for some scheme of values and ideals may have prompted a more critical re-examination of his biological position. Whether this be so is a point that I must leave to the social historians. The fact remains that the pendulum is again on the swing, the man-animal gap again broadening. After Darwin, man could no longer avoid considering himself as an animal; but he is beginning to see himself as a very peculiar and in many ways a unique animal. The analysis of man's biological uniqueness is as yet incomplete. This essay is an attempt to review its present position.

The first and most obviously unique characteristic of man is his capacity for conceptual thought; if you prefer objective terms, you will say his employment of true speech, but that is only another way of saying the same thing. True speech involves the use of verbal signs for objects, not merely for feelings. Plenty of animals can express the fact that they are hungry; but none except man can ask for an egg or a banana. And to have words for objects at once implies conceptual thought, since an object is always one of a class. No doubt, children and savages are as unaware of using conceptual thought as Monsieur Jourdain was unaware of speaking in prose; but they cannot avoid it. Words are tools which automatically carve concepts out of experience. The faculty of recognizing objects as members of a class provides the potential basis for the concept: the use of words at once actualizes the potentiality.

This basic human property has had many consequences.

The most important was the development of a cumulative tradition. The beginnings of tradition, by which experience is transmitted from one generation to the next, are to be seen in many higher animals. But in no case is the tradition cumulative. Offspring learn from parents, but they learn the same kind and quantity of lessons as they, in turn, impart: the transmission of experience never bridges more than one generation. In man, however, tradition is an independent and potentially permanent activity, capable of indefinite improvement in quality and increase in quantity. It constitutes a new accessory process of heredity in evolution, running side by side with the biological process, a heredity of experience to supplement the universal heredity of living substance.

The existence of a cumulative tradition has as its chief consequence—or if you prefer, its chief objective manifestation—the progressive improvement of human tools and machinery. Many animals employ tools; but they are always crude tools employed in a crude way. Elaborate tools and skilled technique can develop only with the aid of speech and tradition.

In the perspective of evolution, tradition and tools are the characters which have given man his dominant position among organisms. This biological dominance is, at present, another of man's unique properties. In each geological epoch of which we have knowledge, there have been types which must be styled biologically dominant: they multiply, they extinguish or reduce competing types, they extend their range, they radiate into new modes of life. Usually at any one time there is one such type—the placental mammals, for instance, in the Cenozoic Epoch; but sometimes there is more than one. The Mesozoic is

4

usually called the Age of Reptiles, but in reality the reptiles were then competing for dominance with the insects:
in earlier periods we should be hard put to it to decide
whether trilobites, nautiloids, or early fish were *the* dominant type. To-day, however, there is general agreement
that man is the sole type meriting the title. Since the
early Pleistocene, widespread extinction has diminished
the previously dominant group of placental mammals, and
man has not merely multiplied, but has evolved, extended
his range, and increased the variety of his modes of life.

Biology thus reinstates man in a position analogous to
that conferred on him as Lord of Creation by theology.
There are, however, differences, and differences of some
importance for our general outlook. In the biological
view, the other animals have not been created to serve
man's needs, but man has evolved in such a way that he
has been able to eliminate some competing types, to en-
slave others by domestication, and to modify physical and
biological conditions over the larger part of the earth's
land area. The theological view was not true in detail or
in many of its implications; but it had a solid biological
basis.

Speech, tradition, and tools have led to many other
unique properties of man. These are, for the most part,
obvious and well known, and I propose to leave them
aside until I have dealt with some less familiar human
characteristics. For the human species, considered as a
species, is unique in certain purely biological attributes;
and these have not received the attention they deserve,
either from the zoological or the sociological standpoint.

In the first place, man is by far the most variable wild
species known. Domesticated species like dog, horse, or

5

fowl may rival or exceed him in this particular, but their variability has obvious reasons, and is irrelevant to our inquiry.

In correlation with his wide variability, man has a far wider range than any other animal species, with the possible exception of some of his parasites. Man is also unique as a dominant type. All other dominant types have evolved into many hundreds or thousands of separate species, grouped in numerous genera, families, and larger classificatory groups. The human type has maintained its dominance without splitting: man's variety has been achieved within the limits of a single species.

Finally, man is unique among higher animals in the method of his evolution. Whereas, in general, animal evolution is divergent, human evolution is reticulate. By this is meant that in animals, evolution occurs by the isolation of groups which then become progressively more different in their genetic characteristics, so that the course of evolution can be represented as a divergent radiation of separate lines, some of which become extinct, others continue unbranched, and still others divergently branch again. Whereas in man, after incipient divergence, the branches have come together again, and have generated new diversity from their Mendelian recombinations, this process being repeated until the course of human descent is like a network.

All these biological peculiarities are interconnected. They depend on man's migratory propensities, which themselves arise from his fundamental peculiarities, of speech, social life, and relative independence of environment. They depend again on his capacity, when choosing mates, for neglecting large differences of colour and appearance which would almost certainly be more than enough to deter more instinctive and less plastic animals. Thus divergence, though it appears to have gone quite a long way in early human evolution, generating the very distinct white, black, and yellow subspecies and perhaps others, was never permitted to attain its normal culmination. Mutually infertile groups were never produced: man remained a single species. Furthermore, crossing between distinct types, which is a rare and extraordinary phenomenon in other animals, in him became normal and of major importance. According to Mendelian laws, such crosses generate much excess variability by producing new recombinations. Man is thus more variable than other species for two reasons. First, because migration has recaptured for the single interbreeding group divergences of a magnitude that in animals would escape into the isolation of separate species; and secondly, because the resultant crossing has generated recombinations which both quantitatively and qualitatively are on a far bigger scale than is supplied by the internal variability of even the numerically most abundant animal species.

We may contrast this with the state of affairs among ants, the dominant insect group. The ant type is more varied than the human type ; but it has achieved this variability by intense divergent evolution. Several thousand species of ants are known, and the number is being added to each year with the increase of biological exploration. Ways of life among ants are divided among different subtypes, each rigidly confined to its own methods. Thus even if ants were capable of accumulating experience, there could exist no single world-wide ant tradition. The fact that the human type comprises but one biological species is a consequence of his capacity for tradition, and also permits his exploitation of that unique capacity to the utmost.

Let us remind ourselves that superposed upon this purely biological or genetic variability is the even greater amount of variability due to differences of upbringing, profession, and personal tastes. The final result is a degree of variation that would be staggering if it were not so familiar. It would be fair to say that, in respect to mind and outlook, individual human beings are separated by differences as profound as those which distinguish the major groups of the animal kingdom. The difference between a somewhat subnormal member of a savage tribe and a Beethoven or a Newton is assuredly comparable in extent with that between a sponge and a higher mammal. Leaving aside such vertical differences, the lateral difference between the mind of, say, a distinguished general or engineer of extrovert type and of an introvert genius in mathematics or religious mysticism is no less than that between an insect and a vertebrate. This enormous range of individual variation in human minds often leads to misunderstanding and even mutual incomprehensibility; but it also provides the necessary basis for fruitful division of labour in human society.

Another biological peculiarity of man is the uniqueness of his evolutionary history. Writers have indulged their speculative fancy by imagining other organisms endowed with speech and conceptual thought—talking rats, rational ants, philosophic dogs, and the like. But closer analysis shows that these fantasies are impossible. A brain capable of conceptual thought could not have been developed elsewhere than in a human body.

The course followed by evolution appears to have been broadly as follows. From a generalized early type, various lines radiate out, exploiting the environment in various ways. Some of these comparatively soon reach a limit to their evolution, at least as regards major alteration. Thereafter they are limited to minor changes such as the formation of new genera and species. Others, on the other hand, are so constructed that they can continue their career, generating new types which are successful in the struggle for existence because of their greater control over the environment and their greater independence of it. Such changes are legitimately called 'progressive.' The new type repeats the process. It radiates out into a number of lines, each specializing in a particular direction. The great majority of these come up against dead ends and can advance no further: specialization is one-sided progress, and after a longer or shorter time, reaches a biomechanical limit. The horse stock cannot reduce its digits below one; the elephants are near the limits of size for terrestrial animals; feathered flight cannot become aerodynamically more efficient than in existing birds, and so on.

Sometimes all the branches of a given stock have come up against their limit, and then either have become extinct or have persisted without major change. This happened, for instance, to the echinoderms, which with their sea-urchins, starfish, brittle-stars, sea-lilies, sea-cucumbers, and other types now extinct had pushed the life that was in them into a series of blind alleys: ,they have not advanced for perhaps a hundred million years, nor have they given rise to other major types.

In other cases, all but one or two of the lines suffer this fate, while the rest repeat the process. All reptilian lines were blind alleys save two—one which was transformed into the birds, and another which became the mammals. Of the bird stock, all lines came to a dead end; of the mammals, all but one—the one which became man.

Evolution is thus seen as an enormous number of blind alleys, with a very occasional path of progress. It is like a maze in which almost all turnings are wrong turnings. The goal of the evolutionary maze, however, is not a central chamber, but a road which will lead indefinitely onwards.

If now we look back upon the past history of life, we shall see that the avenues of progress have been steadily reduced in number, until by the Pleistocene period, or even earlier, only one was left. Let us remember that we can and must judge early progress in the light of its latest steps. The most recent step has been the acquisition of conceptual thought, which has enabled man to dethrone the non-human mammals from their previous position of dominance. It is biologically obvious that conceptual thought could never have arisen save in an animal, so that all plants, both green and otherwise, are at once eliminated. As regards animals, I need not detail all the early steps in their progressive evolution. Since some degree of bulk helps to confer independence of the forces of nature, it is obvious that the combination of many cells to form a large individual was one necessary step, thus eliminating all single-celled forms from such progress. Similarly, progress is barred to specialized animals with no blood-system, like planarian worms; to internal parasites, like tapeworms; to animals with radial symmetry and consequently no head, like echinoderms.

Of the three highest animal groups—the molluscs, the

arthropods, and the vertebrates—the molluscs advanced least far. One condition for the later steps in biological progress was land life. The demands made upon the organism by exposure to air and gravity called forth biological mechanisms, such as limbs, sense-organs, protective skin, and sheltered development, which were necessary foundations for later advance. And the molluscs have never been able to produce efficient terrestrial forms: their culmination is in marine types like squid and octopus.

The arthropods, on the other hand, have scored their greatest successes on land, with the spiders and especially the insects. Yet the fossil record reveals a lack of all advance, even in the most successful types such as ants, for a long time back—certainly during the last thirty million years, probably during the whole of the Tertiary Epoch. Even during the shorter of these periods, the mammals were still evolving rapidly, and man's rise is contained in a fraction of this time.

What was it that cut the insects off from progress? The answer appears to lie in their breathing mechanism. The land arthropods have adopted the method of air-tubes or tracheae, branching to microscopic size and conveying gases directly to and from the tissues, instead of using the dual mechanism of lungs and bloodstream. The laws of gaseous diffusion are such that respiration by tracheae is extremely efficient for very small animals, but becomes rapidly less efficient with increase of size, until it ceases to be of use at a bulk below that of a house mouse. It is for this reason that no insect has ever become, by vertebrate standards, even moderately large.

It is for the same reason that no insect has ever become even moderately intelligent. The fixed pathways of instinct, however elaborate, require far fewer nerve-cells than the multiple switchboards that underlie intelligence. It appears to be impossible to build a brain mechanism for flexible behaviour with less than a quite large minimum of neurones; and no insect has reached a size to provide this minimum.

Thus only the land vertebrates are left. The reptiles shared biological dominance with the insects in the Mesozoic. But while the insects had reached the end of their blind alley, the reptiles showed themselves capable of further advance. Temperature regulation is a necessary basis for final progress, since without it the rate of bodily function could never be stabilized, and without such stabilization, higher mental processes could never become accurate and dependable.

Two reptilian lines achieved this next step, in the guise of the birds and the mammals. The birds soon, however, came to a dead end, chiefly because their forelimbs were entirely taken up in the specialization for flight. The subhuman mammals made another fundamental advance, in the shape of internal development, permitting the young animal to arrive at a much more advanced stage before it was called upon to face the world. They also (like the birds) developed true family life.

Most mammalian lines, however, cut themselves off from indefinite progress by one-sided evolution, turning their limbs and jaws into specialized and therefore limited instruments. And, for the most part, they relied mainly on the crude sense of smell, which cannot present as differentiated a pattern of detailed knowledge as can sight. Finally, the majority continued to produce their young several at a time, in litters. As J. B. S. Haldane has pointed out, this gives rise to an acute struggle for existence in the prenatal period, a considerable percentage of embryos being aborted or resorbed. Such intra-uterine selection will put a premium upon rapidity of growth and differentiation, since the devil takes the hindmost; and this rapidity of development will tend automatically to be carried on into postnatal growth.

As everyone knows, man is characterized by a rate of development which is abnormally slow as compared with that of any other mammal. The period from birth to the first onset of sexual maturity comprises nearly a quarter of the normal span of his life, instead of an eighth, a tenth or twelfth, as in some other animals. This again is in one sense a unique characteristic of man, although from the evolutionary point of view it represents merely the exaggeration of a tendency which is operative in other Primates. In any case, it is a necessary condition for the evolution and proper utilization of rational thought. If men and women were, like mice, confronted with the problems of adult life and parenthood after a few weeks, or even, like whales, after a couple of years, they could never acquire the skills of body and mind that they now absorb from and contribute to the social heritage of the species.

This slowing (or 'foetalization,' as Bolk has called it, since it prolongs the foetal characteristics of earlier ancestral forms into postnatal development and even into adult life) has had other important by-products for man. Here I will mention but one—his nakedness. The distribution of hair on man is extremely similar to that on a late foetus of a chimpanzee, and there can be little doubt that it represents an extension of this temporary anthropoid phase into permanence. Hairlessness of body is not a unique biological characteristic of man; but it is unique among terrestrial mammals, save for a few desert creatures, and some others which have compensated for loss of hair by developing a pachydermatous skin. In any case, it has important biological consequences, since it must have encouraged the comparatively defenceless human creatures in their efforts to protect themselves against animal enemies and the elements, and so has been a spur to the improvement of intelligence.

Now, foetalization could never have occurred in a mammal producing many young at a time, since intra-uterine competition would have encouraged the opposing tendency. Thus we may conclude that conceptual thought could develop only in a mammalian stock which normally brings forth but one young at a birth. Such a stock is provided in the Primates—lemurs, monkeys, and apes.

The Primates also have another characteristic which was necessary for the ancestor of a rational animal—they are arboreal. It may seem curious that living in trees is a prerequisite of conceptual thought. But Elliot Smith's analysis has abundantly shown that only in an arboreal mammal could the forelimb become a true hand, and sight become dominant over smell. Hands obtain an elaborate tactile pattern of what they handle, eyes an elaborate visual pattern of what they see. The combination of the two kinds of pattern, with the aid of binocular vision, in the higher centres of the brain allowed the Primate to acquire a wholly new richness of knowledge about objects, a wholly new possibility of manipulating them. Tree life laid the foundation both for the fuller definition of objects by conceptual thought and for the fuller control of them by tools and machines.

Higher Primates have yet another prerequisite of human intelligence—they are all gregarious. Speech, it is obvious, could never have been evolved in a solitary type. And speech is as much the physical basis of conceptual thought as is protoplasm the physical basis of life.

For the passage, however, of the critical point between subhuman and human, between the biological subordination and the biological primacy of intelligence, between a limited and a potentially unlimited tradition—for this it was necessary for the arboreal animal to descend to the ground again. Only in a terrestrial creature could fully erect posture be acquired; and this was essential for the final conversion of the arms from locomotor limbs into manipulative hands. Furthermore, just as land life, ages previously, had demanded and developed a greater variety of response than had been required in the water, so now it did the same in relation to what had been required in the trees. An arboreal animal could never have evolved the skill of the hunting savage, nor ever have proceeded to the domestication of other animals or to agriculture.

We are now in a position to define the uniqueness of human evolution. The essential character of man as a dominant organism is conceptual thought. And conceptual thought could have arisen only in a multicellular animal, an animal with bilateral symmetry, head and blood system, a vertebrate as against a mollusc or an arthropod, a land vertebrate among vertebrates, a mammal among land vertebrates. Finally, it could have arisen only in a mammalian line which was gregarious, which produced one young at a birth instead of several, and which had recently become terrestrial after a long period of arboreal life.

There is only one group of animals which fulfils these conditions—a terrestrial offshoot of the higher Primates. Thus not merely has conceptual thought been evolved only in man: it could not have been evolved except in man. There is but one path of unlimited progress through the evolutionary maze. The course of human evolution is as unique as its result. It is unique not in the trivial sense of being a different course from that of any other organism, but in the profounder sense of being the only path that could have achieved the essential characters of man. Conceptual thought on this planet is inevitably associated with a particular type of Primate body and Primate brain.

A further property of man in which he is unique among higher animals concerns his sexual life. Man is prepared to mate at any time: animals are not. To start with, most animals have a definite breeding season; only during this period are their reproductive organs fully developed and functional. In addition to this, higher animals have one or more sexual cycles within their breeding seasons, and only at one phase of the cycle are they prepared to mate. In general, either a sexual season or a sexual cycle, or both, operates to restrict mating.

In man, however, neither of these factors is at work. There appear to be indications of a breeding season in some primitive peoples like the Eskimo, but even there they are but relics. Similarly, while there still exist physiological differences in sexual desire at different phases of the female sexual cycle, these are purely quantitative, and may readily be overridden by psychological factors. Man, to put it briefly, is continuously sexed: animals are discontinuously sexed. If we try to imagine what a human society would be like in which the sexes were interested in each other only during the summer, as in songbirds, or, as in female dogs, experienced sexual desire only once every few months, or even only once in a lifetime, as in ants, we can realize what this peculiarity has meant. In this, as in his slow growth and prolonged period of dependence, man is not abruptly marked off from all other animals, but represents the culmination of a process that can be clearly traced among other Primates. What the biological meaning of this evolutionary trend may be is difficult to understand. One suggestion is that it may be associated with the rise of mind to dominance. The bodily functions, in lower mammals rigidly determined by physiological mechanisms, come gradually under the more plastic control of the brain. But this, for what it is worth, is a mere speculation.

Another of the purely biological characters in which man is unique is his reproductive variability. In a given species of animals, the maximum litter-size may, on occasions, reach perhaps double the minimum, according to circumstances of food and temperature, or even perhaps threefold. But during a period of years, these variations will be largely equalized within a range of perhaps fifty per cent. either way from the average, and the percentage of wholly infertile adults is very low. In man, on the other hand, the range of positive fertility is enormous—from one to over a dozen, and in exceptional cases to over twenty; and the number of wholly infertile adults is considerable. This fact, in addition to providing a great diversity of patterns of family life, has important bearings on evolution. It means that in the human species differential fertility is more important as a basis for selection than is differential mortality; and it provides the possibility of much more rapid selective change than that found in wild animal species. Such rapidity of evolution would, of course, be effectively realized only if the stocks with large families possessed a markedly different hereditary constitution from those with few children; but the high differential fertility of unskilled workers as against the professional classes in England, or of the French Canadians against the rest of the inhabitants of Canada, demonstrates how rapidly populations may change by this means.

Still another point in which man is biologically unique is the length and relative importance of his period of what we may call 'post-maturity.' If we consider the female sex, in which the transition from reproductive maturity to non-reproductive post-maturity is more sharply defined than in the male, we find, in the first place, that in animals a comparatively small percentage of the population survives beyond the period of reproduction; in the second place, that such individuals rarely survive long, and so far as known never for a period equal to or greater than the period during which reproduction was possible; and thirdly, that such individuals are rarely of importance in the life of the species. The same is true of the male sex, provided we do not take the incapacity to produce fertile gametes as the criterion of post-maturity, but rather the appearance of signs of age, such as the beginnings of loss of vigour and weight, decreased sexual activity, or greying hair.

It is true that in some social mammals, notably among ruminants and Primates, an old male or old female is frequently found as leader of the herd. Such cases, however, provide the only examples of the special biological utility of post-mature individuals among animals; they are confined to a very small proportion of the population, and it is uncertain to what extent such individuals are post-mature in the sense we have defined. In any event, it is improbable that the period of post-maturity is anywhere near so long as that of maturity. But in civilized man the average expectation of life now includes over ten post-mature years, and about a sixth of the population enjoys a longer post-maturity than maturity. What is more, in all advanced human societies, a large proportion of the leaders of the community are always post-mature. All the members of the British War Cabinet are in their post-maturity.

This is truly a remarkable phenomenon. Through the new social mechanisms made possible by speech and tradition, man has been able to utilize for the benefit of the species a period of life which in almost all other creatures is a mere superfluity. We know that the dominance of the old can be over-emphasized; but it is equally obvious that society cannot do without the post-mature. To act on the slogan 'Too old at forty'—or even at forty-five—would be to rob man of one of his unique characteristics, whereby he utilizes tradition to the best advantage.

We have now dealt in a broad way with the unique properties of man both from the comparative and the evolutionary point of view. Now we can return to the present and the particular and discuss these properties and their consequences a little more in detail. First, let us remind ourselves that the gap between human and animal thought is much greater than is usually supposed. The tendency to project familiar human qualities into animals is very strong, and colours the ideas of nearly all people who have not special familiarity both with animal behaviour and scientific method.

Let us recall a few cases illustrating the unhuman characteristics of animal behaviour. Everyone is familiar with the rigidity of instinct in insects. Worker ants emerge from their pupal case equipped not with the instincts to care for ant grubs in general, but solely with those suitable to ant grubs of their own species. They will attempt to care for the grubs of other species, but appear incapable of learning new methods if their instincts kill their foster children. Or again, a worker wasp, without food for a hungry grub, has been known to bite off its charge's tail and present it to its head. But even in the fine flowers of vertebrate evolution, the birds and mammals, behaviour, though it may be more plastic than in the insects, is as essentially irrational. Birds, for instance, seem incapable of analysing unfamiliar situations. For them some element in the situation may act as its dominant symbol, the only stimulus to which they can react. At other times, it is the organization of the situation as a whole which is the stimulus: if the whole is interfered with, analysis fails to dissect out the essential element. A hen meadow-pipit feeds her young when it gapes and squeaks in the nest. But if it has been ejected by a young cuckoo, gaping and squeaking has no effect, and the rightful offspring is neglected and allowed to die, while the usurper in the nest is fed. The pipit normally cares for its own young, but not because it recognizes them as such.

Mammals are no better. A cow deprived of its calf will be quieted by the provision of a crudely stuffed calf-skin. Even the Primates are no exception. Female baboons whose offspring have died will continue carrying the corpses until they have not merely putrefied but mummified. This appears to be due not to any profund-

20

ity of grief, but to a contact stimulus: the mother will react similarly to any moderately small and furry object.

Birds and especially mammals are, of course, capable of a certain degree of analysis, but this is effected, in the main, by means of trial and error through concrete experience. A brain capable of conceptual thought appears to be the necessary basis for speedy and habitual analysis. Without it, the practice of splitting up situations into their components and assigning real degrees of significance to the various elements remains rudimentary and rare, whereas with man, even when habit and trial and error are prevalent, conceptual thought is of major biological importance. The behaviour of animals is essentially arbitrary, in that it is fixed within narrow limits. In man it has become relatively free—free at the incoming and the outgoing ends alike. His capacity for acquiring knowledge has been largely released from arbitrary symbolism, his capacity for action, from arbitrary canalizations of instinct. He can thus rearrange the patterns of experience and action in a far greater variety, and can escape from the particular into the general.

Thus man is more intelligent than the animals because his brain mechanism is more plastic. This fact also gives him, of course, the opportunity of being more nonsensical and perverse: but its primary effects have been more analytical knowledge and more varied control. The essential fact, from my present standpoint, is that the change has been profound and in an evolutionary sense rapid. Although it has been brought about by the gradual quantitative enlargement of the association areas of the brain, the result has been almost as abrupt as the change (also brought about quantitatively) from solid ice to liquid water. We should remember that the machinery of the change has been an increase in plasticity and potential variety: it is by a natural selection of ideas and actions that the result has been greater rationality instead of greater irrationality.

This increase of flexibility has also had other psychological consequences which rational philosophers are apt to forget: and in some of these, too, man is unique. It has led, for instance, to the fact that man is the only organism normally and inevitably subject to psychological conflict. You can give a dog neurosis, as Pavlov did, by a complicated laboratory experiment: you can find cases of brief emotional conflict in the lives of wild birds and animals. But, for the most part, psychological conflict is shirked by the simple expedient of arranging that now one and now another instinct should dominate the animal's behaviour. I remember in Spitsbergen finding the nest of a Red-throated Diver on the shore of an inland pool. The sitting bird was remarkably bold. After leaving the nest for the water, she stayed very close. She did not, however, remain in a state of conflict between fear of intruders and desire to return to her brooding. She would gradually approach as if to land, but eventually fear became dominant, and when a few feet from the shore she suddenly dived, and emerged a good way farther out—only to repeat the process. Here the external circumstances were such as to encourage conflict, but even so what are the most serious features of human conflict were minimized by the outlet of alternate action.

Those who take up bird-watching as a hobby tend at first to be surprised at the way in which a bird will turn, apparently without transition or hesitation, from one activity to another—from fighting to peaceable feeding, from courtship to uninterested preening, from panic flight to unconcern. However, all experienced naturalists or those habitually concerned with animals recognize such behaviour as characteristic of the subhuman level. It represents another aspect of the type of behaviour I have just been describing for the Red-throated Diver. In this case, the internal state of the bird changes, presumably owing to some form of physiological fatigue or to a diminution of intensity of a stimulus with time or distance; the type of behaviour which had been dominant ceases to have command over the machinery of action, and is replaced by another which just before had been subordinate and latent.

As a matter of fact, the prevention of conflict between opposed modes of action is a very general phenomenon, of obvious biological utility, and it is only the peculiarities of the human mind which have forced its partial abandonment on man. It begins on the purely mechanical level with the nervous machinery controlling our muscles. The main muscles of a limb, for instance, are arranged in two antagonistic sets, the flexors bending and the extensors straightening it. It would obviously be futile to throw both sets into action at the same time, and economical when one set is in action to reduce to the minimum any resistance offered by the other. This has actually been provided for. The nervous connections in the spinal cord are so arranged that when a given muscle receives an impulse to contract, its antagonist receives an impulse causing it to lose some of its tone and thus, by relaxing below its normal level, to offer the least possible resistance to the action of the active muscle.

23

Sherrington discovered that the same type of mechanism was operative in regard to the groups of muscles involved in whole reflexes. A dog, for instance, cannot very well walk and scratch itself at the same time. To avoid the waste involved in conflict between the walking and the scratching reflex, the spinal cord is constructed in such a way that throwing one reflex into action automatically inhibits the other. In both these cases, the machinery for preventing conflicts of activity resides in the spinal cord. Although the matter has not yet been analysed physiologically, it would appear that the normal lack of conflict between instincts which we have just been discussing is due to some similar type of nervous mechanism in the brain.

When we reach the human level, there are new complications; for, as we have seen, one of the peculiarities of man is the abandonment of any rigidity of instinct, and the provision of association-mechanisms by which any activity of the mind, whether in the spheres of knowing, feeling, or willing, can be brought into relation with any other. It is through this that man has acquired the possibility of a unified mental life. But, by the same token, the door is opened to the forces of disruption, which may destroy any such unity and even prevent him from enjoying the efficiency of behaviour attained by animals. For, as Sherrington has emphasized, the nervous system is like a funnel, with a much larger space for intake than for outflow. The intake cone of the funnel is represented by the receptor nerves, conveying impulses inward to the central nervous system from the sense-organs: the outflow tube is, then, through the effector nerves, conveying impulses outwards to the muscles, and there are many more of the former

24

than of the latter. If we like to look at the matter from a rather different standpoint, we may say that, since action can be effected only by muscles (strictly speaking, also by the glands, which are disregarded here for simplicity's sake), and since there are a limited number of muscles in the body, the only way for useful activity to be carried out is for the nervous system to impose a particular pattern of action on them, and for all other competing or opposing patterns to be cut out. Each pattern, when it has seized control of the machinery of action, *should* be in supreme command, like the captain of a ship. Animals are, in many ways, like ships which are commanded by a number of captains in turn, each specializing in one kind of action, and popping up and down between the authority of the bridge and the obscurity of their private cabins according to the business on hand. Man is on the way to achieving permanent unity of command, but the captain has a disconcerting way of dissolving into a wrangling committee.

Even on the new basis, however, mechanisms exist for minimizing conflict. They are what are known by psychologists as suppression and repression. From our point of view, repression is the more interesting. It implies the forcible imprisonment of one of two conflicting impulses in the dungeons of the unconscious mind. The metaphor is, however, imperfect. For the prisoner in the mental dungeon can continue to influence the tyrant above in the daylight of consciousness. In addition to a general neurosis, compulsive thoughts and acts may be thrust upon the personality. Repression may thus be harmful; but it can also be regarded as a biological necessity for dealing with inevitable conflict in the early years of life, before rational judgment and control are possible. Better to have the capacity for more or less unimpeded action, even at the expense of possible neurosis, than an organism constantly inactivated like the ass between the two bundles of hay, balanced in irresolution.

In repression, not only is the defeated impulse banished to the unconscious, but the very process of banishment is itself unconscious. The inhibitory mechanisms concerned in it must have been evolved to counteract the more obvious possibilities of conflict, especially in early life, which arose as by-products of the human type of mind.

In suppression, the banishment is conscious, so that neurosis is not likely to appear. Finally, in rational judgment, neither of the conflicting impulses is relegated to the unconscious, but they are balanced in the light of reason and experience, and control of action is consciously exercised.

I need not pursue the subject further. Here I am only concerned to show that the great biological advantages conferred on man by the unification of mind have inevitably brought with them certain counterbalancing defects. The freedom of association between all aspects and processes of the mind has provided the basis for conceptual thought and tradition; but it has also provided potential antagonists, which in lower organisms were carefully kept apart, with the opportunity of meeting face to face, and has thus made some degree of conflict unavoidable.

In rather similar fashion, man's upright posture has brought with it certain consequential disadvantages in regard to the functioning of his internal organs and his proneness to rupture. Thus man's unique characteristics are by no means wholly beneficial.

In close correlation with our subjection to conflict is our

proneness to laughter. So characteristic of our species is laughter that man has been defined as the laughing animal. It is true that, like so much else of man's uniqueness, it has its roots among the animals, where it reveals itself as an expression of a certain kind of general pleasure—and thus in truth perhaps more of a smile than a laugh. And in a few animals—ravens, for example,—there are traces of a malicious sense of humour. Laughter in man, however, is much more than this. There are many theories of laughter, most of them containing a partial truth. But biologically the important feature of human laughter seems to lie in its providing a release for conflict, a resolution of troublesome situations.

This and other functions of laughter can be exaggerated so that it becomes as the crackling of thorns under the pot, and prevents men from taking anything seriously; but in due proportion its value is very great as a lubricant against troublesome friction and a lightener of the inevitable gravity and horror of life, which would otherwise become portentous and overshadowing. True laughter, like true speech, is a unique possession of man.

Those of man's unique characteristics which may better be called psychological and social than narrowly biological spring from one or other of three characteristics. The first is his capacity for abstract and general thought: the second is the relative unification of his mental processes, as against the much more rigid compartmentalization of animal mind and behaviour: the third is the existence of social units, such as tribe, nation, party, and church, with a continuity of their own, based on organized tradition and culture.

There are various by-products of the change from pre-human to the human type of mind which are, of course, also unique biologically. Let us enumerate a few: pure mathematics; musical gifts; artistic appreciation and creation; religion; romantic love.

Mathematical ability appears, almost inevitably, as something mysterious. Yet the attainment of speech, abstraction, and logical thought, bring it into potential being. It may remain in a very rudimentary state of development; but even the simplest arithmetical calculations are a manifestation of its existence. Like any other human activity, it requires proper tools and machinery. Arabic numerals, algebraic conventions, logarithms, the differential calculus, are such tools: each one unlocks new possibilities of mathematical achievement. But just as there is no essential difference between man's conscious use of a chipped flint as an implement and his design of the most elaborate machine, so there is none between such simple operations as numeration or addition and the comprehensive flights of higher mathematics. Again, some people are by nature more gifted than others in this field; yet no normal human being is unable to perform some mathematical operations. Thus the capacity for mathematics is, as I have said, a by-product of the human type of mind.

We have seen, however, that the human type of mind is distinguished by two somewhat opposed attributes. One is the capacity for abstraction, the other for synthesis. Mathematics is one of the extreme by-products of our capacity for abstraction. Arithmetic abstracts objects of all qualities save their enumerability; the symbol π abstracts in a single Greek letter a complicated relation between the parts of all circles. Art, on the other hand, is an extreme by-product of our capacity for synthesis. In one unique production, the painter can bring together form, colour, arrangement, associations of memory, emotion, and idea. Dim adumbrations of art are to be found in a few creatures such as bower-birds; but nothing is found to which the word can rightly be applied until man's mind gave the possibility of freely mingling observations, emotions, memories, and ideas, and subjecting the mixture to deliberate control.

But it is not enough here to enumerate a few special activities. In point of fact, the great majority of man's activities and characteristics are by-products of his primary distinctive characteristics, and therefore, like them, biologically unique.

On the one hand, conversation, organized games, education, sport, paid work, gardening, the theatre; on the other, conscience, duty, sin, humiliation, vice, penitence —these are all such unique by-products. The trouble, indeed, is to find any human activities which are not unique. Even the fundamental biological attributes such as eating, sleeping, and mating have been tricked out by man with all kinds of unique frills and peculiarities.

There may be other by-products of man's basic uniqueness which have not yet been exploited. For let us remember that such by-products may remain almost wholly latent until demand stimulates invention and invention facilitates development. It is asserted that there exist human tribes who cannot count above two; certainly some savages stop at ten. Here the mathematical faculty is restricted to numeration, and stops short at a very rudimentary stage of this rudimentary process. Similarly, there are human societies in which art has never been developed beyond the stage of personal decoration. It is probable that during the first half of the Pleistocene period, none of the human race had developed either their mathematical or their artistic potentialities beyond such a rudimentary stage.

It is perfectly possible that to-day man's so-called supernormal or extra-sensory faculties are in the same case as were his mathematical faculties during the first or second glaciations of the Ice Age—barely more than a potentiality, with no technique for eliciting and developing them, no tradition behind them to give them continuity and intellectual respectability. Even such simple performances as multiplying two three-figure numbers would have appeared entirely magical to early Stone Age men.

Experiments such as those of Rhine and Tyrrell on extra-sensory guessing, experiences like those of Gilbert Murray on thought transference, and the numerous sporadic records of telepathy and clairvoyance suggest that some people at least possess possibilities of knowledge which are not confined within the ordinary channels of sense-perception. Tyrrell's work is particularly interesting in this connection. As a result of an enormous number of trials with apparatus ingeniously designed to exclude all alternative explanation, he finds that those best endowed with this extra-sensory gift can guess right about once in four times when once in five would be expected on chance alone. The results are definite, and significant in the statistical sense, yet the faculty is rudimentary: it does not permit its possessor to guess right all the time or even most of the time—merely to achieve a small rise in the percentage of right guessing. If, however, we could discover in what this faculty really consists, on what mechanism it depends, and by what conditions and agencies it can be influenced, it should be capable of development like any other human faculty. Man may thus be unique in more ways than he now suspects.

So far we have been considering the fact of human uniqueness. It remains to consider man's attitude to these unique qualities of his. Professor Everett, of the University of California, in an interesting paper bearing the same title as this essay, but dealing with the topic from the standpoint of the philosopher and the humanist rather than that of the biologist, has stressed man's fear of his own uniqueness. Man has often not been able to tolerate the feeling that he inhabits an alien world, whose laws do not make sense in the light of his intelligence, and in which the writ of his human values does not run. Faced with the prospect of such intellectual and moral loneliness, he has projected personality into the cosmic scheme. Here he has found a will, there a purpose; here a creative intelligence, and there a divine compassion. At one time, he has deified animals, or personified natural forces. At others, he has created a superhuman pantheon, a single tyrannical world ruler, a subtle and satisfying Trinity in Unity. Philosophers have postulated an Absolute of the same nature as mind.

It is only exceptionally that men have dared to uphold their uniqueness and to be proud of their human superiority to the impersonality and irrationality of the rest of the universe. It is time now, in the light of our knowledge, to be brave and face the fact and the consequences of our uniqueness. That is Dr Everett's view, as it was also that of T. H. Huxley in his famous Romanes lecture. I agree with them; but I would suggest that the antinomy between man and the universe is not quite so sharp as they have made out. Man represents the culmination of that process of organic evolution which has been proceeding on this planet for over a thousand million years. That process, however wasteful and cruel it may be, and into however many blind alleys it may have been diverted, is also in one aspect progressive. Man has now become the sole representative of life in that progressive aspect and its sole trustee for any progress in the future.

Meanwhile it is true that the appearance of the human type of mind, the latest step in evolutionary progress, has introduced both new methods and new standards. By means of his conscious reason and its chief offspring, science, man has the power of substituting less dilatory, less wasteful, and less cruel methods of effective progressive change than those of natural selection, which alone are available to lower organisms. And by means of his conscious purpose and his set of values, he has the power of substituting new and higher standards for change than those of mere survival and adaptation to immediate circumstances, which alone are inherent in pre-human evolution. To put the matter in another way, progress has hitherto been a rare and fitful by-product of evolution. Man has the possibility of making it the main feature of his own future evolution, and of guiding its course in relation to a deliberate aim.

But he must not be afraid of his uniqueness. There may be other beings in this vast universe endowed with reason, purpose, and aspiration: but we know nothing of them. So far as our knowledge goes, human mind and personality are unique and constitute the highest product yet achieved by the cosmos. Let us not put off our responsibilities onto the shoulders of mythical gods or philosophical absolutes, but shoulder them in the hopefulness of tempered pride. In the perspective of biology, our business in the world is seen to be the imposition of the best and most enduring of our human standards upon ourselves and our planet. The enjoyment of beauty and interest, the achievement of goodness and efficiency, the enhancement of life and its variety—these are the harvest which our human uniqueness should be called upon to yield.

II

EUGENICS AND SOCIETY

EUGENICS, Dean Inge writes in one of his essays, is capable of becoming the most sacred ideal of the human race, as a race; one of the supreme religious duties. In this I entirely agree with him. Once the full implications of evolutionary biology are grasped, eugenics will inevitably become part of the religion of the future, or of whatever complex of sentiments may in the future take the place of organized religion. It is not merely a sane outlet for human altruism, but is of all outlets for altruism that which is most comprehensive and of longest range.

However, in addition to holding out these emotional possibilities, the eugenic movement must obey practical necessities. If it is to grow into a soul-compelling ideal, it must first achieve precision and efficiency as a branch of applied science.

At the moment, it is idle to pretend that it has advanced very far in either direction. True that to a limited number of men and women, it is already an inspiring ideal: but for the bulk of people, if not a subject for a jest, it remains either mistrusted or wholly neglected. True that, thanks to the genius of Darwin and his cousin Galton, the notion of evolutionary improvement through selection has provided a firm scientific base for eugenics, and that in recent years distinct progress has been made in applying the triumphant discoveries of modern genetics to the human

34

species: yet for the bulk of scientists, eugenics is still hardly reckoned as a science.

It may be that, as a scientist myself, I overrate the importance of the scientific side. At any rate, it is my conviction that eugenics cannot gain power as an ideal and a motive until it has improved its position as a body of knowledge and a potential instrument of control: and in this essay I shall endeavour to point out what, in my opinion, is the next step towards the graduation of eugenics into the dignity of an established science. It will be an inquiry into the methodology of our subject.

Eugenics falls within the province of the Social Sciences, not of the Natural Sciences. It shares with the rest of them a suspicion, often very frankly expressed by the pundits of more respectable branches of study, such as physics or pure biology, of being not quite scientifically respectable. Some, indeed, go as far as to assert that the social sciences can never be truly scientific, and imply that they have illegitimately used the word *science* in their title in order to exploit the prestige attaching to it in this scientific age.

Personally, I do not think that this criticism is justified. All young sciences are attacked by their elders on the ground of irregularity in their canons of scientific behaviour: but they cannot expect to establish rigorous canons until they are no longer young, any more than an untried adolescent can be expected to possess the assurance and practical skill of a man in the prime of life. In addition, young sciences are not merely young like young human beings owing to the accident of the date of their birth. The date of their birth is no accident: they are young because they are more complex and more difficult.

Physics is an older science than biology because in physics it is easier to isolate phenomena and to discover simple but fundamental laws. The social sciences are younger than the natural sciences because of the appalling complexity of variables which make up their subject-matter.

This, however, is not all. The social sciences in certain respects differ radically from the natural sciences; they cannot expect to achieve success by applying the same simple methods as served their elder sisters, but must work out new methods of their own. In the natural sciences, we isolate phenomena in order to analyse them. If possible we isolate them in the form of a controlled experiment, as in physics or genetics; if this cannot be achieved, we isolate them in thought, make deductions, and test our conclusions by empirical observations, as in astronomy or stratigraphical geology. By refinements of technique, we can eliminate for practical purposes all irrelevant variables; the geneticist wanting to understand some new type which has appeared in his cultures can eliminate, say, the variable of environment, then the variable of single-gene mutations, then the variable of addition or subtraction of whole chromosomes, and finally pin responsibility for the phenomenon on, for example, the inversion of a particular chromosome-section.

But the social scientist cannot do this sort of thing: he can at the best find a correlation between several variables. In terms of causation, the natural scientist can sometimes find a single definite cause for a phenomenon; the social scientist must always be content with several partial causes. He has to work out a system based on the idea of multiple causation. The attractive simplicity of simple and single causation is for him a false simplicity:

36

he needs a different intellectual technique. Anyone who asserts that so-and-so is *the* cause of a social phenomenon is bound to be wrong: it can at best be *a* cause. Let us as eugenists therefore beware of making such assertions as that the celibacy of the clergy was *the* cause of the decadence of Spain, or that the differential birth-rate is *the* cause of the increase of feeble-mindedness: for by so doing we are being scientifically disreputable.

And, of course, the inevitable obverse of the principle of multiple cause is the principle of multiple effect. I need not labour the point, save to stress the need for the working out of suitable methods, of partial correlation and the like, to deal with this multiple complexity.

Another peculiarity of the social sciences, closely linked with the first, is that we cannot make rigorous and repeatable experiments, because we cannot isolate our material or control all its variables. Again a different technique from that of the natural sciences has to be worked out—here a different practical technique. Properly planned regional experiments are an example.

But perhaps the most fundamental difference between natural and social science is that the social scientist is himself part of his own material, and that the criteria for judging the outcome of an experiment are partially subjective. Thus the social scientist cannot escape bias, and he cannot hope to check his work against objective criteria that will be accepted by all normal men.

As regards bias, we may compare this with experimental error in natural science. Just as it is possible to reduce experimental error, but never entirely to eliminate it, so it is clearly possible to a large extent to discount and reduce bias. Discovering the technique of reducing bias

37

will be as important in social science as has been in natural science the long and often tiresome process of discovering the technique of reducing experimental error.

The difficulty of finding an objective criterion of truth in social science cuts deeper. But it is based upon an intellectualist philosophy which hankers after abstract truth. It largely disappears if we take the more robust view that science is control as well as knowledge, and that these two aspects cannot be separated. There can be some measure of general agreement on the practical results of social experiments, especially if these are properly planned. Thus in social science, experiment is not the remote preliminary to action that it is in natural science, but is itself partly action—both pure and applied science simultaneously. *Solvitur operando* should be the working principle of the social sciences. It implies that progress in social science and its applications will be slower and more sprinkled with practical mistakes than progress in natural science; but it does not mean that we should deny its possibility.

These general considerations have many particular applications to our subject. Eugenics is not, as some of its devotees have perhaps unconsciously assumed, a special branch of natural science: it is a branch of social science. It is not merely human genetics. True that it aims at the improvement of the human race by means of the improvement of its genetic qualities. But any improvement of the sort can only be realized in a certain kind of social environment, so that eugenics is inevitably a particular aspect of the study of man in society.

Up to the present, eugenics has concerned itself primarily with a study of the hereditary constitution, and with deductive reasoning on the effects of selection. It was rightly shocked at the intellectual excesses of the perfectionists and sentimental environmentalists, who adhered to the crudest form of Lamarckism and believed that improvements in education and social conditions would be incorporated in an easy automatic way into human nature itself and so lead to continuous and unlimited evolutionary progress. As a result, it converted the distinction between nature and nurture into a hard antithesis, and deliberately or perhaps subconsciously belittled or neglected the effects of the environment and the efforts of the social reformers —except in so far as their real or alleged dysgenic effects might be used to point a moral or provide a horrid warning.

This was natural, and perhaps necessary; but it was neither scientific nor sufficient. It was an example of the error to which I have already referred, the error of assuming that the methods of the natural sciences will serve for the social sciences. The pure natural science of genetics was able, at least during its early career, to neglect consideration of the environment. It could do this because in its experiments it can and does control the environment in order to deal solely with constitutional factors. By this means it has succeeded (and by no other means could it have succeeded) in making those spectacular discoveries about chromosomes and their doubling and halving, about the existence, number and localization of the genes or hereditary units, their mutation and its effects, which in a brief quarter-century have raised it to the position of being that branch of biology which in its method and its progress most nearly conforms to the standard set by physics.

But in eugenics this is not possible. The purpose of eugenics is on the one hand to study the presence of different inherited types and traits in a population, and the fact that these can be increased or diminished in the course of generations as the result of selection, unconscious or deliberate, natural or artificial, and on the other, eventually to use the results of this study for control. Eugenics studies the selective implications of human genetic differences.

However, these implications may and often indeed must differ in different environments. Since the social environment is now by far the most important part of the environment of man; and since the social environment differs from one nation to another, one period to another, one class to another, and its differences are outside the control of the eugenist, he must not neglect it. Its uncontrolled variables bring the eugenist face to face with the principle of multiple causation, at work here as in all the social sciences.

The study of the environment is necessary for the eugenist on a number of counts. First, because he cannot equalize it experimentally, he must learn to discount its effects if he is not to mistake their pinchbeck glitter (as he would be apt to think it) for the true gold of genetic influence. If, for instance, the observed lower stature of the so-called lower classes should prove to be due to an inadequate diet, it is eugenically of no significance. Secondly, because by the limited control of social conditions which is open to us already, it is often possible to alter the effect of a genetic factor. Inherited eye-defects, once a grave handicap in almost every walk of life, are now, in most cases, thanks to the progress of the science of optics and the art of spectacle-making, no more than a minor inconvenience.

Thirdly, the environment itself exercises a selective influence. This fundamental truth, long axiomatic in evolutionary biology, has not been properly recognized in human biology so far as the social environment is concerned. A young pioneer civilization, for instance, will both initially attract and later encourage different types from those attracted and encouraged by a civilization that is old and settled.

Fourthly, in planning a eugenic programme, the eugenist must take account of the social system in which he hopes or expects his improved race to live. Cattle-breeders will set about their work quite differently according to whether they are building up a stock for use in a rich pasture country where winter feed is provided, or one for an undeveloped and semi-arid land, like parts of Africa. Similarly the eugenist must adopt different aims according as to whether he envisages a world of nationalism and war or one of peace and cultural progress. This is already patent in the crude eugenic efforts of to-day—in the encouragement of high fecundity in Fascist Italy and Nazi Germany, together with the persecution of so-called 'non-Aryans' and the glorification of the Nordics in the latter.

Finally, there is the question of bias. It is probably inevitable that most men who come fresh to a problem in social science, however scientifically-minded they may be by nature and training, will have some bias due to their own social environment. This bias in social outlook which besets the pioneers in the social sciences is comparable to the bias in favour of common sense and accepted modes of thought which equally inevitably beset the pioneers in the early stages of the natural sciences. And just as in the natural sciences men had to develop the technique of controlled experiment and verified prophecy and to be willing to follow their findings wherever they might lead, far away from the beaten track of common sense if need be, so in the social sciences a means must be found to detect and discount bias in the observer himself, even though this lead him far from the comfortable road of his preconceived notions.

Let me develop these points a little more fully, one by one. In the first place, one and the same genetic outfit will give different effects in different environments. This is so elementary and fundamental a fact that it has often been neglected, by the geneticist as well as the eugenist. In the early literature of modern genetics, you will often find references to the inheritance of such and such characters. But characters are not and cannot be inherited, in the sense in which inheritance is used by the geneticist. What are inherited are genes, factors, genetic outfit. Any character whatsoever can only be a resultant between genes and environment. A given character expresses the interaction between a particular set of genes and a particular set of environmental conditions. Thus at the outset we see that the old question, whether nature or nurture is the more important, is meaningless. It is like the question 'When did you stop beating your wife?' in conveying implications which do not correspond with reality. In general, neither nature nor nurture can be more important, because they are both essential.

You will note that I say 'in general.' In particular cases, one or the other may be more important. Do not let us forget that all genetics depends on a study of differences. We take two individuals and strains, and ask what is the cause of the difference between them. By adjusting the conditions of our experiment, we find that this is due either to a difference in their environment or to a difference in their inherited constitution (or, often, to a difference in both). We then proceed further and find out, say, that the genetic difference is due primarily to a difference in a single gene. Let us suppose that the difference was one between red and white flowers in a plant. Then we say, if the white-flowered variety is the aberrant one, that we have discovered 'a gene for white flower-colour.' But this is a shorthand notation. Scientifically, we have discovered that the main cause of the difference in flower-colour is a difference in the nature of one unit-section of the chromosome outfit. That is why certain authors tried at one time to substitute the term *differential* for *gene*.

This rather tedious argument has two corollaries of immediate eugenic importance. The first is this. The more similar are the environments of two human samples, the more likely are the observable differences between the samples to be inheritable. The opposite is also true in theory, that the more similar are their genetic constitutions, the more likely are any differences to be environmental and non-inheritable; but in view of our ignorance of the precise genetic constitution of human populations, this has little applicability save in special cases like that of identical twins.

When on the other hand there are obvious differences in environment between two groups, there is a strong presumption that many of the differences between them will turn out to be mere modifications, which would disappear if the environmental conditions were equalized. This is not, of course, to say that the groups will not differ genetically also: merely that the observed differences in characters are not likely to be wholly inherited.

43

Genetics can provide interesting examples in which certain conditions of environment may wholly mask the effect of a gene. The classical case is that of *Primula sinensis*. In this plant there is a white-flowered variety and a red-flowered variety, which differ in regard to a single Mendelian gene. The white remains white at all temperatures; but the red variety when raised at a high temperature produces white flowers. A hot-house will thus entirely mask the perfectly real genetic difference between the two.

Even more significant for our purpose is the case of the mutant of the fruit-fly Drosophila known as *abnormal abdomen*, which depends on a single recessive gene. Flies characteristic of this strain show a bloated and rather abnormal-looking abdomen, with an extremely poor and irregular development of the normal pattern of black bands. However, all gradations from this to normal appearance are found. Analysis has shown that in moist conditions the character manifests itself fully, while in very dry conditions it does not show at all, and the flies resemble the normal wild type. Environment may thus wholly mask the effect of a pathological gene.

These cases introduce us to the further principle, somewhat paradoxical at first sight, that equalizing the environment may either increase or decrease the amount of visible variation in a group. In a universe containing both dry and moist conditions, a mixture of wild-type and abnormal-abdomen strains of fruit-fly would show a certain range of variation. Equalize the environment by making the universe wholly dry, and the population becomes uniform: but equalize it by making the universe wholly moist, and the variability is increased. Hogben has drawn attention to the importance of this point.[1]

In various biometric studies, it has been shown that unfavourable conditions tend to increase the degree of observed variation. But the attempt to erect this into a general principle cannot be correct, since the opposite may in other cases hold good. This is so, for instance, in our fruit-fly example—moist conditions, being associated with abundance and availability of food, are favourable; yet they here increase variability. A human example of the same sort, also cited by Hogben,[2] concerns education. 'The effect of extending to all classes of society the educational opportunities available to a small section of it would presumably be that of increasing variability with respect to educational attainment. The effect of depriving the more favoured of their special advantage would be to diminish variability in educational attainments.' Either policy would result in an equalization of environment; but equalizing it by making it more favourable would bring out genetic differences more fully, while the reverse process would mask them.

However, whether equalizing the environment will in this or that case increase or decrease variability, what differences then remain *must* be genetic in their origin. Thus without either equalizing or discounting the effect of environment, we cannot be sure what differences between groups are due to inheritance.

This point is of extreme importance in eugenics. For instance, it is well known that members of different social classes differ in their average of stature, physique and intelligence—all of them characters of the greatest evolu-

[1] Hogben, 1933, p. 115.   [2] *Op. cit.*, p. 115.

tionary importance. I take one or two examples from Carr-Saunders.[1] In a sample of fourteen-year-old Liverpool schoolboys, the boys from a secondary school were on the average no less than $6\frac{1}{2}$ inches (over 10 per cent.) taller than those from a council school in a poor neighbourhood; and differences in weight were equally marked. In a similar investigation in London, the 'mental age' (as determined by intelligence tests) of boys from a superior school was far above that of boys from a school in a poor neighbourhood. Twelve-year-olds from the superior school had a mental age nearly a year above their real age, while those from the poor school were a whole year behind their real age—a difference of 15 per cent.

Such differences are usually cited by eugenists as proof of a real and considerable difference in genetic qualities. For instance, Professor Carr-Saunders, after quoting these facts, concluded that 'so far as persons in this country are concerned, the mental differences which we observe, after stripping off the obvious acquirements in the form of knowledge of facts, habits, customs, manners, are due only in very small part to differences in the physical environment, and in a varying though never to a large degree to differences in the social environment, and for the greater part to inherited differences.' And he draws the same general conclusion with regard to the physical differences. Yet in the few years since Professor Carr-Saunders' book was written, this conclusion has become extremely unlikely. For recent work has shown that vitamins and other accessory food-factors have physical and mental effects far transcending what we originally thought possible.

[1] Carr-Saunders, 1926, pp. 97, 105, 126.

In the early years of vitamin research, attention was concentrated upon the definitely pathological states resulting from total or almost total deprivation. During the last ten years, it has been shown that moderate insufficiency of these accessory food-factors will result in retardation of growth, stunting, lack of physical and mental energy, and reduced resistance to infectious disease. Even boys who by all ordinary canons were regarded as in fine health and well above the average in physique were shown to benefit both in growth and in energy from the addition of extra milk to their diet. Sir John Orr has shown that the diet actually consumed by the poorer classes in Aberdeen, when given in unlimited quantities to rats, results in poor physique, small litters, low expectation of life, and proneness to numerous diseases, while the same diet with the addition of various vitamins and mineral salts kept the animals in tip-top condition.[1]

In the face of such facts, it is no longer legitimate to attribute the observed differences in physique and intelligence between social classes mainly to genetic factors. Genetic differences may of course exist; but the strong probability is that most of the differences are dependent on differences in nutrition. Further, the defective nutrition of the poorer classes is in part due to ignorance, but in a large measure to mere poverty. Until we equalize nutrition, or at least nutritional opportunity, we have no scientific or other right to assert the constitutional inferiority of any groups or classes because they are inferior in visible characters.

The extreme importance of applying accurate methods to the problem is shown by the results of recent investiga-

[1] Cited in Orr, 1936.

tions on twins. As is well known, twins may be identical or monozygotic, always of the same sex and both derived from the same fertilized egg; or they may be fraternal or dizygotic, either of like or unlike sex, and derived from two separate eggs. The former will have identical hereditary outfits, the latter will have hereditary outfits as different as those of members of the same family born at different times.

Yet it is true that in regard to intelligence tests, fraternal twins of like sex, though as we would expect they show considerably less resemblance than identical twins, are more alike than pairs of brothers or pairs of sisters born at different times. The additional similarity of their environment, due to their developing pre-natally and post-natally in more similar conditions, has assimilated them.

Writing of these results, Hogben [1] says that 'the ambiguity of the concept of causation' inherent in classical biometrical method has 'completely obscured the basic relativity of nature and nurture.' The difficulties inherent in multiple causation are here pithily summed up, and attention also drawn to the practical impossibility of comparing results obtained on material from different environments, and drawing genetic conclusions on their face value.

The same is true of racial differences. It seems clear that the very idea of race as applied to man is a misnomer under present conditions. Professor Gates has indeed recently asserted [2] that the major races (colour varieties) of man should be regarded as true species. This appears to me to be a grave error, arising from a failure to recognize the biological peculiarities of the human species, as

[1] *Op. cit.*, p. 95.   [2] Gates, 1934.

a species. These are due to man's mobility and his tradition, and result in a unique degree of variability combined with a failure of the usual tendencies to speciation: the incipient species are brought together again by migration and mingled by inter-crossing before any mutual infertility has been established.

While, however, modern genetics has shown that the term *race* only has meaning as a description of somewhat hypothetical past entities or as a goal for even more hypothetical future ideals,[1] yet it is of course clear that different ethnic groups (to use the most general and non-committal phrase) differ in genetic characters. Ethnic groups obviously differ in regard to the mean values, and also the range and type of variability, of physical characters such as stature, skin-colour, head- and nose-form, etc.: and these differences are obviously in the main genetic. There is every reason to believe that they will also be proved to differ genetically in intellectual and emotional characters, both quantitatively and qualitatively. But— and this cannot be too strongly emphasized—we at present have on this point no evidence whatever which can claim to be called scientific. Different ethnic groups have different languages and cultures; and the effects of the cultural environment are so powerful as to override and mask any genetic effects.

Most so-called racial traits are in point of fact national traits; and being so, they have no genetic or eugenic significance. In illustration we may think of those chief contributors to our own ancestry, the ancient Britons and the even less civilized Picts and Scots, of the Roman Imperial period. They were truly described by the

[1] Huxley and Haddon, 1935, especially chapter iv.

Romans as barbarians. It is obvious that the difference between their then barbaric state and our present level of relative civilization is due entirely or almost entirely to changes in tradition and culture, material and other. The genetic basis on which this progress has been erected was doubtless a good one; but the only way to see whether other ethnic groups now in the barbaric stage of culture, such as the Bantu, differ in their genetical quality is to give them a similar opportunity. To assert, as is often done, that the present barbarism of, say, the Bantu is proof of their genetic inferiority is a gross error of scientific method.

The dangers of pseudo-science in these matters are being illustrated on a large scale, and with the accompaniment of much individual suffering and political danger, in present-day Germany. The Nazi racial theory is a mere rationalization of Germanic nationalism on the one hand and anti-Semitism on the other. The German nation consists of Mendelian recombinations of every sort between Alpine, Nordic, and Mediterranean types. The theory of Nordic supremacy and initiative is not true even for their own population:[1] it is a myth like any other myth, on which the Nazis are basing a pseudo-religion of nationalism.

When we come to the distinction between Aryan and non-Aryan, the scientific error is magnified; for the very term Aryan denotes the speakers of a particular type of language, and can by definition have no genetic significance. As Max Müller himself wrote in a belated recantation:[2] 'To me an ethnologist who speaks of

[1] Huxley and Haddon, *op. cit.*, chapters iii, vi, vii, ix.
[2] Müller, M., 1888, p. 245.

50

Aryan race, Aryan blood, Aryan eyes and hair, is as great a sinner as a linguist who speaks of a dolichocephalic dictionary or a brachycephalic grammar.'

And when it comes to anti-Semitic measures, we must remember the elementary fact that the Jews are primarily a pseudo-national group, with a cultural and religious basis, not primarily an ethnic group with a genetic basis. Laws that lay down the amount of Jewish 'blood' permissible in an 'Aryan' have no quantitative basis and no real biological meaning.

The alleged inferiority of half-castes between whites and black or browns is another case in point. If the inferiority really exists, it is much more likely to be the product of the unfavourable social atmosphere in which they grow up than to any effect (which would be biologically very unusual) of their mixed heredity.

The results of intelligence tests applied to different ethnic stocks are for the same reason devoid of much value. Intelligence tests are now very efficient when applied to groups with similar social environment; they become progressively less significant as the difference in social environment increases. Again, we must equalize environment upwards—here mainly by providing better educational opportunity—before we can evaluate genetic difference.

To sum up, in the practical handling of every so-called racial problem, the error seems invariably to have been made of confusing genetic with cultural factors. The former alone could legitimately be called racial: but indeed the very term race disintegrates when subjected to modern genetic analysis. The net results are, firstly that it would be best to drop the term *race* from our vocabulary, both scientific and popular, as applied to man; and secondly, and more importantly for our present purpose, that until we equalize environmental opportunity, by making it more favourable for those now less favoured, we cannot make any pronouncements worthy to be called scientific as to genetic differences in mental characters between different ethnic stocks.

In point of fact, so-called racial problems on analysis invariably turn out to be problems of culture-contact. A dominant civilization or class desires to continue its dominance over a civilization or class of different colour or ethnic type, or is afraid that its values will be impaired if it tries to assimilate those of the other group. These are very real problems: but let us tackle them as such, sociologically, not on the basis of a false appeal to genetic science.

My readers must not imagine that I underrate the extent of the genetic differences between human groups, be they classes or so-called races. Man as an animal organism is unique in several respects: and one of them is his abnormal range of genetic variability. A reminder of the basic nature of this variability is given by the recent work of Blakeslee on taste and smell.[1] He finds that a number of substances which have a strong taste to some people, are not tasted at all by others. Thus the perceptual worlds inhabited by different human beings may be different on account of differences in genetic make-up. What far greater differences in conceptual worlds must be due to genetic differences in intelligence and emotion!

It would be most unlikely that this variability should be evenly distributed between different social and ethnic

[1] Blakeslee and Fox, 1932.

groups. As regards the latter, indeed, the existence of marked genetic differences in physical characters (as between yellow, black, white and brown) make it *prima facie* likely that differences in intelligence and temperament exist also. For instance, I regard it as wholly probable that true negroes have a slightly lower average intelligence than the whites or yellows. But neither this nor any other eugenically significant point of racial difference has yet been scientifically established.

Further, even were the probability to be established that some 'races' and some classes are genetically inferior to others as a fact, it seems certain, on the basis of our present knowledge, that the differences would be small differences in average level, and that the ranges would overlap over most of their extent—in other words, that a considerable proportion of the 'inferior' group would be actually superior to the lower half of the 'superior' group. Thus no really rapid eugenic progress would come of encouraging the reproduction of one class or race against another: striking and rapid eugenic results can be achieved only by a virtual elimination of the few lowest and truly degenerate types and a high multiplication-rate of the few highest and truly gifted types.

Do not let us forget that the over-believers in genetics are not the only ones in error. While the view that the observed differences in achievement and behaviour between class and class, nation and nation, are primarily genetic, is untrue and unscientific, the opposite view that opportunity is all, and that we need only work at reforming the social environment, is precisely as unscientific and untrue. For instance, up to the present, the theoretical foundations of Communism have prevented the Russians, in spite of their great achievements in pure genetics, from paying proper attention to eugenics. It now appears, however, that they are being confronted with problems, such as the rarity of qualities making for leadership and the inherent difference between a born leader and an ordinary man, which are bound to bring them face to face with eugenics. Here we see a social bias operating in the first place, to be checked later by the realities emerging from the social situation.

But while the enormous differences in social environment between nation and nation, class and class, normally mask any genetic differences that may exist, and, so far as visible and effective characters are concerned, largely override constitutional influences, it is clear that the social environment itself often exercises a selective influence which may be of great importance.

This selective influence is of two distinct kinds, which we may call pre-selective and post-selective. In simplest terms, pre-selective influences are those which attract certain types into an environment and discourage others. Post-selective influences are those which act on the population subjected to the environment, favouring certain evolutionary trends within it at the expense of others.

As a biological example, think of the assemblage of animals found living in caves. They are characterized broadly by poor eyesight and reliance on touch; the extreme types are eyeless, and pale or even colourless. It seems clear that both pre- and post-selective processes must have here been at work. Animals with somewhat poorly developed eyes, which shun the light and normally live in dark corners, will more frequently find themselves in caves, and will be likely to survive there better than more active and more 'normal' types. But once a cave-population is established, selection will be at work to encourage the development of tactile and other organs for use in the dark; it will also cease to operate strongly or at all on the genes responsible for keeping up full pigmentation or perfect eyes, so that these will in many cases degenerate.

A striking example is that concerning the selective influence of the environment provided by fields of cultivated cereals. As Vavilov has shown,[1] this favoured certain other plants, which could then flourish as what the farmer calls weeds, in association with the crop. Among these weeds were wild grasses related to the cultivated cereal; and in certain climatic conditions, these weeds flourished relative to the crop, became the dominant species, and were then used by man as the basis for a new crop-plant.

Just as cultivation of one crop-plant here provided the basis for the later development of another, so the social environment appropriate to one stage of human culture gives opportunities for the expression of human traits which may be destined to become dominant at a later stage. The eliciting effect of environment is in both cases essential.

The United States furnishes a classical human example. Pre-selection was at work on the pioneers. The human cargo of the *Mayflower* was certainly not a random sample of the English population. Religious zeal, independence of character, perhaps a tendency to fanaticism, together with courage, must have been above the average among the leaders, and probably in the whole band. The early

[1] Vavilov, 1926.

settlers in Virginia and Carolina were pre-selected on other lines, though some of the characters involved were the same. After the first settlements were made, further immigrants until near the end of the nineteenth century were pre-selected for restlessness, initiative, adventurousness, and the qualities making up the pioneer spirit. The easily contented, the unadventurous and the timid, were pre-selected to remain behind. So, too, on the average, must have been those with artistic, philosophic, literary, or mathematical gifts. Even if the mean differences between those who went and those who stayed were not large, they must have been significant.

Once the immigrants were established in the country, selection continued. This post-selection, so long as there was an open physical frontier to the west, and an open economic frontier in the more settled regions, must on the whole have encouraged and discouraged the same qualities favoured by pre-selection: in addition, assertiveness and ambition were encouraged in the acute phase of 'rugged individualism,' while artistic and literary endowment still were at a discount. Of course the direct moulding effect of the social environment must have acted in the same sense as its selective effect; so that here again genetic differences would be masked. Yet on deductive grounds we can be certain that the selective effect would be at work, and would produce genetic differences: the only question is the extent of those differences.

Whenever there are mass-movements of population, we are sure to find similar selective effects. The difference between the southern Irish in America and in Ireland strikes every observer: we can hardly doubt that it is due in part (though doubtless not entirely) to a sifting of more from less adventurous types. And the same holds true of the obvious differences between rural and urban population in a country like our own. Whatever be the effect of country life and labour on a man's temperament, we can be sure that those who stayed behind were not as a group genetically identical with those who ventured away into the new life of the towns.

One of the profoundest selective influences ever brought to bear on the human population of the globe must have been that exerted by the invention and spread of agriculture, as has been well stressed by Ellsworth Huntington.[1]

A settled agricultural civilization demands qualities in its members very different from those demanded by a nomadic or a hunting existence. Agriculture demands constant application; the pastoral life is freer, and hunting demands rather occasional outbursts of maximum energy. Agriculture demands foresight and the sacrificing of present comfort to future benefit; in the more primitive modes of life, activity springs more immediately from events. Agriculture demands steady routine in one spot; the nomad and the hunter can profitably indulge the spirit of restlessness.

Inevitably, it would seem, where early agricultural civilizations were growing up, there must have been a considerable drift of the more restless types out of them into the nomad and hunting cultures on their borders; and quite possibly there occurred also a converse movement inwards of more calculating and less restless types.

Further, once the agricultural civilizations were well established, a dominant class always appeared whose in-

[1] Huntington, 1928, chapter xiv.

57

terests were bound up with the success of the group. The members of this class therefore were bound to encourage submissiveness and industry in the cultivators of the soil: and although much was in fact accomplished by purely environmental means, such as religion and law, there must again have been a selective effect, so that the level of inherent docility would tend to rise in the peasant class. Thus in the long run, agriculture must have markedly increased the selective value of tendencies making for the humdrum hard-working human virtues, and in its secondary effects, as in the birth of the merchant class and in other ways, have encouraged foresight and calculation.

Class differences in environment may also be selective. It seems to be established that the inhabitants of our industrial towns are on the average smaller and darker than those of the rural and small-town population.[1] It may well be that there is a selection against tall and therefore rapidly-growing types on account of the unfavourable diet and living conditions of the slum dweller, since slow growth makes less demands upon a low supply of vitamins: and that tall stature is on the whole correlated with fair complexion. But whatever the cause, the fact remains, and can only be due to selection of some sort.

A recent report of the Industrial Health Research Board[2] points out that in the early part of the industrial era, the demand in factories was for men of good physique irrespective of build, while appearance or presence counted for more in shops and offices. This may have laid the basis for the observed fact that manual workers average

[1] Carr-Saunders, 1926, pp. 195-6.
[2] Ind. Health Res. Bd. Rept., 1935.

shorter than blackcoated workers, but are stronger. It is quite likely that with the recent introduction of more automatic machinery, which does not demand strength, the type of selection will alter, and the factory workers come to lose their better physique.

The same report mentions that a fairly large sample of unemployed, contrasted with a large sample of employed men, were slightly less tall and distinctly less strong. These were mainly men who would be the first to be turned off and the last to be taken on, so that selection seems definitely to have been at work here.

This brings up the large and important question of the selective effect of the class system as a whole in an industrial capitalist society. As many writers have pointed out, in so far as there is any ladder of opportunity by which men may rise or sink in the social scale, there must be some selective action. With the passage of time, more failures will accumulate in the lower strata, while the upper strata will collect a higher percentage of successful types.

This would be good eugenically speaking *if* success were synonymous with ultimate biological and human values, or even partially correlated with them; *and if* the upper strata were reproducing faster than the lower. However, we know that reproduction shows the reverse trend, and it is by no means certain that the equation of success with desirable qualities is anything more than a naïve rationalization.

Before, however, we discuss this further, let us look at some other effects of our pattern of class-system. Once we begin to reflect, we see that certain qualities are more favoured, often much more favoured, in some classes than in others. For instance, initiative and independence have less opportunity among unskilled labourers than elsewhere. Inclinations to art, science, or mathematics will be more favoured in the upper and upper-middle classes than elsewhere. The result may be truly selective, for instance by encouraging types genetically above the average in submissiveness among the proletariat. For the most part, however, it is likely merely to mask genetic differences. The fact that an undue proportion of artists, writers and scientists spring from the upper strata of society would then not mean that these strata were proportionately well endowed by heredity—merely that in the rest of society the Darwins and the Einsteins, like the Miltons, were mute and inglorious.

Two interesting recent studies by Gray and Moshinsky[1] confirm and extend this conclusion. They show, on the basis of intelligence tests, and without discounting any of the superior performance of upper-class children as partly due to their superior environment, that our present educational system leaves vast reservoirs of innate intelligence untrained in the children from lower social strata. Contrary to usual belief, only about a third of the children whose performance is in the top thousandth, come from the higher social and the professional classes, while wage-earners contribute 50 per cent. of these children of 'exceptional intelligence.' Thus our society is not utilizing the innate intelligence of its members as it might, nor does the system give adequate opportunity for intelligence to rise.

Again, highly-strung types are less likely to achieve success in the lower economic strata, more likely to become

[1] Gray and Moshinsky, 1935, *a* and *b*.

neurotic or insane. People from the lower-middle and working classes who are apparently mentally deficient or abnormal have often reached their unfortunate condition because they have not had either the care or the opportunities for self-expression which would have been available in a more generous social environment.

Let us also remember that society as a whole can have a similar effect. Those same types which in Siberian tribes would achieve prestige and power as shamans and medicine-men, or in the medieval world would have become candidates for sainthood, would here and to-day often find their way into asylums.

This brings us on to a biological point whose importance has not always been realized. It is that selection is theoretically meaningless and practically without value except in relation to a particular environment. The practical implications are both the easiest to grasp and the more important for our purpose. In breeding domestic animals, as Hammond of Cambridge has so well stressed,[1] selection and breeding will not produce the desired results so quickly, and may not produce them at all, if they are conducted in the unreal environment of an academic breeding station where optimum conditions are provided. They should be conducted in an environment similar to that in which the animals are destined to be used.

An extreme illustration of this is provided by cattle. In various parts of tropical Africa, the semi-arid bush country provides but scanty nutriment, and erosion has led to various mineral deficiencies. The native cattle are scrubby little beasts, no bigger than ponies, yielding not more than two gallons of milk a day, and growing so

[1] Hammond, 1932 (pp. 251-2), 1935.

slowly that they do not breed until four to five years old.
Contrasted with cows of a good modern British milking
breed, which are double the size, give up to nine gallons
of milk daily, and breed at two to three years of age, they
are, you would say, very inefficient bits of biological machinery. Yet if we try to introduce European breeds into
such areas, they are a complete failure. They make demands which are greater than can be met by the environment. And it is they which suffer; they become stunted,
rickety or otherwise diseased, and cannot hold their own
in competition with the native breeds. The native stock
will stand a little genetic grading up in present conditions;
but the only chance for radical improvement is to begin
with improvement of the environment—the provision of
mineral fertilizers, salt-licks, watering facilities, and so
on—and then practise genetic selection to keep pace with
the environmental change.

Another example is that of Stapledon's remarkable
work on moorland grazings.[1] By his methods, rough hill
grazings can be converted into real pastures, capable of
carrying many more sheep, and carrying them all the year
round instead of only in the summer. But this can only
be done by the simultaneous transformation of the environment and of the herbage stocks. The environmental
transformation consists in breaking up the soil, followed
by the application of certain mineral fertilizers. The
genetic transformation consists first in the destruction of
the original plant covering, brought about by the break-
ing-up of the soil, followed by the sowing of more nutri-
tious pasture grasses and clovers. Furthermore, the new
plants must be of special strains, previously bred and

[1] Stapledon, 1935.

selected to resist the climatic conditions of the higher alti-
tudes; the ordinary strains that give good lowland pastures will not maintain themselves.

Precisely the same considerations apply to the improvement of man. Our schemes for improving the genetic
qualities of the nation or the species are meaningless
except in relation to some particular environment, present
or future. Our eugenic ideals will be different according
as we relate them to a slave order or a feudal order of
things, a primitive industrial or a leisure order, a this-
worldly or an other-worldly order, a capitalist or a socialist
order, a militarist or a peaceful internationalist order.
Even if we imagine we are working to absolute genetic
standards, we are in reality thinking of them, albeit unconsciously, in relation to some ideal environment of the
future, or to the needs and realities of the present social
environment, or, very frequently, to our bias and *a priori*
views about this present environment and how in our
opinion it ought to be changed. If we were really treating
of absolute genetic standards, we should have deserted
reality for a metaphysical vacuum, and our reasoning and
deductions would have even less value than a discussion
of, say, eugenics in heaven. (Even in this latter case, be
it noted, the discussion would inevitably be related to the
environment which we supposed was awaiting us in the
next world!)

Now all such unconscious thinking is inevitably irrational or at best non-rational: if it had been submitted
to the light of reason, it would no longer be unconscious.
So that a prime task before eugenists is the reasoned
formulation of their views on the environment to which
their schemes of genetic betterment are to be related.

There are, it seems to me, three possible courses to be pursued. Either we may accept as given our present type of social environment, and adjust our eugenic programme to it. In practice we shall of course be forced to take a dynamic instead of a purely static point of view, and consider the trends of change within that environment, while assuming that the social system will not be fundamentally altered. Or, going to the opposite extreme, we may assume an ideal social environment—more scientifically, one which is the optimum we can imagine—and plan our eugenic measures in relation to that, piously hoping that in the long run social change will adjust itself to our ideal or to whatever measure of genetic change we may have brought about. Or finally we may envisage, as in Stapledon's grassland work, a joint attack upon environment and germ-plasm. Assuming that we have some measure of control over the social environment, we shall adjust our genetic programme to that programme of environmental change which represents, both in direction and tempo, a happy mean between the ideal and the immediately practical, between what we should like and what we are likely to get.

Let us look at these three alternatives and their implications. First, however, it should be pointed out that they are not wholly alternative to each other. Even if we take the environment for granted, we must face the fact of social change and attempt to meet it eugenically; and in so doing we shall find it difficult to avoid giving some play to our wishes, fears, and hopes. Even if we assume an optimum environment, our ideal must be based on our conscious or unconscious estimate of what developments are inherently possible to the present system. We shall, in effect, be attempting to forecast social improvement, and we shall prove, we can be sure, as widely out in our forecasts as if we were attempting to prophesy the future of scientific discovery. And the third method, of necessity, must take into account both the hard fact of the present and the ideal of wishes and hopes for the future.

None the less, there are real differences between the three; and we must consider these more in detail.

To accept the continuance of the present type of social environment as essentially given (whether given in reality or in our hopes and fears will make no difference to our eugenic plans) means, I take it, two main things. It means that we must plan for a capitalist class-system, and for a nationalist system. We accept the division of society into economic strata, with large differences in standard of living, outlook, and opportunity between the different classes; and we accept all the implications of the principle that the earning of a return on capital is the primary aim and duty of business and finance, whatever minor modifications and regulations may be found desirable or opportune. We accept individualist competition, however much toned down in practice, as essential. Further, we accept the division of the world into nationalist states, which, however their sovereignty and independence of action may be modified or curtailed by international agreements, will be competing as well as co-operating with each other, and must in certain eventualities be prepared to resort to war.

Coming down to results, we accept the economic and spiritual frustrations of the system also—that is to say, we accept the necessity of some degree of unemployment, for without that there can be no approach to a free market for labour; we accept the continuance of trade cycles of boom

E   65

and slump, even though they may be toned down in amplitude. We accept the need for restriction of output whenever surplus interferes with profit. We accept the existence of a cheap supply of unskilled and semi-skilled workers; we accept the need for man-power in case of war.

If so, then we must plan our eugenic policy along some such lines as the following:

First comes the prevention of dysgenic effects. The upper economic classes are presumably slightly better endowed with ability—at least with ability to succeed in our social system—yet are not reproducing fast enough to replace themselves, either absolutely or as a percentage of the total population. We must therefore try to remedy this state of affairs, by pious exhortation and appeals to patriotism, or by the more tangible methods of family allowances, cheaper education, or income-tax rebates for children. The lowest strata, allegedly less well-endowed genetically, are reproducing relatively too fast. Therefore birth-control methods must be taught them; they must not have too easy access to relief or hospital treatment lest the removal of the last check on natural selection should make it too easy for children to be produced or to survive; long unemployment should be a ground for sterilization, or at least relief should be contingent upon no further children being brought into the world; and so on. That is to say, much of our eugenic programme will be curative and remedial merely, instead of preventive and constructive.

Then, in systems like the present, man-power is important, and for man-power, quantity of population above a certain minimum qualitative standard is as essential as higher quality; and if the two conflict, quantity supply must not be interfered with. For qualitative change, a dual standard is indicated—docility and industrious submissiveness in the lower majority; intelligence, leadership and strength of character in the upper few. Since a high degree of intellect and imagination, of scientific and artistic ability and other qualities, cannot be adequately expressed or utilized, under any system resembling the present, in the great majority of the lower strata, it is useless to plan for their genetic increase in these strata. Indeed, it is more than useless, it is dangerous; for the frustration of inherent capacity leads to discontent and revolution in some men, to neurosis and inefficiency in others. The case is strictly analogous to that of cattle in Africa; in an unfavourable environment, too drastic genetic improvement is worse than none.

Next we come to planning for an ideal or optimum environment. An obvious difficulty here is that the various optima conceived by different minds, or groups of minds, will be so different as to be irreconcilable. Putting this on one side, however, it is I think possible to state the sort of optimum which would commend itself to the mass of what we may call 'men of goodwill.' It would, I take it, be a social environment which gave the opportunity, first of work which was not excessive, which was felt to be useful, and whose rewards would provide not only the necessities but a reasonable supply of the comforts and amenities of life: secondly, of a reasonable amount of leisure: thirdly, the opportunity to everyone of expressing whatever gifts of body and mind they might possess, in athletics or sport; in art, science or literature, passive or actively enjoyed; in travel or politics, in individual hobbies or in social service.

If so, then we should plan a eugenic programme with a single and very high standard. We should aim at a high level of inherent physical fitness, endurance and general intelligence; and we should encourage the breeding of special talent of any and every sort, for mathematical as much as for business success, artistic as much as administrative. We should realize that, if we succeeded, our genetic results would over a great range of the population be out of harmony with their social surroundings, and would either be wasted or lead to friction and discontent, or might express themselves in characters such as neurosis or a sense of maladjustment which would represent a lower level than that from which we started. For ultimate success we should rely on creating a demand for changing the environment towards our optimum. The supply of genetic types which could only reach proper expression in such an environment would help to create the demand; the friction and discontent would add themselves to the forces of change.

It will, however, by now have become clear that neither of these approaches is so satisfactory as the third. Indeed, neither is methodologically sound. If the aim of eugenics be to control the evolution of the human species and guide it in a desirable direction, and if the genetic selection should always be practised in relation to an appropriate environment, then it is an unscientific and wasteful procedure not to attempt to control environment at the same time as genetic quality. Science is simultaneously both theory and practice, both knowledge and control. For the applied science of eugenics to neglect the environment is a source both of confusion and of practical weakness. I would go further: I would say that we cannot succeed

68

in achieving anything in the nature of adequate positive eugenics unless we attempt the control of the social environment simultaneously with the control of the human germ-plasm, any more than Stapledon could have improved his rough mountain grazings save by a similar double attack.

Let us then look more in detail into this third or dual method of approach. It has two facets, theoretical and practical. On the theoretical side, we shall only progress in our attempt to disentangle the effects of nature from those of nurture in so far as we follow the footsteps of the geneticist and equalize environment. We shall never be able to do this in the same radical way as the pure scientist, by testing out a whole range of controlled and equalized environments on selected stocks. We must therefore concentrate on producing a single equalized environment; and this clearly should be one as favourable as possible to the expression of the genetic qualities that we think desirable. Equally clearly, this should include the following items. A marked raising of the standard of diet for the great majority of the population, until all should be provided both with adequate calories and adequate accessory factors; provision of facilities for healthy exercise and recreation; and upward equalization of educational opportunity. The further we move in this direction, the more readily shall we be able to distinguish inherent physical and mental defects from environmental stunting and frustration; the higher we raise the average, the more certain shall we be that physical or mental performance above the average is dependent upon genetic endowment and therefore provides the raw material for positive eugenics. Not only this, but we know from various sources that raising the standard of life among the poorest classes almost invariably results in a lowering of their fertility. In so far, therefore, as differential class-fertility exists, raising the environmental level will reduce any dysgenic effects which it may now have.

Returning, however, to the more important aspect of the eugenic knowledge to be gained by levelling up the social environment, I anticipate that at the bottom, the social problem group, though shrinking in size, will be left, clearly marked out by its inadequate performance in the new and favourable conditions, as a well-defined target for measures of negative eugenics such as segregation and sterilization; and that minor targets of the same nature will emerge out of the present fog, in the shape of nests of defective germ-plasm inspissated by assortative mating and inbreeding, such as have been imaginatively glimpsed by Lidbetter and others. I further anticipate that the professional classes will reveal themselves as a reservoir of superior germ-plasm, of high average level notably in regard to intelligence, and therefore will serve as a foundation-stone for experiments in positive eugenics. But I anticipate that society will tap large resources of high ability that are at present unutilized, thus facilitating the social promotion of at least certain fitter elements; and without social promotion we cannot proceed to reproductive encouragement. This is the scientific ideal at which we should aim. Like many other ideals, we shall not achieve it; but any approach to it will help us towards a more certain knowledge.

Science, however, is control as well as knowledge; and new practice may advance theory as much as new theory lay the basis for practice. This is especially true for the social sciences, where, as we have seen, rigorously controlled experiment, on the pattern of pure physics or physiology, is impossible, and problems must frequently be solved *ambulando*. We make a partial experiment which is simultaneously pure and applied science. The experiment is both an attempt to gain knowledge and an effort to realize a wish, a desired control. It is planned, like more crucial experiments in the natural sciences, to verify deductions from known facts. In so far as the desired end is attained, the deductions are verified and knowledge is increased: and even if the control is not attained, knowledge is increased, though not to the same extent.

This more empirical mode of attack must also be used in eugenics. We must attempt to control the change of social environment and at the same time to control the change of human germ-plasm, along lines which appear likely to yield tangible and desirable results. It is the results which interest us. Admirable germ-plasm unable to realize itself owing to unfavourable conditions does not interest us: nor do the most alluring social conditions, if they permit or encourage the deterioration of the germ-plasm. Thus the two attacks must be planned in relation to each other, and also in relation to practicability.

When we think along these lines, we shall find, I believe, that a system such as ours, a competitive and individualist system based on private capitalism and public nationalism, is of its nature and essence dysgenic. It is dysgenic both in the immediate respect of failing to utilize existing reservoirs of valuable genes, and also in the long-range tasks of failing to increase them, failing to trap and encourage favourable mutations, and failing to eliminate harmful mutations.

Under our social system, the full stature or physique of the very large majority of the people is not allowed to express itself; neither are the full genetic potentialities of health permitted to appear except in a small fraction of the whole, with a consequent social waste of energy and time, not to mention a waste of individual happiness which is formidable in extent; and finally, innate high ability is encouraged or utilized only with extreme inadequacy. For the first two wastes, ignorance is partly responsible, but in the lower economic strata, poverty is the chief cause. For the last, our inadequate educational system is chiefly responsible.

Then R. A. Fisher has brilliantly and devastatingly shown [1] the relentless way in which such a system as ours promotes both infertility and certain types of talent, and in so doing ties together the genetic factors responsible. In the course of the generations genes making for small families become increasingly bound up with those making for social and economic success; and conversely those making for social and economic failure become bound up with those making for high reproduction rates. Eugenically speaking our system is characterized by the social promotion of infertility and the excess fertility of social failure.

If this be true, then so long as we cling to a system of this type, the most we can hope to do is to palliate its effects as best we may, by extending birth-control facilities downwards, instituting graded systems of family allowances, providing for sterilization here and financial relief for children there. But even if we thus reduce the distortion we cannot hope to change its sign.

[1] Fisher, 1930, chapter xi.

Then, in so far as our system remains nationalist, the demand for man-power and quantity will continue to interfere with the higher aim of quality. Furthermore, modern war itself is dysgenic. This has often been pointed out as regards its direct effects. It appears, however, also to hold for its indirect effects; many among the more imaginative and sensitive types are to-day restricting their families, sometimes to zero, because they feel that they cannot bear to bring children into a world exposed to such a constant risk of war and chaos.

As eugenists we must therefore aim at transforming the social system. There may of course be those amongst our ranks who prefer the not disagreeable rôle of a Jeremiah darkly prophesying gloom to settling down at the more prosaic job of constructive work. But as a body, we shall wish, I take it, to see at least the possibility of our dreams coming true.

What sort of practical changes, then, should we as eugenists try to encourage in the social and economic system? In the first place—what we have already noted as desirable on theoretical grounds—the equalizing of environment in an upward direction. For this, by permitting of more definite knowledge as to the genetic constitution of different classes and types, will at once give us more certainty in any eugenic selection, negative or positive, upon which we may embark. And secondly, we must aim at the abandonment of the idea of national sovereign states, and the subordination of national disputes to international organization and supernational power.

But we need something more radical than this—we must try to find a pattern of economic and communal life which will not be inherently dysgenic; and we must also try to find a pattern of family and reproductive life which will permit of more rapid and constructive eugenics.

On the first point, it seems clear that the individualist scramble for social and financial promotion should be dethroned from its present position as main incentive in life, and that we must try to raise the power of group-incentives. Group-incentives are powerful in tribal existence, and have been powerful in many historical civilizations, such as the old Japanese. What interests us chiefly, however, is to find that they have been to a large extent effective in replacing individualist money incentives, or at least diminishing their relative social importance, in several modern States, notably Germany and the U.S.S.R.

It is not for a biologist to discuss the purely social merits of different political philosophies: but he may be allowed to point out that not all group-incentives are equally valuable from the eugenic standpoint. Those of Nazi Germany, for instance, presuppose an intensification of nationalist feeling and activity instead of their diminution: and this, we have concluded, is actually anti-eugenic. It may of course be urged that it is in its immediate effect eugenic; and there will be many to uphold the value of the eugenic measures recently adopted in Germany under the stimulus of National-Socialist ideas and emotions, even if some of them be crude and unscientific. But if in the long run it leads to over-population and war, it is essentially dysgenic, and in matters of evolution we must, I think, take the long view.

Further, if the social environment is such as to give satisfaction to the possessors of social traits such as altruism, readiness to co-operate, sensitiveness, sympathetic enthusiasm, and so forth, instead of, as now, putting a premium on many antisocial traits such as egoism, low cunning, insensitiveness, and ruthless concentration, we could begin to frame eugenic measures for encouraging the spread of genes for such social virtues. At the moment this is hardly possible, for the expression of such genes is so often inhibited or masked by the effects of the environment. This is a human illustration of Hammond's general principle, that breeding and selection for a given type can only be efficiently carried out in an environment favouring the fullest development of the type.

There is no doubt that genetic differences of temperament, including tendencies to social or antisocial action, to co-operation or individualism, do exist, nor that they could be bred for in man as man has bred for tameness and other temperamental traits in many domestic animals; and it is extremely important to do so. If we do not, society will be continuously in danger from the antisocial tendencies of its members.

Just as the basic structure of our present social system is essentially dysgenic, so we may say that the genetic composition of our present population is largely and perhaps essentially antisocial. Thus both environmentally and genetically the present state of mankind is unstable, at war with itself.

Another important point to remember, especially in these days when the worship of the State is imposing a mass-production ideal of human nature, is the fact and the significance of human variability. The variability of man, due to recombination between divergent types that have failed to become separated as species, is greater than that of any wild animal. And the extreme variants thrown up by the constant operation of this genetic kaleidoscope have proved to be of the utmost importance for the material and spiritual progress of civilization. Whatever bias or prejudice may beset the individual eugenist, eugenics as a whole must certainly make the encouragement of diversity one of its main principles. But here again the environment comes in. If extreme types are to be produced, especially gifted for art, science, contemplation, exploration, they must not be wasted. The social system must provide niches for them.

As a special and important special case of providing for variability, there are the needs of the educational profession. At the moment, this social category seems definitely selective in that it attracts and encourages men and women of an intellectualist and academic type. This is partly because there are not sufficient outlets provided elsewhere in our social system for such types, partly because the educational profession as at present constituted does not provide sufficient attraction for contrasted types. This restriction of type among those responsible for the upbringing of the next generation cannot be satisfactory, and an altered status for the educational profession so that its genetic basis is broadened is an important task for social biology, and, since it involves genetics, legitimately part of the eugenic movement.

Still more important for the comparatively immediate future is the relation of the dominant group-incentive to reproductive morality, law, and practice. We all know that certain schools of Christian thought to-day are opposed on grounds of religious principle to birth-control, that indispensable tool of eugenics as well as of rational control of population, and even to the very notion of eugenics itself. But even if this opposition could be overcome, there would remain in this field grave obstacles, both to the spread of the eugenic idea and to the rate of its progress in practice. These are the prevailing individualist attitude to marriage, and the conception, based on this and on the long religious tradition of the West, of the subordination of personal love to procreation. The two influences together prevent us collectively from grasping the implications of the recent advances in science and technique which now make it possible to separate the individual from the social side of sex and reproduction. Yet it is precisely and solely this separation that would make real eugenics practicable, by allowing a rate of progress yielding tangible encouragement in a reasonable time, generation by generation.

The recent invention of efficient methods on the one hand of birth-control and on the other of artificial insemination have brought man to a stage at which the separation of sexual and reproductive functions could be used for eugenic purposes. But it is of real interest to note that these inventions represent merely the last steps in an evolutionary process which started long before man ever existed.

In lower mammals, the existence of limited breeding seasons, and, during these, the restriction of mating to the oestrous phase in the female's reproductive cycle, do in fact link sexual behaviour firmly with reproduction. But in the great primate stock to which we belong, a new trend early becomes apparent. Breeding seasons are less definite, and mating may occur at any time during the female cycle, so that most acts of union are in fact and of necessity infertile, without reproductive consequences. This trend becomes more marked as we ascend the evolutionary scale, and culminates in man. In civilized man, the faint traces of a breeding season apparent in certain primitive ethnic stocks have wholly disappeared, and there is no greater readiness to mate during the short period when alone conception is possible than at most other times of the female cycle.[1]

This has already led in point of fact to the widespread separation of the personal function of sexual union from its racial consequences, of love from reproduction. It is true that some persons and bodies on theological or metaphysical grounds either ostrich-like deny the existence of this separation, or assert that it ought not to be practised; but this does not alter the fact.

The perfection of birth-control technique has made the separation more effective; and the still more recent technique of artificial insemination has opened up new horizons, by making it possible to provide different objects for the two functions. It is now open to man and woman to consummate the sexual function with those they love, but to fulfil the reproductive function with those whom on perhaps quite other grounds they admire.

This consequence is the opportunity of eugenics. But the opportunity cannot yet be grasped. It is first necessary to overcome the bitter opposition to it on dogmatic theological and moral grounds, and the widespread popular shrinking from it, based on vague but powerful feelings, on the ground that it is unnatural.

We need a new attitude to these problems, an attitude which for want of another term we may still call religious. We need to replace the present attitude fostered by established religions by a new but equally potent attitude.

As regards the sense of salvation, we need to substitute

<hr>

[1] Zuckerman, 1932, p. 73 f.

social salvation for individual salvation; and as regards the need of some escape-mechanism from the pressure of present difficulty, we need to substitute the real possibility of evolutionary progress for other-worldly phantasies. Once this possibility of true human progress, both social and genetic, is generally apprehended, and the social system remodelled so that individual success does not conflict with communal welfare, and self-expression and personal satisfaction can be largely achieved in serving society, then sex and reproduction can take their due places as individual and social functions respectively. Gone will be many of the conflicts inherent in present-day marriage: any sacrifice involved in parenthood will be made on the altar of the race, and in the knowledge that it will be acceptable. Those who wish to pursue further the possibilities of such a step should consult Mr Brewer's recent article on Eutelegenesis [1] and Professor Muller's book *Out of the Night*.[2] Here it must suffice to point out that unless we alter the social framework of law and ideas so as to make possible the divorce between sex and reproduction, or if you prefer it between the individual and the social sides of our sexual functions, our efforts at evolutionary improvement will remain mere tinkering, no more deserving the proud title of eugenics than does the mending of saucepans deserve to be called engineering.

That consummation, you will perhaps say, is impossibly remote from our imperfect present, hardly to be affected by any of our little strivings to-day. That may be so: but I am not so sure. Let us remember that modern science is a mere three centuries old: yet it has already achieved changes in outlook that are of comparable magnitude.

[1] Brewer, H., 1935.   [2] Muller, H. J., 1935.

Biological science is only now attaining its maturity, and the social sciences are mere infants. Looked at in the long perspective of evolution, the present phase of human activity is one of transition between that of acceptance and that of control of destiny, between magic and science, between unconsciously-nurtured phantasy and consciously-faced reason. It is, in the sense of the word used in physics, a critical phase: and being so, it cannot be either stable or long-enduring.

It is to my mind not only permissible but highly desirable to look far ahead. Otherwise we are in danger of mistaking for our eugenic ideal a mere glorification of our prejudices and our subjective wish-fulfilments. It is not eugenics but left-wing politics if we merely talk of favouring the survival and reproduction of the proletariat at the expense of the bourgeoisie. It is not eugenics but right-wing politics if we merely talk of favouring the breeding of the upper classes of our present social system at the expense of the lower. It is not eugenics but nationalist and imperialist politics if we speak in such terms as subject races or miscegenation. Our conclusions in any particular case *may* be on balance eugenically correct (though the correlation between broad social or ethnic divisions and genetic values can never be high), yet they will not be based primarily upon eugenic considerations, but upon social or national bias. The public-school ideal, or that of the working-class movement, or that of colonial imperialism, may be good ideals; but they are not eugenic ideals.

Before concluding, I should like to draw attention to one eugenically important consequence of recent progress in pure genetics. In all organisms so far investigated, deleterious mutations far outnumber useful ones. There is an inherent tendency for the hereditary constitution to degrade itself. That man shares this tendency we can be sure, not only from analogy but on the all-too-obvious evidence provided by the high incidence in 'civilized' populations of defects, both mental and physical, of genetic origin.

In wild animals and plants, this tendency is either reversed or at least held in check by the operation of natural selection, which here again proves itself to be, in R. A. Fisher's words, a mechanism capable of generating high degrees of improbability. In domestic animals and plants, the same result is achieved by our artificial selection. But in civilized human communities of our present type, the elimination of defect by natural selection is largely (though of course by no means wholly) rendered inoperative by medicine, charity, and the social services; while, as we have seen, there is no selection encouraging favourable variations. The net result is that many deleterious mutations can and do survive, and the tendency to degradation of the germ-plasm can manifest itself.

To-day, thanks to the last fifteen years' work in pure science, we can be sure of this alarming fact, whereas previously it was only a vague surmise.[1] Humanity will gradually destroy itself from within, will decay in its very core and essence, if this slow but relentless process is not checked. Here again, dealing with defectives in the present system can be at best a palliative. We must be able to pick out the genetically inferior stocks with more certainty, and we must set in motion counter-forces making for faster reproduction of superior stocks, if we are to reverse or even arrest the trend. And neither of these,

[1] Muller, H. J., 1935.

as we have seen, is possible without an alteration of social system.

Whether or not I have been asking you to accompany me too far into the visionary future, I will end this essay with a very concrete suggestion for the present, backed by a warning from the immediate past.

Twenty-five years ago, when I had just taken my degree, the field of heredity was still a battle-field. The Mendelians and the Biometricians were disputing for its possession, and in the heat of the struggle little mercy was shown by either side to the other. In the last dozen years or so, however, the apparent conflict of principle has been shown not to exist, and now, thanks to the work of such men as R. A. Fisher and J. B. S. Haldane, we realize that the two methods of approach are complementary, and that certain important problems can only be solved by their simultaneous employment.

The present position of eugenists appears to me to be closely parallel with the position of the Mendelians a quarter of a century ago. They find themselves in apparent conflict with the environmentalists and the protagonists of social reform. Speaking broadly, the field of human improvement is a battle-field between Eugenists and Sociologists, and the battle is often as violent as that between the Mendelians and Biometricians—or between Swift's Big-endians and Little-endians. In my opinion, it is also as unreal and useless. We eugenists must no longer think of the social environment only in its possible dysgenic or non-eugenic effects, but must study it as an indispensable ally. Changes in social environment are needed both for the adequate expression of eugenic progress, and as a means for its realization.

The next step for eugenics is, as I urged at the beginning of this essay, a methodological one. We eugenists must familiarize ourselves with the outlook and the concepts of sociology, with the technique and practice of social reform; for they are an indispensable part of the machinery we need to realize our aims.

REFERENCES

Blakeslee, A. F., and Fox, A. L. 1932. 'Our different taste worlds.' *J. Hered.*, *23*.

Brewer, Herbert. 1935. 'Eutelegenesis,' *Eugenics Review*, *27*, 121.

Carr-Saunders, A. M. 1926. *Eugenics*. Home University Library. Williams & Norgate. London.

Fisher, R. A. 1930. *The Genetical Basis of Natural Selection*. Clarendon Press. Oxford.

Gates, R. R. 1934. 'Racial and Social Problems in the Light of Heredity,' *Population*, *1* (2).

Gray, J. L., and Moshinsky, P. 1935. (*a*) 'Ability and Opportunity in English Education,' *Sociological Review*, 27 (2), 1935. (*b*) 'Ability and Educational Opportunity in Relation to Parental Occupation,' *Sociological Review*, *27* (3), 1935.

Hammond, J. 1932. *Growth and Development of Mutton Qualities in the Sheep*. Oliver & Boyd. Edinburgh.

Hammond, J. 1935. 'Inheritance of Productivity in Farm Livestock. I. Meat,' *Empire Jour. Exper. Agric.*, *3*, 1.

Hogben, L. T. 1933. *Nature and Nurture*. Williams & Norgate. London.

Huxley, J. S., and Haddon, A. C. 1935. *We Europeans*. Cape. London.

Huntington, E. 1928. *The Human Habitat.* Chapman & Hall. London.

Industrial Health Research Board, *Fifteenth Annual Report*, 1935. H.M. Stationery Office. London.

Muller, H. J. 1935. *Out of the Night.* Vanguard Press. New York.

Müller, Max. 1888. *Biographies of Words and the Home of the Aryas.* Longmans. London.

Orr, Sir J. B. 1936. *Food, Health and Income.* Macmillan. London.

Stapledon, R. G. 1935. *The Land Now and To-morrow.* Faber & Faber. London.

Vavilov, N. I. 1926. *Bull. Appl. Bot., Leningrad, 16,* 139.

Zuckerman, S. 1932. *The Social Life of Monkeys and Apes.* Kegan Paul. London.

CLIMATE AND HUMAN HISTORY

O F late years a determined attempt has been made to rewrite history in economic terms. But this does not go deep enough. Man's thought and social life are built on his economic life; but this, in its turn, rests on biological foundations. Climate and geology between them decide where the raw materials of human industry are to be found, where manufactures can be established; and climate decides where the main springs of human energy shall be released. Changes of climate cause migrations, and migrations bring about not only wars, but the fertilizing intermingling of ideas necessary for rapid advance in civilization.

Disease and hygiene play as important a part; half the population of the world is permanently below par on account of animal parasites such as the hookworm and the microscopic malaria germ; and disease may bring about the rise or fall of empires. Nor has selection ever ceased its rigorous activity. To pass from one mode of life to another is not a simple affair for a people; a settled agricultural life demands a very different temperament from hunting, and the hereditary make-up of the race must be altered if a people is to pass successfully from one to the other. Most migrations, too, are selective; to take but one example, the Puritans who first colonized Massachusetts did not bring with them a random sample of the genes responsible for the qualities of the English people.

But selection is altered and reduced. The better care of the young and the elaboration of social life allow all sorts of variations, which otherwise would be snuffed out, to survive and often to play an important part in progress. Knowledge for knowledge's sake is out of place in a primitive hunting tribe.

When the world's climatic belts are sharply marked (as they are to-day, in contrast to epochs like the late Eocene, when climate was much more uniform), the temperate zones, flanked poleward by the subarctic and the arctic, are separated from the tropics by two dry belts, along which all the world's great deserts are strung. The only zones where vegetation is abundant and man can easily flourish are the temperate and the tropical. But the temperate has another advantage. It contains the belt of cyclonic storms—in other words, of rapid and frequent changes of weather. And this type of climate, as Ellsworth Huntington has shown, is the one most stimulating to human energy and achievement.

We are still so ignorant of the earliest steps in the evolution of man from his simian ancestors that ideas as to the influence of climate on this phase of his history are highly speculative. It can scarcely be doubted, however, that the progressive desiccation of the world that took place in the late Cenozoic Epoch helped to drive our ancestors down from the trees and out into the plains. We know that the Himalayas were elevated at this time; and it has been plausibly suggested that man originated to the north of them. For, as the land here grew drier, the forests shrank southward, where they were met by the impassable mountain barrier, and disappeared from Central Asia. Their anthropoid inhabitants were therefore forced either to disappear too or to become adapted to the new conditions, growing more terrestrial and more carnivorous. However this may be, men of a sort were undoubtedly in existence before the beginning of the Ice Age, over half a million years ago. But until we shall have found more traces of Eolithic and Lower Paleolithic man in other parts of the world than Europe (which was doubtless a mere outlier of human development) we shall not be able to piece together the fascinating story of the influence of the different advances and retreats of the ice, or the slow progress of Old Stone Age man. Pekin man and recent discoveries in Africa show how complex the picture was.

When the ice of the glacial period was still in the early stages of its last retreat, the storm belt must have lain over North Africa, making what is now the Sahara green and fertile. It was through Africa, and perhaps eventually from southern Asia, that Europe received its modern men, perhaps about 20,000 B.C. (Until about 4000 B.C. our dating must be regarded as provisional only; for the most part the chronology of Peake and Fleure, in their series, *The Corridors of Time*, is here followed.)

Gradually, as the ice withdrew northward, the belts of climate followed it up. The Sahara began to come within the limits of the dry belt. To-day, in certain parts of the Sahara, crocodiles and certain fresh-water fish exist in scattered oases. But these oases are isolated, without possible connections with other bodies of water. The water beasts that inhabit them are living in the sparse remnants of the well-watered, and indeed probably swampy, expanse of verdure that once spread over the Great Desert. This drying of the Sahara must have sent wave after wave of migrating men out of it, both northward and southward.

II

Meanwhile the zone of greatest fertility and greatest human vigour came to lie along the Mediterranean, through Mesopotamia and across to Turkestan. This again set great movements afoot. The Magdalenians, last of the Old Stone Age men, pushed northward with the forests in the wake of the retreating game of the treeless plains; till eventually, hemmed in between forest and sea, they were forced to lead a wretched existence as gatherers of shellfish and berries on the Baltic coast. The descendants of the other Stone Age peoples, who had remained behind in North Africa and Spain, evolved what is called the Caspian Culture; later they too trekked northward and eventually fetched up in western Asia.

As the open plains shrank before the advance of the forests, big game grew scarce, and men turned to other sources of food. They became food-gatherers as well as hunters, eating nuts and berries and wild grain. This must have seemed a misfortune to those early hunters. But it was the spur to progress, for from food-gathering to food-growing, to real agriculture, was a natural step. It seems to have been somewhere before 5000 B.C., in the Near East, that the art of agriculture was discovered. Legend has it that Isis, the great goddess, found corn on Mount Hermon in Syria, and gave it to her sacred son. The legend may well contain two kernels of truth. It is probable that women rather than men first hit on the idea of planting grain, for the men's work would still be afield, hunting; and it is probable that it was discovered somewhere in Syria or its near neighbourhood. By 5000 B.C. grain-growing had spread round from Palestine to Mesopotamia, and permanent settlements had come into being. The polish gained by stone implements used for hoeing probably gave men the idea of deliberately polishing their tools; if so, agriculture was the cause of the change to the Neolithic Culture. In any case, agriculture and polished neolithic stone implements appear at about the same time.

The arts of pottery and weaving were in all probability discovered about the same time as that of grain-growing, and the first permanent houses were built. Domestic animals followed soon after; domestication seems first to have been learned by hunters, but the art spread rapidly and was extended and improved by the settled agriculturists. Metal-working was not long behind, though for centuries only copper and gold were employed—copper for use and gold solely for ornament.

The glacial period did not die steadily away; it left the earth in a series of spasms or oscillations, a time of rapid retreat being followed by a standstill or even an advance of the ice, brought about, it would seem, by an elevation of the land. For a century or so about 4500 B.C., there was such an elevation. This seems to have had two interesting consequences. For one thing, the increased snowfall round the Mesopotamian basin gave rise to such violent spring floods, year after year, that some towns were abandoned, and the memory of the disastrous time has been preserved, it seems, in the story of Noah's flood and the corresponding Mesopotamian legends. But more important was its effect on Egypt. In the centuries before this time, the Nile Valley seems to have been marshy and largely uninhabitable; the elevation must have drained it. And the long ribbon of marvellously fertile land thus provided for the use of man tempted in the agriculturists of neighbouring countries. This, it appears, was the real beginning of the civilization of Egypt; but, once started on its career, its geographical position was such that it soon outstripped its rivals.

Thus, largely as a result of the pressure of changing climate on early man, hunting gave place to agriculture. Well before 4000 B.C. what we may call the Archaic Civilization, based on corn and a settled life,—with houses and pottery, woven fabrics and metal work, in addition,—was fully established, from Egypt round by Syria to the Tigris and Euphrates. This corner of the globe was predestined to be the cradle of the modern world—by its climate, by its great rivers, by the fact of its being the original home of wheat, by its being a natural meeting-place for different streams of culture brought by different migrations of men, east and west as well as north and south.

Before 4000 B.C. there had been added to the achievements of settled man the art of writing, the framing of a calendar, irrigation, the wheel, and the making of fermented liquor. Through the whole of the next millennium this remarkable civilization was free to develop its own potentialities. It was a time of depression of land, a moist time over the steppes and the Arabian peninsula, and so a time when the nomad inhabitants of these regions could thrive and multiply in their own homes, not driven by drought to irrupt into the lands of their richer neighbours. To what height the Mesopotamian civilization reached is attested by the marvellous workmanship of the objects from Ur of the Chaldees, which date from about 3500 B.C. The organization of the State under a priest-king, even the welding of empires a million strong, stone architecture, the arch, written codes of law, sea-going ships—these were some of the achievements of this millennium.

But the available land in this corner of the world was being filled up by the natural increase of population; and this filling up coincided with a new elevation of the land and a new period of drought. Between them, the two caused such a movement in the world of man that the Archaic Culture, though made to totter in its original home, was forced to spread its influence far and wide over Europe, Africa, and Asia.

III

The new millennium dawned favourably enough. Egyptian civilization, borne along on its own momentum, reached new successes. Beautiful temples of stone, and the pyramids, with their astounding exactitude and colossal size, date from its earliest centuries. Mathematics and astronomy take their rise; the State is run by a regular bureaucracy. A little later, in Mesopotamia, King Sargon comes on the scene, the first of the great conquerors to build an empire with armies.

For armies were another new invention. The primitive hunters had doubtless fought, but it had probably never been organized fighting; and the early food-gatherers and cultivators seem to have been peaceable on the whole. There was assuredly never any Golden Age of Peace, as Perry and other enthusiasts imagine, but the early ages of human life were probably on the whole peaceful, because deliberate and organized warfare was not necessary and did not pay. War began as settled man quarrelled over his property and his privileges. The idea of war soon spread to the less civilized peoples who fringed the settled lands;

and it became possible for these peoples to practise war efficiently because they had passed from the state of hunters to that of nomads, disciplined herdsmen, and horsemen. The horse must have been domesticated on the steppes somewhere before 3000 B.C. A little later, drought began, and the nomads, lacking food at home, poured down on the settled lands with their horses. These were as terrible an innovation in warfare then as were the tanks in the wars of our own day some 4500 years later; and both Egypt and Mesopotamia were overrun and their civilization put in peril.

Meanwhile the pressure of population, of climatic changes, of invasions in the rear, forced the grain-growers out in all directions. Not till about 3000 B.C. did any settle on the continent of Europe; but well before the close of the succeeding millennium they had spread over its greater part, to Thrace, to Germany, to Belgium, to France. And the push was felt by sea as well as by land. The whole Mediterranean became a great trade-lake, and the Ægean sailors had reached the Atlantic at latest by 2200 B.C. At the same time a great wave of migration spread eastward, and a new culture reached northern India and right across to China, which thus seems to have received the first rude germs of her culture. It is possible that the American continent also received its first dose of civilization during this period, by a migration over the land-bridge where now are the Behring Straits.

The maritime expansion continued into the next millennium, and so did the dry climate, which was especially marked in north-western Europe. Sea trade reached Ireland and Scandinavia. Ireland attained a very high level of culture, which was probably only made possible by this dry and bracing climate, before the excessive moisture of later centuries damped the energies of her inhabitants.

About 1800 B.C. there was again a change. The climate became gradually moister and cooler. From about 1200 B.C. to A.D. 200 there was a new cycle of wet and cold, reaching its maximum about 400 B.C. and then gradually falling off, to pass over to drought about A.D. 500. The belt of storm-tracks again passed through the Mediterranean, giving opportunity for the rise of Babylonia and Assyria, Canaan and Phoenicia, of latter-day Crete and Egypt, of Mycenae and Troy, Greece, Carthage, and Rome. North Africa was then the granary of the world. The Mediterranean was the focus of human energy, and, since the nomads could live comfortably on their steppes while the wet time continued, could pursue its destiny little troubled by barbarian invasions.

But the change of climate was disastrous to the northern lands. On them, cold and wet descended; the peat bogs spread; the forests died off as the swampy moors extended. There was a marked falling off of culture in Ireland and Scandinavia; and the worst cold spell, in the fifth and fourth centuries B.C., has apparently left its permanent trace in the northern legend of the Twilight of the Gods, which pictures a disastrous world bound in the grip of snow and ice.

After this, the classical Mediterranean civilization began to fail. Jones, some twenty-five years ago, suggested in a remarkable book that the downfall of Greece was due to malaria imported from Africa. Now that we know that a progressive desiccation was in progress at the time, the idea gains in probability. The rivers, drying up to a series of pools in summer, would afford countless new breeding-places for the larvae of the malaria-carrying mosquitoes. Malaria probably contributed to the downfall of Rome as well; but since Italy has more rainfall than Greece, the malaria-spreading change would have struck her later. But in addition the yield of agriculture in the Mediterranean began to grow less; and about the same time the first of a new series of barbarian invasions poured in.

For the period from A.D. 500 to 1000 was definitely a dry one. This it seems to have been which in the South drove the Huns and Goths to the limits of Europe, and stimulated the expansion of Islam from drought-stricken Arabia. But it brought new life to the swampy North. The culture of Ireland revived. In Scandinavia this was the great age of the Vikings, the Norsemen. As toward its close it grew less dry, the wet began to rob the Vikings of their livelihood and their lands as surely as the drought had robbed the steppe dwellers of theirs; and they poured forth in a burst of migration which took them across the Atlantic, and eventually, in the guise of Normans, as far as Sicily.

IV

In the New World too the climatic changes were similar and had the same general effects, notably upon the story of the remarkable Maya civilization of Yucatan. The huge monuments of the Mayas are now buried in dense tropical jungle, which no primitive people could hope to keep at bay. After the first flourishing period of the Mayas, civilization retreated for centuries from Yucatan, but recolonized its northern part for a short time about A.D. 1000. The two flourishing periods of Maya history correspond with what we have called cold, wet

94

periods. But these were wet only in regions at a certain distance from the poles. During these times, the storm tracks shifted further toward the equator; and accordingly the dry belts between temperate and tropical were shifted equatorward too. To-day, Yucatan lies just south of where the northern dry zone passes over into the tropical. When the temperate rainy zone shifted south, the margin of the dry zone also was forced southward over Yucatan, the forest melted, and the Mayas could build an empire there.

In the temperate zones, after the short wet period of the eleventh century, there followed a series of minor and drier fluctuations. There was one cold spell in the thirteenth century. There was another in the first half of the seventeenth, in which the tradition of the 'old-fashioned' severe winter probably takes its origin (though doubtless perpetuated by the common failing of age to decry the present in favour of the past). Since then there has not been any great change. True, there have been shiftings of sea currents, such as that which brought the herrings to the Baltic, or that which sent the cod away from the coast of Brittany; but there have been no marked movements of the storm belt.

This long string of conclusions is drawn from the most diverse sources—from the deposits in northern peat bogs, from the old shore lines of the Caspian, from the salt lakes of Central Asia, from the now waterless cities, such as Palmyra, that once lay on great trade routes, from legend and historical record. But they find a wonderful corroboration within the trunks of the big trees of the western United States. Rain is the limiting factor of the tree's summer growth, and so the size of the growth ring in its wood preserves for us the record of the season. By measuring the growth rings of over two thousand big trees, Douglass has given us a curve of climate which corresponds with remarkable accuracy with what we have deduced from other sources. Some of these trees date back four thousand years. In their trunks we can read of the dry periods which spread civilization over the world but spelled the ruin of the first Archaic Culture; of the 'classical' rainfall maximum, as Brooks calls it, which allowed Greece and Rome and Yucatan to achieve their destiny; of the new drought which brought the barbarians into the Holy City and raised the Norsemen to their first height of activity. And they record for us the final settling of the fertilizing, energy-giving belt of cyclonic weather in its present place, a thousand miles and more northward of its old position.

Thus climatic belts have not shifted seriously for almost a thousand years. What will happen to civilization when they move again we can hardly foresee; but we cannot suppose that shifting climate will respect our modern balance of power, any more than it spared the civilizations of Mesopotamia. Climate is inexorable.

V

The question of the effects of climate and other natural phenomena on human history is not all speculative. We can see some of its very practical ramifications in the problems of cattle, soil, and grasslands. Here the chemistry of soils enters in as well as climate, but the two are not without relation.

From time to time, in different parts of the world, cattle exhibit perverted appetites. They take to chewing bones, and will sometimes even devour the carcasses of other cattle that have died. These abnormal instincts are invariably the prelude to grave disorders. In typical cases the bones grow soft, the joints become swollen, the animals get thin and feeble and move stiffly and awkwardly; their hoofs grow abnormally long; sterility and abortion are common. Milch cows and young growing beasts are invariably the most seriously affected; and imported modern breeds suffer worse than the poorer native types. Sheep may be affected in the same sort of way; and horses too, though more rarely.

These outbreaks, which may inflict severe losses, may only recur every few years ; or they may continue unabated for long periods. In every case they are confined to particular regions. In such a region, even in years when there is no actual disease, the animals are generally below par. Their fertility is very low; there is much infant mortality among the calves; growth is slow and stunted; milk yield is subnormal.

Much search has been made for the causes of this state of affairs. Bacteria have been blamed, and other parasites, and poisonous plants. But all these were gradually eliminated. It became more and more evident that the cause was some deficiency in the beasts' food; and since the food they eat draws all its supplies (save carbon and oxygen from the inexhaustible air) from the soil, the deficiency must ultimately lie in the soil.

Chemical analysis has confirmed this verdict. The cause of this poor performance and actual loss, specially grave in dry countries like Africa and Australia, is a deficiency of one or more of the elements supplied to plants from the mineral salts of the soil. The commonest deficiency is that of phosphorus or of calcium—or of both at once. Since both are necessary ingredients of bone, a shortage of either will prevent proper bone growth. Both are also necessary for the universal processes of metabolism in the body; and if the supply falls short of the vital minimum needed for tissue life, the tissues draw on the reserves held in the skeleton. The mineral framework of the bones is redissolved to be used up by the living cells, hungry for the missing elements, and the skeleton grows weak and soft. The milk too grows poor in calcium and phosphorus, the calf has to go short of them, and, as he is a rapidly growing organism, feels the lack even more acutely than his parents.

The depraved appetite for carcasses and bones is a last resort for getting back some of the missing elements into the system. It is, however, often disastrous, for many animals thus eat disease-producing bacteria in the decaying bones, and develop serious illness from this cause; and even if they avoid poisoning, the mineral shortage eventually becomes so acute that the animal sickens and dies. In other cases, mere stunting is the chief result. In the Falkland Islands, for example, whose pastures are very short of calcium, an ox will hardly reach five hundred pounds in weight, and the offspring of good breeds of horses grow up no bigger than ponies.

The symptoms vary a good deal from place to place, largely according as the defect is a defect mainly of phosphorus,—perhaps the commonest condition,—or of calcium, or of both. But they all agree in taking origin in a lack of necessary bone-building elements.

Here and there, though much more rarely, the cattle farmer attempts to ply his trade on areas where there is a shortage of other mineral constituents. When the missing element is iron, as in parts of Kenya and New Zealand, the animals suffer from a progressive anaemia; they grow thinner and thinner, and finally lose control of their limbs. In certain parts of the plains region of the United States and Canada, on the other hand, iodine is the defaulter, and farm animals (like the human population) suffer from the swelling of the thyroid known as goitre, with all the attendant symptoms of low chemical activity and stunted growth. In some areas, the lack of iodine is so pronounced that the young pigs lose all their hair and hardly any of them survive.

VI

The shortages, as we have said, are primarily due to a deficiency native to the soil. It is surprising but true that there are great stretches of country which from the outset are unsuitable (without special treatment) for stock-raising on any large scale, because the ground simply does not have enough of one or another chemical element. Countries composed of igneous rock often have a shortage of calcium. In much of the west of Scotland, where the soil is poor in calcium and phosphorus and the pastures have long been depleted by grazing without any return in the shape of artificial manure, the sheep are frequently afflicted with disease, there is a high rate of mortality among growing lambs, and the carrying capacity of the land is falling. Iodine is generally low in limestone districts, or where, as in parts of North America, the great meltings that followed the Ice Age have leached it out of the soil.

Phosphorus is the trickiest of all these elements. It is the one which usually is nearest to the border line, and there are very big tracts of phosphorus-poor soil. In addition, drought apparently makes it harder for plants to get phosphorus out of the ground, so that an arid climate will turn a soil that elsewhere would be adequate into a phosphorus-deficient one.

Why, then, are these regions of the earth's surface not bare of wild animals? And how is it that man can generally thrive where his cattle sicken? The answer is that the demands are a matter of degree. No region is entirely without any of the essential elements. In nature, a balance is soon struck. The country supports what it can support. If animals fall sick, they are speedily eliminated; as soon as overmultiplication of any grazing animal brings down the supply of any element per individual to the danger point, migration relieves the pressure. Man, on the other hand, attempts more intensive operations. He wants the land to carry the maximum amount of stock, and to carry it all the time. Furthermore, different animals make very different demands on the mineral resources of the soil. It is the quick-growing beast which suffers, because it has to lay by a large quantity of calcium and phosphorus in its skeleton, of iron in its blood, of iodine in its thyroid, all in a short time; while the slower-growing kinds escape—just as in man a degree of shortage of vitamins which is almost without effect on grown men and women may produce serious rickets in growing children.

Now cattle are in any case quick-growing animals. A human infant takes six months to double his weight after birth; a calf, in spite of his much greater size, takes only about a month and a half. And in domestic breeds of cattle man has intensified this quick growth, since his prime aim is the biggest possible return of meat in the shortest possible time. Besides, he breeds for milk-yielding capacities so enlarged as to be almost unnatural. Whereas, for instance, in the natural state cows at one lactation produce two or three hundred gallons of milk, we ask the best modern breeds to give us up to a thousand gallons. The native cattle of Nigeria have their first calf at about six years; a well-fed cow of a modern breed has hers at three. In beef breeds, the rate of putting on flesh has been doubled. In all these ways, domesticated cattle have been deliberately bred to make more demands upon the soil than other beasts, and the better they are as cattle, the more demands they must make. Accordingly, when good European bulls have been used to grade up native cattle in India or Africa, the result has frequently been merely that the sickness and mortality due to mineral deficiencies have leaped up.

Man the stock-breeder has thus been putting new and unprecedented demands upon the mineral resources of the world's soil. But that is not all. He has also been depleting those resources without making any return. As Sir John Orr says in his book, *Minerals in Pastures*: 'Accompanying the visible movement of milk and beef, there is a slow invisible flow of fertility. Every cargo of beef or milk products, every ship ton of bones, leaves the exporting country so much the poorer.' For, in nature, animals die where they live, and the constituents of their bodies are returned to their native soil. But man changes all that. He ships off the bodies of his animals or the products of those bodies to distant countries, and in every exported pound of meat or cheese or bone meal so much phosphorus and so much calcium and iron and mag-

161328

nesium have been extracted from the soil and removed from the country's shores. Richardson calculates that since 1870 the export of animals from Victoria alone has taken out of its soil the equivalent of two million tons of superphosphates.

As we are now beginning to see, man's difficulties about grassland and the products of grassland are not merely due to local and natural deficiencies. They are due too to deficiencies of his own making, and these artificial deficiencies are cumulative and world-wide. In old days, the cattle of mineral-deficient areas would make periodic journeys to salt-licks, where the instinctive cravings for the elements they lacked would save them from disease and death. It is interesting to find the same instinctive cravings in man. In some parts of Africa, where mineral deficiency is serious, the black children spend their pennies, not on sweets, but on lumps of unpurified salt, imported from distant salt-pans and full of all the elements for which their systems are crying out. To-day, fencing has often made the cattle's annual ' cure' impossible. In one part of Kenya, for instance, the settling of the country happened to put an important salt-lick on to land allocated to whites, to the great detriment of the native cattle, which either could not get at their necessary supply of minerals, or strayed and trespassed in search of it, and were lost to their owners. Economic restrictions may have the same effect. In the old days of the heavy French tax on salt, you could tell without a map when you crossed the boundary in the Jura from France to Switzerland by looking at the cattle. The French cows looked poorly, the Swiss beasts fine and healthy.

The next step was the discovery that the amount of

mineral which would prevent disease in a pasture was not enough to give the best results. By adding more, up to a definitely ascertainable point, sheep and cattle could be made to grow faster, to yield more milk, and especially to be more fertile.

Thus what began as a study of local cattle diseases has turned into a problem of the soil chemistry of grasslands. The problem is one of first-rate importance. Cereals may be the staff of life; but the products of grass are more varied. Grass gives us not only meat, but also wool, leather, milk, butter, cheese, and various valuable by-products from bones and hides and horns. The value of the products of grass consumed annually in Britain alone is over £400,000,000, and the quantity of this which is imported makes nearly a quarter of the country's total imports. And some countries, like New Zealand, live almost wholly by grass.

VII

The question at issue becomes the question of the future of the world's grass. We have spent an enormous amount of energy on improving wheat and maize, and have hardly given a thought to grass; but there is little doubt that by proper attention to the ecology and genetics of grasses we could double the output of the world's pastures.

For one thing, proper dosing with mineral salts helps the growth of plants which make greater demands on the soil, and so takes the ecological succession a stage further to a richer herbage. In dry areas it often helps also by conserving more moisture in the soil. Then there are strange and subtle interrelations between grass and the beasts that eat it. Their trampling and their browsing alter conditions for the herbage. Too little grazing may allow scrub or moor to invade the pasture; too much may impoverish the sward. Such problems are especially prominent in new countries—in New Zealand, for instance, there seem to have been no indigenous grazing creatures, save possibly the giant flightless bird, the moa; yet to-day 94 per cent. of the country's exports are the products of grass-eating animals. Here, to clear scrubland for sheep, not only must the scrub be cut and rooted up and burned, but cattle must be introduced to keep the bracken and brush from winning back the land they have lost. As Dr Stapledon says, 'Cattle, no matter how prices rule, are essential to the reclamation and maintenance of scrublands. They are implements as necessary to the wool grower on hilly, scrubby country as the plough to the producer of wheat on the plains.' Trampling, too, prevents the grass from getting coarse and rough. The amount of grazing a pasture will stand depends a good deal on climate. If grassland (as in so much of Europe and New Zealand) is not the natural climax of plant life, but is only a 'sub-climax,' which would go on to a richer type of vegetation, such as forest, if left to itself, then it will stand very heavy grazing. If, however, the climate is so dry that grass of sorts is the natural climax, it has fewer reserves, so to speak, and heavy grazing may seriously damage it.

But the amount of grazing will also depend on the kinds of grasses there are to be grazed. In New Zealand the native vegetation, unused to being nibbled down to the ground, succumbs to this new treatment. A judicious mixture of the right grasses and clovers from all over the world (only we must remember that what is right for one place may be very wrong for another!) is rapidly raising the productive power of grass. This will soon get to a limit; but then the geneticist can step in and continue the process by deliberately breeding richer and more resistant pasture plants. A beginning has been made with this at places like the Grass Research Station at Aberystwyth, and the results already obtained, together with the comfortable knowledge of what has been actually achieved with wheat, warrant great hopes for the future.

We could vastly increase the productive power of the world's grasslands by deliberately working for types of beast that make greater demands on the grass, and types of grass that make greater demands on the soil. We have only got to make sure that we can continue to provide the soil with the necessary chemical ingredients. But to achieve this result we need the services, not only of the farmer and the scientific agriculturist, but of the plant and animal geneticist, the soil chemist, the systematic botanist, and the ecologist; nature cannot be improved upon without the amassing of a deal of knowledge and the expenditure of a deal of pains.

THE CONCEPT OF RACE
IN THE LIGHT OF MODERN GENETICS

RACE and its problems are playing an important rôle on the world's political stage at the present time. But the race concept as employed by the politician, or even in most cases by the anthropologist, is a product of the pre-Mendelian era. How does it look to that infant prodigy of biological science, modern genetics? Does it stay as it was, does it alter its lineaments, or does it tend to fade away into nothingness? Should we perhaps banish the very word *race* from any scientific or accurate vocabulary? These are questions of the utmost urgency in national and international affairs.

The fundamental thesis of modern genetics is that the hereditary constitution of any organism (man, animal, or plant) consists of a large number of discrete units or genes, which normally perpetuate themselves *ad infinitum* by self-reproduction. When different gene-outfits are mixed in a cross, while there may be blending of visible characters, there is no blending or modification of the genes themselves. The only alteration of the genes is due to the rare and infrequent process of mutation.

The gene-outfit of an organism is double, one set from the father, one from the mother. When the time comes for the formation of reproductive cells, the two members of each gene-pair separate in a clean-cut way from each other, so that each reproductive cell has one or the other member of each pair. This is what we call segregation.

With certain minor restrictions, each pair of genes segregates independently of every other. The result is that when a cross is made involving differences in several pairs of genes, in the second and later generations every possible combination of the different genes will occur. This is the principle of independent assortment.

In the third place, we are coming to a more exact comprehension of the rôle played by environment. Genes remain unaltered but their expression will change according to the circumstances. In other words, any character is the product of an interaction between heredity and environment.

Most important for our purpose perhaps, modern genetics clears up our ideas on the subject of variation. Variation merely implies difference, and the differences between two individuals or strains of men or other organisms may be due to three essentially distinct factors:

First: to differences in environment, as when differences in exposure to sunlight tan one child and leave the other bleached and pallid.

Second: to differences caused by mutation of genes, as between bearded and beardless varieties of grain; the accumulation of mutations is responsible for most differences brought about in evolution.

Third: to recombination—*i.e.* to reshuffling of old genes in new constellations owing to independent assortment after a cross. This accounts for most of the differences observed between brothers and sisters in the same family.

Man, owing to crossing of different stocks, shows an unusual degree of recombinative variation; further, owing to the plasticity of his mind, he shows an unusual degree of environmentally produced variation. Let us, in the light of these facts, consider some human characteristics. Stature will serve as an excellent example.

In man, as in other animals, various degrees of stunting can be produced by various degrees of underfeeding and other unfavourable conditions (disease, lack of exercise or sunlight, etc.). The effect will also vary according to the time at which the unfavourable conditions were operative. As shown by recent experiments in which the growth of healthy boys was still further increased by the addition of milk to an abundant and varied diet, 'underfeeding' is a relative term, and apparently normal conditions may not provide the optimum.

This provides an excellent example of the interaction of genetic and environmental factors, and is also important from the standpoint of so-called 'racial' differences. The fact that stature can be altered by feeding and other environmental conditions does not mean that it cannot also be altered by change in genetic make-up, or *vice versa*. To believe that one alternative excludes the other (as many popular writers appear to do) is to fall into an elementary logical and biological error.

As a matter of fact, marked genetic differences in stature do occur in man. No amount of extra feeding could raise the stature of a Pigmy to that of a normal European. The average height of Scots is considerably higher than that of, say, southern Frenchmen, and the difference is almost wholly due to differences in genetic make-up. The Scots possess genes which make for height; the Pigmies, genes which keep them small; but the height of both races could be considerably modified by feeding and other environmental conditions.

This will show the complexity of even such an apparently simple question as that of human stature. Let me illustrate this complexity by two particular problems in this field. In the first place, it is known that the average stature of various industrial nations has increased quite definitely within the last half-century or so: does this mean an alteration in the character of the 'race' (national stock), as has been frequently asserted? In the second place, it is a fact that the average stature of different social-economic classes in most nations of western civilization is different, being highest in the upper social classes: is this because the upper classes contain genetically different stock from the others?

With regard to the first question—concerning the increase in average national stature—the answer is fairly clear. The increase is due in the main to better food and better conditions of life, and not to any permanent change in the constitution. In other words, the national stock has not altered appreciably. Put it back in the old conditions, and it would once more shrink to its old stature, as our red-flowered Chinese primrose would produce white flowers on being transferred to a hot-house (p. 44).

The second question is harder to answer. It is clear that much of the difference must be due to the better conditions enjoyed by the children of the richer classes. But it is quite possible that there also exists an average genetic difference between different classes; *e.g.* in Britain there may be more genetically short stock in the lower classes, derived from the early Mediterranean-type inhabitants of the country, or selection may have been at work favouring tall types in the upper classes (*e.g.* by sexual selection of tall women), or short types in the proletariat (*e.g.* short types may be better suited to town life or factory conditions, and therefore be favoured in an urban-industrial civilization). It is probable that both sets of causes, genetic and environmental, are at work. At the moment, however, it is impossible to evaluate their exact share, though the environmental is doubtless the more important.

·II

What is true of stature applies with far greater force to psychological characters—of intelligence, special aptitude, temperament, and character. In the first place, such characters are far more susceptible to changes in environment (here of course predominantly social environment) than are physical characters. Second, the social environment shows a greater range of difference than the physical environment. High innate mathematical ability would be unable to express itself in paleolithic society or among present-day savages. The most consummate artistic gifts would find little scope on a desert island. The temperament which gives its possessor the capacity for going into a trance or seeing visions is in our modern western world likely to land its possessor in an asylum, whereas in various Australian and Asiatic tribes it will further his attainment of power and practising as a medicine-man or shaman. A warlike temperament which would have expressed itself adequately in the early days of Jewish history would have been at a discount during the Captivity. The same capacities, of inventiveness and initiative, which would be expressed to the full in a pioneer country tend to remain latent in conditions of unskilled factory labour. Certain economic and social conditions favour the expression of the tendencies to individualism and self-assertion, other conditions favour the reverse; we can think of early industrialism on the one hand, the Authoritarian State on the other.

In general, the expression of temperamental tendencies seems to be determined mostly in the very early years of life, so that changes affecting the atmosphere of the home and the theories and practice of children's upbringing will have large effects.

Similarly, the sweeping assertions often made as regards the differences of women's aptitudes and character from men's undoubtedly refer in the main to differences brought about by differences in the upbringing of boys and girls and by the different social and economic status of the sexes. An amusing example is the exclamation of the third-century Greek gossip-writer Athenaeus, 'Who ever heard of a woman cook?'

While it is clear that individuals endowed with exceptional combinations of genes will often rise superior to all obstacles, it is equally clear that the quantity of innate talent which a person possesses depends for its realization and expression upon adequate facilities for its cultivation; and that these again depend upon environmental factors such as financial resources, social outlook, and existing educational systems. The chief reason why children from the upper social classes obtain proportionately more scholarships than those from the lower classes is because they have better educational opportunities, not because they are better endowed by heredity.

The bearing of such facts upon problems of race and nationality is obvious. With the best will in the world it is, in the present state of knowledge, impossible to disentangle the genetic from the environmental factors in

matters of 'racial traits,' 'national character,' and the like.
Such phrases are glibly used. In fact they are all but
meaningless, since they are not properly definable. Further, in so far as they are capable of definition, the common
presupposition that they are entirely or mainly of a permanent or genetic nature is unwarranted.

Do not let me be misunderstood. It is clear that there
must exist innate genetic differences between human
groups in regard to intelligence, temperament, and other
psychological traits. There do exist genetic differences in
physical characters; there is every reason to believe that
similar differences in psychical characters also exist. However, in the first place this need not mean that the mental
differences are highly correlated with the physical—that a
dark skin, for instance, automatically connotes a tendency
toward low intelligence or irresponsible temperament.
Second, the mental differences must be expected to be like
the physical, mere matters of general averages and proportions of types—in every social class or ethnic group there
will be a great quantitative range and a great qualitative
diversity of mental characters, and different groups will
very largely overlap one another. Finally, and perhaps
most important of all, there exist as yet no means for
assigning the shares of genetic constitution and of environment in producing the observed difference of type.

All the evidence we possess goes to show that the expression of such mental characters is to a very high degree
dependent on the social environment. Let us first take
so-called 'national character.' There was a time when
England was called 'merry'; during the nineteenth century that epithet was not applicable. In Elizabethan
times the English were among the most musical of the

European nations; the reverse is generally held to have been true in late Victorian times. Again, as Hume shrewdly notes in his *Essay of National Characters*, the Spaniards were in earlier times restless and warlike; whereas in his day and the period immediately preceding it the reverse was the case.

Were these changes due to alteration in the genes or to such influences as the difference between the social atmosphere of the Renaissance and that of early industrialism? The social answer is here far the more likely. In other cases it is manifestly the correct one. For instance, in Carlyle's time, the German 'national character' was supposed to be peaceable, philosophic, musical, and individualist. After the Franco-Prussian War it became arrogant and militarist. Now we are witnessing the blossoming of tendencies to state-worship, mass-enthusiasm, and the like which we are once more assured are inherent in it. But it would be inconceivable on any biological theory whatsoever, let alone on that of modern genetics, to believe that the inherent constitution of the German people could change so rapidly. We are, therefore, driven to believe that the change, where it has not been merely an apparent one, due to the bias of the recorder, has been brought about by changes in social atmosphere and institutions.

Let us now examine the problem from a different angle, 'racial' rather than 'national.' It is often asserted that the Nordic 'race' is gifted above all others with initiative, originality, and that all the great advances in civilization have been due to the Nordic genius.

What are the facts? The fundamental discoveries on which civilization is built are the art of writing, agriculture, the wheel, and building in stone. All these appear to have originated in the Near East, among people who by no stretch of imagination could be called Nordic or presumed to have but the faintest admixture of genes from Nordic or even Proto-Nordic germ-plasm.

In the classical period, Aristotle (*Politics VII*) gave what appeared even to that great thinker cogent reasons for believing the Nordic barbarians as well as the Asiatic peoples inherently incapable of rising to the level of Greek achievements. The inhabitants of northern climates, he says, though endowed with plenty of spirit, are wanting in intelligence and skill, while the reverse is true of the Asiatics. The Greeks, on the other hand, are endowed with both sets of qualities. The attitude of the Roman invaders of this island toward the ancient Britons must have been very similar to that of the British and Dutch invaders of South and Central Africa toward the Bantu. We have as yet no means of learning whether this latter attitude will be any more justified than that of the dominant peoples of classical times to the barbarian tribes which they subdued.

When we come to matters of detail, facts are equally hostile to the myth of Nordic superiority. For instance, exploration certainly demands initiative. But far from Nordic types being pre-eminent in that domain, Havelock Ellis, in his *Study of British Genius*, has shown that hardly any of the great British explorers were fair-haired or in other ways of Nordic type.

The Nordic myth has many upholders in the United States; but, as Hrdlička has shown in his book *The Old Americans*, the early colonists were mostly round-headed and dark or medium in complexion.

Again, the orthodox Nazi view is that Germany owes her chief achievements to the 'Aryan' or Nordic elements in her population. As we shall see later, the Nordic type, besides being fair and tall, is long-headed. But as Weidenreich has shown, the greatest Germans, including Beethoven, Kant, Schiller, Leibnitz, and Goethe, were all moderately or extremely round-headed (cephalic indices 84 to 92)! Already the difficulties in the way of a simple Nordic explanation are apparent to the Nazi 'intelligentsia' and they are now introducing such terms as *Nordic-Dinaric* and *Baltic-Nordic* to denote certain very numerous Germans of obviously mixed type,—a procedure which at once robs the 'pure race' concept of its meaning. The influential German anthropologist Kossina, in his *Ursprung der Germanen*, says that 'Nordic souls may often be combined with un-Nordic bodies, and a decidedly un-Nordic soul may lurk in a perfectly good Nordic body.' This may be a convenient method of disposing of certain awkward facts, but it assuredly has no point of contact with biological science: the implication that the genes responsible for 'the soul' segregate *en bloc* from those responsible for 'the body' is more medieval than Mendelian.

One final example, and I have done. In so far as the Jews constitute a 'racial type,' they should be long-headed, since this is a distinctive Semite character. But Einstein is, like a large proportion of Jews, extremely broad-headed. The Jewish problem indeed is, from the standpoint of biology, a particularly illuminating one. The ancient Jews were formed as the result of crossing between several groups of markedly distinct types. Later there has always been a certain amount of crossing between the Jews and the non-Jewish inhabitants of the countries where they settled, the most striking example being the black Jews of Northern Africa and the famous historical case of the

Chazars of South Russia. The result is that the Jews of different areas are not genetically equivalent, and that in each country the Jewish group overlaps with the non-Jewish in every conceivable character. The word *Jew* is valid more as a socio-religious or pseudo-national description than as an ethnic term in any genetic sense. Many 'Jewish' characteristics are without doubt much more the product of Jewish tradition and upbringing, and especially of reaction against extreme pressure and persecution, than of heredity.

III

Man is unique in the extent to which the expression of the characteristics most important to him as a species—intelligence, mentality, and temperament—can be influenced by the character of his environment. He is also unique in respect of his purely biological variation. The nature of such biological variation we must briefly consider.

In most wild species of animals, especially those with wide distribution, two types of genetic phenomena are found. In the first place, a population from any one locality presents relatively little range of variability. Of this, some is non-genetic, due to environmental and nutritional differences; but a large amount is due to differences in genetic composition between different individuals. Usually this genetic variability is continuous, because of gene-differences with slight and quantitative effects—so that some individuals are slightly darker, others slightly lighter than the mean; some slightly bigger, others slightly smaller; and so on. Occasionally, however, larger or more definite individual differences occur, as for instance between the blue and the white types of Arctic fox, or between the normal and so-called bridled variety of the guillemot, which latter has a white spectacle-mark round the eye. Such differences usually depend on differences in very few genes, and often involve only one.

Beside differences of this kind, there are differences distinguishing populations from different localities. These are often quite marked, and constitute the diagnostic characters of 'geographical races,' or, as they are now usually and more satisfactorily called, *subspecies*. Well-marked subspecies may be connected with one another by every gradation or they may be sharply distinct. Gradation is usually found when the range of the two is continuous, discontinuity when the ranges are isolated. The latter is most clearly manifested in island races, for instance the St Kilda Wren, or the British Pied Wagtail.

A third kind of variation may sometimes be recognized, as when markedly different subspecies (or mutually fertile species) have overlapping ranges. Then, while the two types present constant and characteristic differences over most of the ranges along the region of overlap, individuals are found with every possible combination of these characters. Classical examples of this are the Eastern and Western Flickers of North America, and the Hoodie and Carrion Crows of northern Europe. This effect seems to be produced when considerable differentiation has taken place in the two types while isolated, and when after this they extend their ranges so as to meet. Interbreeding then produces every variety of Mendelian recombination. This type of variation, due to the wholesale crossing of distinct and differentiated types, is much rarer in animals than the geographical variation due to the divergent differentiation of groups wholly or largely isolated from one another geographically.

In man conditions are quite different. In this as in numerous other respects, man is a unique animal. In the first place, his tendency to migrate from one more or less permanent habitat to another [1] is much stronger than in any other animal and has become progressively more manifest in the later stages of his history. In the second place, because of more plastic mating reactions, physical differentiation of local types has been able to go much further than in almost any other wild species without leading to the development of mutual sterility—*i.e.* to fully differentiated species, sterile *inter se*. An African Pigmy, a Chinese, and a typical Scandinavian Nordic, in spite of their striking differences, are mutually fertile.

The result is that crossing of types with the production of much variation by recombination is incomparably more frequent in man than in any other species. This crossing has occurred between the major as well as the minor subdivisions of man, between groups that show large physical differences as well as between those that approximate in type. The great majority of native Africans, the reader may be surprised to learn, are not pure negroes, but have an admixture of Caucasian genes from crosses with Hamitic stocks. India is more of a racial melting-pot than the United States. Mongolian invasions from the East have left their physical traces in eastern Europe: there is an increasing gradient of Mongol genes, from Prussia eastward across European Russia into Central Asia. How the major subdivisions of man may have originated is a

[1] As contrasted with the *seasonal* migration found in birds or the *reproductive* migration of various fish.

large problem which I have no space to discuss here. But however they originated and whatever degree of difference they may show, they have been intercrossing for tens of thousands of years, and this fact has had various important results.

On simple Mendelian principles, the first result of a cross between groups differing in average physical type will be to increase variability by producing a large number of hitherto non-existent recombinations, quite different from either of the original types or from the intermediate between them.

Next, it should be remembered that after crossing, selection may play a very important rôle. For instance, it appears that after the irruption of light-skinned conquerors from temperate latitudes into more tropical areas inhabited by darker-skinned peoples, natural selection has seen to it that combinations with darker skins survive the excessive intensity of the sunlight,[1] while those with fair skin tend to die out, for instance in Greece and in India. In India especially, the social selection brought about via the caste system seems to have exerted pressure for the retention in the highest castes of the general features of the conquering group—'Aryan,' as they used to be called (and perhaps rightly in that particular land); but there seems little doubt that the genes for these are now associated with a different set of pigmentation-genes from those present in the original invaders. Similarly, in Greece to-day the average distribution of genes and the most frequent types of gene-combination must be very different

---

[1] This is so even when there has been counter-selection of a social nature against dark skin, *e.g.* in the higher castes of India. These are on the average much lighter in skin-colour than the lower castes, but are clearly darker than the original stock from which they trace descent.

not only from those found either in the Achaeans or in the indigenous Pelasgian population before the irruption of the former in the second millennium B.C., but also from those characteristic of the mixed population in early classical times.

It must further be emphasized that, after crossing, the various gene-combinations will, in the absence of selection, automatically maintain themselves in proportions which depend on the proportions of the different genes originally contributed to the cross. There will not be a uniform mixed type, but the same general tendency to form recombinations will occur, generation after generation. Those who have been to Sicily know how types immediately classifiable as 'Greek,' 'Moorish,' and 'Norman,' and those with certain negroid characters, still crop up strikingly in the more mixed general population after centuries of crossing. The same phenomenon occurs in Britain, where we still find men of well-marked Mediterranean type, dark and small and swarthy. In Germany too men with dark and fair hair, round and long head, tall and stumpy stature regularly recur as segregation-types from the mixture of Nordic, Eurasiatic (Alpine), and numerous other stocks, which constitutes the general population. There is no sign of a tendency towards a uniform blend.

In addition to the variation produced by the crossing of already differentiated groups, which in man thus appears to be basic and not merely of the secondary importance that it assumes in other species, the general variability inherent in most animal populations is also to be found in *Homo sapiens*. For instance, some, at all events, of the variation in stature, proportions, pigmentation, intelligence, etc., which are to be found in all human groups must be ascribed to this type of variation. I may stress the fact that the main types of body-build and temperament recur in all ethnic groups, black, white, brown, or yellow.

It will thus be clear that the picture of the hereditary constitution of human groups which can now be drawn in the light of modern genetics is very different from any which could be framed in the pre-Mendelian era. Populations differ from one another with respect to the genes which they possess. Sometimes certain genes are wholly absent from a group—*e.g.* that for light eye-colour among Central African tribes, or for frizzy hair among the Eskimos. Most frequently, however, the difference is a quantitative one, in regard to the proportions of genes present and in the frequency of certain main types of gene-combinations. This is eminently characteristic of the populations of western Europe.

To sum the matter up, intercrossing between differentiated types is frequent as the aftermath of large-scale migration and gives rise to many previously unrealized gene-combinations. Infiltrative individual migration also takes place very frequently and leads to the steady diffusion of genes from one region to another. There is no such thing as blending inheritance, which would cause gene-recombinations to disappear gradually after crossing: in the absence of selection, the various types of combination will tend to recur in the same proportion, generation after generation.

IV

It follows that practically all human groups are of decidedly mixed origin. Within any one group we should, therefore, expect the variation due to recombination to be great. This last point is of great importance. The expectation of the anthropologist of the Darwinian era, when the *a priori* idea of blending inheritance was in fashion, was of groups with well-marked characteristics, and a not large range of chiefly quantitative variation; the expectation of the Mendelian geneticist, knowing the facts of inheritance and the migratory habits of·man, is of groups possessing a large range of variation, often of striking extent, and only capable of being distinguished by statistical methods. In such groups the *mean values* for characters, though still useful, no longer have the same theoretical importance. The *range of variation* of characters is of far greater practical importance, as is also the range of qualitatively different recombination-types. The two resultant race-concepts are fundamentally dissimilar.

To these considerations derived from the modern study of inheritance may be added others due to the historical progress of ethnology. The modern outlook had its beginnings in the Renaissance. In its growth the exploration of the planet, first geographical and then scientific, went hand in hand with the liberation of thought and the transformation of social and economic structure. In the earliest part of this modern period the voyages of the great explorers and of the traders and colonizers who succeeded them brought home to man a new realization of the variety of the human race and the marked distinction between its types. The red man of the New World, the black man of Africa, the yellow man of the Far East, the brown man of the East Indies—it was the *differences* between human types which impressed themselves upon general thought.

The patient labours of anthropological science during

the last hundred years or so, however, have given us a wholly different picture. The different main types exist, but they are vaguer and less well-defined than was at first thought. Within each main type there are geographical trends of variation and there are connecting links even between the most distinct major types. Quite apart from the results of very recent crossings, every gradation exists between the Negro and the European along several different lines, via Hamite, Semite, and Mediterranean; every gradation exists between the white man and the yellow, through east-central Europe, across Russia, to Mongolia and China; every gradation exists between the yellow man and the already mixed dark-brown Asiatic. Even among the Eskimos and the Pigmies we find evidence of crossing with other types. The same process, of course, is continuing to-day and at an increasing rate. New links, often along new racial lines, are yearly being forged between negro and white in countries like the United States, Brazil, Portugal, and Africa; new links between yellow and white and between brown and white in various parts of the world; new links between yellow and brown all over the East.

We can thus no longer think of common ancestry, a single original stock, as the essential badge of a 'race.' What residuum of truth there is in this idea is purely quantitative. Two Englishmen, for instance, are almost certain to have more ancestors in common than an Englishman and a negro. For the sharply defined qualitative notion of common ancestry we must substitute the statistical idea of the probable number of common ancestors which two members of a group may be expected to share in going back a certain period of time. Being quantitative and statistical, this concept cannot provide any sharp definition of race, nor do justice to the results of recombination. If, however, concrete values for the probability could be obtained for various groups (which would be a matter of great practical difficulty) it would provide a 'coefficient of common ancestry' which could serve as the only possible measure of their biological relationship.

The result is that the popular and the scientific views of 'race' no longer coincide. The word 'race' as applied scientifically to human groupings has lost any sharpness of meaning. To-day it is hardly definable in scientific terms, except as an abstract concept which may under certain conditions, very different from those now prevalent, have been realized approximately in the past, and might, under certain other but equally different conditions, be again realized in the distant future.

In spite of the work of the geneticist and anthropologist there is still a lamentable confusion between the ideas of *race*, *culture*, and *nation*. In this respect anthropologists themselves have not been blameless, and therefore the formidable amount of loose thinking on the part of writers, politicians, and the general public is not surprising. In the circumstances, it is very desirable that the term *race* as applied to man should be dropped from our scientific and general vocabulary. Its employment as a scientific term had a dual origin. In part it represents merely the taking over of a popular term, in part the attempt to apply the biological concept of variety or geographical race to man. But the popular term is so loose that it turns out to be unworkable, and the scientific analysis of human populations shows that the variation of man has taken place on quite other lines than those characteristic of other animals. In

124

other animals the term *subspecies* has been substituted for race. In man migration and crossing have produced such a fluid state of affairs that no such clear-cut term, as applied to existing conditions, is permissible. What we observe is the relative isolation of groups, their migration and their crossing.

Scientifically, there are only two methods of treatment which can be used for the genetic definition of human groups. One is to define them by means of the characters which they exhibit, the other to define them by means of the genes which they contain. In both cases the procedure must be primarily quantitative. In any group certain characters or genes may be totally absent, and when this is so we can make a qualitative distinction. More generally the distinction will be quantitative. The characters or genes which are present will be present in different proportions in different groups: their most frequent combinations will also differ from one group to the next. It is only by means of this quantitative difference in representation that, in the main, we can hope to define the difference between one group and another.

The method of characters and the method of genes differ in their scientific value and in their practicability. It is much easier to attempt a classification in terms of characters, and indeed this is the only method that is immediately practicable (as well as providing a necessary first step toward the classification in terms of genes).

But it is less satisfactory from the scientific point of view. This is partly because apparently similar characters may be determined by different genes and, conversely, because the same gene in combination with different constellations of other genes may produce very different characters. It is also less satisfactory because a character is always the result of an interaction between constitution and environment. To disentangle the genetically unimportant effects of environment from the genetically essential action of genes is difficult in all organisms and especially so in man, where the social and cultural environment—that unique character of the human species—plays a predominant part. Until we have invented a method for distinguishing the effects of social environment from those of genetic constitutions we shall be unable to say anything of scientific value on such vital topics as the possible genetic differences in intelligence, initiative, and aptitude which may distinguish different human groups.

It would be highly desirable if we could banish the question-begging term 'race' from all discussions of human affairs and substitute the noncommittal phrase 'ethnic group.' That would be a first step toward rational consideration of the problem at issue.

V

THE SIZE OF LIVING THINGS

THE size of things has a fascination of its own. There is a certain thrill in hearing that a fish weighing hundreds of pounds has been caught with rod and line; that one of the big trees of California has an archway cut through its bole capable of letting a stagecoach pass; that the bulkiest of men have attained a quarter of a ton weight; that it takes two harvest mice to weigh as much as a halfpenny; that an average man contains only about two and a half cubic feet; or that many bacteria, capable of producing virulent diseases, are so small that it would take over three hundred, end to end, to get from one side to the other of the full stop at the end of this sentence.

But when we look into the subject more systematically, the passing thrill of surprise gives place to a deeper interest. For one thing, we shall find ourselves confronted by the problem of the limitations of size. Why has no animal ever achieved a weight of much more than a hundred tons? Why are the predatory dragon-flies never as large as eagles, or these social beings, the ants, as big as those other social beings, men? Why do lobsters and crabs manage to reach weights more than a hundred times greater than the biggest insect, but more than a thousand times smaller than the biggest vertebrates? Why, to choose something which at first sight seems to have nothing to do with size—why do you never see an insect drinking from a pool of water? As we follow up the clues, we

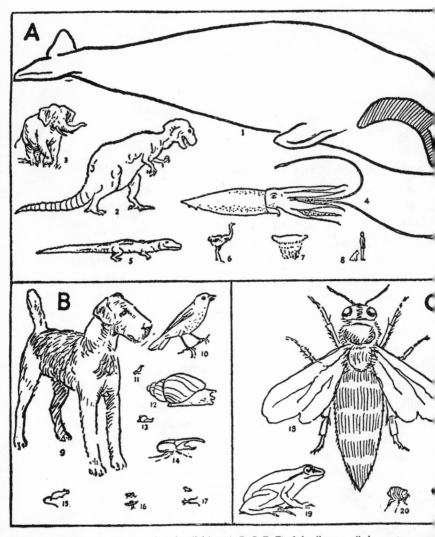

A diagram of relative sizes. In each major division (A, B, C, D, E) of the diagram, all the creatures are to the same scale. The smallest of each division is enlarged to make the largest of the division foll

A	B	C
1. A very large whale.	9. The dog (8) enlarged.	18. The queen bee (16) enlarg
2. The largest known land carnivore, the extinct reptile Tyrannosaurus.	10. A thrush.	19. The frog (17) enlarged.
3. A large elephant.	11. A humming-bird.	20. A flea.
4. A giant cuttlefish.	12. A giant land snail.	21. A very large single-celled (Bursaria).
5. The largest recorded crocodile.	13. The common snail.	
6. An ostrich.	14. The bulkiest insect.	
7. The largest known jellyfish.	15. A mouse.	
8. A man and a dog.	16. A queen bee.	
	17. The smallest vertebrate	

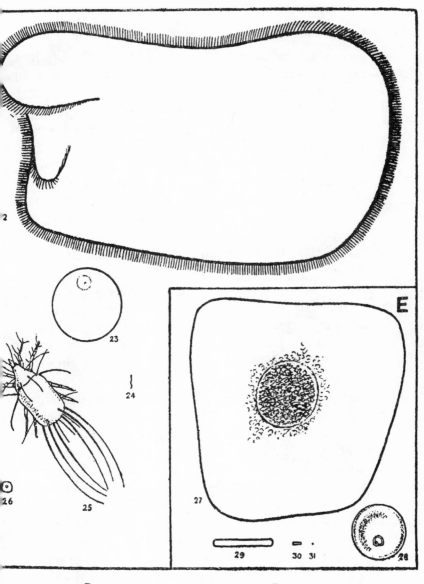

D

22. Bursaria (21) enlarged.
23. A human unfertilized ovum.
24. A human sperm.
25. A cheese-mite.
26. A human gland-cell

E

27. The gland-cell (26) enlarged.
28. A human red blood-corpuscle.
29. A very large bacterium.
30. A small bacterium.
31. An ultramicroscopic filter-passing virus.

shall begin to understand some of life's difficulties in a new way—the difficulties attendant upon very small size, the quite different difficulties attendant upon great bulk; and we shall realize that size, which we are so apt to take for granted, is one of the most serious problems with which evolving life has had to cope.

Reflection upon our own size will also help us toward an estimate of our position in the universe—of how we stand between the infinitely big and the infinitely little. It has been only in the last few decades that this estimate could be justly made. We knew the bulk of the big trees and whales; but not till quite recently did the existence of filter-passing viruses reveal to us the lower limit of size in life. And when we pass to the lifeless background, we seem, in discovering the electron, to have attained to the ultimate degree of smallness, to the indivisible unit of world stuff; and the development of Einstein's theory has made it possible to state at least a minimum weight for the entire universe. Where does the physical body of man stand? Is he nearer in size to whale or to bacterium? How many electrons are there in a man? And how does this number compare with the number of men it would take to weigh down the earth?—the sun?—the entire universe?

Let us begin with a foundation of hard fact, giving the weights in grams. · A gram is about $\frac{1}{28}$ of an ounce; a thousand grams make a kilogram, close to $2\frac{1}{5}$ pounds; a thousand kilograms make a metric ton, almost identical with an English ton. A milligram is a thousandth part of a gram. But both upward and downward the weights prolong themselves to regions where we have no units to deal with them. The simplest way to bring them home is to express them all in grams, but in powers of ten. The exponent, or little number after and above the ten, represents the number of ciphers to put into the figure for grams. When, for instance, the weight of the moon is given as 7×10^{24} g., this means $7 \times 1,000,000,000,000,-000,000,000,000$ grams, or, since there are one million grams to the ton, seven million million million tons—that is, seven trillion tons. When the exponent has a minus sign in front of it, it denotes a fraction of a gram, and again the number of ciphers in the denominator of the fraction is given by the exponent. Thus one of the insulin-secreting cells of our pancreas weighs about 10^{-9} gram. This is $\frac{1}{1,000,000,000}$ gram, or one millionth of a milligram.

In most cases, since the specific gravity of protoplasm is very close to that of water, the weight in grams is close to the volume in cubic centimetres. With trees, this volume will be considerably greater than the weight; while with armoured creatures like crabs or some dinosaurs the weight in grams will exceed the volume in cubic centimetres. Let us also remember that volumes go up as the cube of the linear dimensions. An animal weighing a ton, for instance, would be just balanced by a cubic vessel full of water measuring one metre each way. The corresponding cube of water which would balance a human insulin-producing cell would measure 10^{-3} centimetre along each side, which is $\frac{1}{1000}$ centimetre, or $\frac{1}{100}$ millimetre, or 10μ, one μ being $\frac{1}{1000}$ millimetre.

Since the weights of animals and plants are variable, since many are not very accurately known, and others have to be calculated, with a certain unavoidable margin of error, from their linear dimensions, we do not pretend to give precise weights, but only put organisms between certain limits of weight, the upper limit of each pigeon-hole being ten times as heavy as the lower. Thus most men come in the class between 10^4 and 10^5 grams—between ten and a hundred kilograms. Men are near the upper limit of the class; in the same class, in descending order, come sheep, swans, and the largest known crustaceans.

II

So much for necessary introduction; now for the facts. The largest organisms are vegetables, the big trees of California, with a weight of nearly a thousand tons. A number of other trees exceed the largest animals in weight, and a still greater number in volume. The largest animals are whales, some of which considerably exceed one hundred tons in weight. They are not only the largest existing animals, but by far the largest which have ever existed, for the monstrous reptiles of the secondary period, which are often supposed to hold the palm for size, could none of them have exceeded about fifty tons. Some of the lazy great basking sharks reach about the same weight; so, since we shall never know the exact size of the dinosaurs, the second prize must be shared between reptiles and elasmobranch fish.

The largest invertebrates are to be found among the molluscs; some of the giant squids weigh two or three tons. The runner-up among invertebrate groups is a dark horse; very few even among professional zoologists would guess that it is the coelenterates. But so it is. In the northern seas, specimens of the jellyfish *Cyanea arctica* have been found with a disc over seven feet across and eighteen inches thick, and great bulky tentacles five feet long hanging down below. One of these cannot weigh less than half a ton, with bulk equal to that of a good-sized horse. The clams come next, if we take their shell into account, for Tridacna may weigh nearly as much as a man. If, however, we go by bulk of living substance, the giant clam is beaten by a crustacean, the giant spider crab from Japanese seas.

Then come a number of groups, all of which manage to exceed one kilogram, but fall short of ten. There are the hydroid polyps, with the deep-water Branchiocerianthus which, rooted in the mud, and with gut subdivided into hundreds of tiny tubes for greater strength, stands over a yard high and sifts the slow-passing deep-sea currents for food with its net of tentacles, adjusted by being hung from an obliquely-set disc. There are the largest marine snails; the largest lamp-shells; the largest sea-urchins, starfish, sea-cucumbers, and sea-lilies; and, rather surprisingly, the largest bristle-worms, both marine forms and earth-worms. Possibly the largest tapeworms, such as *Bothrio-cephalus latus*, which may reach a length of over seventy feet of coiled living ribbon in human intestines, just come into this class, though their flatness handicaps them.

The insects and spiders come far below, the largest beetles and tarantulas not exceeding two or three ounces. The pigmy among animal groups is that of the rotifers or wheel animalcules, the most gigantic among which fails to weigh ten milligrams! They comprise, too, the smallest of all multicellular animals, some of their adult males weighing considerably less than a thousandth of a milli-gram, so that it would take about a thousand of them to equal one of our striated muscle fibres, and over a million of them to weigh as much as a hive-bee.

Even the biggest rotifers are much smaller than the biggest among the Protozoa, or single-celled animals. Some of the extinct nummulites, flattened disc-shaped Foraminifera, were bigger than a shilling, and must have weighed well over a gram. They easily beat many small fish and frogs in size, and were bigger than the largest ants, which, though the most successful of all invertebrates, never reach one gram in weight, and are usually much less. The largest ant colonies known possess a million or so inhabitants. This whole population would weigh about as much as one large man. Indeed, the small size of most insects is at first hearing barely credible. Three average fleas go to a milligram. If you bought an ounce of fleas, you would have the pleasure of receiving over eighty thousand of them. Even the solid hive-bee weighs less than a gram—over five hundred bees to the pound, nearly a hundred thousand to outweigh a single average man!

The lower limit of size among the various groups is much more constant than the upper. The smallest insects, crustacea, most groups of worms, and coelenterates, all lie between one hundredth and one thousandth of a milligram. Some very primitive worms run down one class further, and rotifers two. The smallest molluscs, lampshells, and echinoderms are between ten and a thousand times larger, while the smallest vertebrate is four classes up—ten thousand times as big. Even so the difference between the maximum sizes attained by different main groups is greater by a hundred thousand times than the difference between their minima.

There is clearly a lower limit set to a multicellular animal by the fact that it must consist of at least several hundred cells. But it seems to be impossible or unprofitable to construct a vertebrate out of less than several hundred million cells. The vertebrates, both at top and at bottom, are the giants of the animal kingdom.

It is a surprise to find a frog that weighs as much as a fox-terrier. It is a still greater surprise to know that there exist fully formed adult insects—a beetle or two, and several parasitoid wasplike creatures—of smaller bulk than the human ovum and yet with compound eyes, a nice nervous system, three pairs of jaws and three pairs of legs, veined wings, striped muscles, and the rest! It is rather unexpected that the smallest adult vertebrate is not a fish, but a frog; and it is most unexpected to find that the largest elephant would have ample clearance top and bottom inside a large whale's skin, while a full-sized horse outlined on the same whale would look hardly larger than a crest embroidered on the breast pocket of a blazer.

Then we come to single cells. By far the largest is—or was—the yolk of the extinct Aepyornis's egg, which must have weighed some ten pounds. But eggs are exceptional cells; so are multinucleated cells like striated muscle fibres and the biggest nummulites. Of cells with a single nucleus, some protists such as Foraminifera may reach over a milligram—gigantic units of protoplasm; and the ciliate Bursaria is nearly as big. But among ordinary tissue cells of Metazoa the largest are only about one hundredth of a milligram, while average cells of a mammal range between a thousandth and a ten-millionth of a milligram. In our own frames, the body of a large nerve-cell is well over ten thousand times bulkier than a red blood-corpuscle or a spermatozoon—a difference five or ten times greater than that between the largest whale and the average man. (In these calculations the outgrowths of the nerve-cells have been left out of account, as peculiar products of cell activity. If they are included, then the spinal sensory and motor nerve-cells, supplying the limbs of the giant dinosaurs and of giraffes, take the palm for size; but even they can only reach a few milligrams, in spite of being over ten feet long.)

The smallest free-living true cells are in the same size-class with the smallest tissue cells; but parasitic Protozoa, which live inside other cells, may be a hundred times smaller. Bacteria are built on a different scale. The largest of them are little bigger than the smallest tissue cell, and the average round bacterium or coccus is a thousand times smaller. These finally pass below the limits of microscopic vision, until, with the filter-passers, such as the virus of distemper or yellow fever, we reach organisms with only about a thousand protein molecules. Somewhere near these we may expect to find the lower limit of size proscribed to life; for several hundred molecules are probably as necessary in the construction of an organic unit as are several hundred cells for the construction of a multicellular animal.

III

Having made a little voyage of discovery among the bare facts, it is time to begin a quest for principles. The great bulk of land vertebrates range from ten grams to a hundred kilograms. What is it that has led to this comparatively narrow range of weight—not a fifth of that found in animal life as a whole—being most popular in the dominant group?

A disadvantage in being *very* small is that you are not

big enough to be out of reach of annoyance by the mere inorganic molecules of the environment. The molecules of a fluid like water are rushing about in all directions at a very considerable speed. They run against any object in the water, and bounce off again. When the surface of the object is big enough for there to be thousands of such collisions every second, the laws of probability will see to it that the number of bumps on one side will be closely equal to that on the other; and the steady average effect of the myriad single bumps we know and measure as fluid pressure. But when the diameter of the object falls to about 1μ, it may quite easily happen that one side of it momentarily receives an unusually heavy rain of bumps while the other is spared, and the object will be pushed bodily in one direction. The result is that the smallest organisms (like the old lady in the nursery rhyme) can never keep quiet; they are in a constant St Vitus's dance, christened Brownian movement after its discoverer.

Such hectic existences are only possible when the surface is absolutely very small; but let us not forget that an absolutely very small surface must be *relatively* a big one. This question of relative surface is perhaps the most important single principle involved in our dealings with size. Simply magnify an object without changing its shape, and, without meaning to, you have changed all its properties. For the surface increases as the square of the diameter, the volume as its cube; and so the amount of surface relative to bulk must diminish with size. Let us take an example or so. The filter-passing organisms photographed by Barnard with ultra-violet light are $\frac{1}{10}\mu$ across; the yolk or true ovum of an emu's egg is about 10 centimetres across —a million times greater. Both are of the same shape;

137

but the proportion of surface to bulk is one million times greater in the filter-passer than in the bird's egg. In other words, if the substance of the bird's egg were divided into round pieces each as big as one of the filter-passers, the same weight of material would have a million times more surface than before. Or again, a big African elephant is roughly one million times as heavy as a small mouse. The amount of surface for each gram of elephant is only one-hundredth of what it is in the mouse.

The most familiar effect.of this surface-volume relation is on the rate of falling. The greater the amount of surface exposed relative to weight, the greater the resistance of the air. So that it comes about that the spores of bacteria or ferns or mushrooms, or the pollen-grains of higher plants, are kept up by the feeblest air currents; and even in still air they cannot fall fast. They float down, like Alice down the well, rather than fall. If a mouse is dropped down the shaft of a coal-mine, the acceleration due to gravity soon comes up against the retardation due to air resistance, and after a hundred feet or so a steady rate is reached, which permits it to reach the bottom dazed but unhurt, however deep the shaft. A cat, on the other hand, is killed; a man is not only killed, but horribly mangled; and if a pit pony happens to fall over, the speed at the bottom is so appalling that the body makes a hole in the ground, and is so thoroughly smashed that nothing remains save a few fragments of the bones and a splash on the walls.

The same principles hold good for the much slower rate of falling through water; and consequently the microscopic animal will have to make much less effort to prevent itself sinking than any fish unprovided with a gas-bladder.

Relative surface is also important for temperature regu-

138

lation in warm-blooded animals; for the escape of heat must be proportional to the surface, through which it leaks away. As the heat is derived from the combustion of the food, a mouse must eat much more than a man in proportion to its weight to make up for this extra heat-loss which its small size unavoidably imposes upon it. The reason that children need proportionately more food than grown-ups is not only due to the fact that they are growing, but also to the fact that their heat-loss is relatively greater. A baby of a year old loses more than twice as much heat for each pound of its weight than does a twelve-stone man. For this reason, it is doubtful whether the attempt should be made to harden children by letting them go about with bare legs in winter; their heat-requirements are greater than their parents', not less.

IV

The intake of food and oxygen is another function with which surfaces are concerned. When a cell doubles its linear size, the bulk to be nourished increases eightfold, but the surface through which nourishment is to be absorbed increases only fourfold. It is obvious that such a process could not go on indefinitely, any more than could the growth of a nation dependent on foreign trade if its ports and harbour facilities fell progressively behind the increase of its population. The biggest single cells (excluding such mere storehouses as egg-yolks) have only attained their size by adopting some device for increasing relative surface—they are flattened, or cylindrical, or, like Foraminifera, have much of their substance in the form of a network of fine living threads, or possess long thin processes, like nerve-cells.

With many-celled animals, similar considerations still hold good. Food must be absorbed from a surface—the surface of the intestine. In small forms, enough surface is provided by a straight, smooth tube, but this would never work in larger animals. To get over the difficulty, all sorts of dodges have been adopted. In large flatworms, the whole gut is branched; in large Crustacea like lobsters and crabs, absorption mostly goes on in the feathery 'liver,' which provides thousands of tubes instead of one; in the earthworm, the absorptive surface of the intestine is nearly doubled by a projecting fold; in ourselves, not only is the effective inner surface of the intestine multiplied many times by the myriads of miniature finger-like villi, but the intestine itself is coiled; and in some herbivores the coiling is prodigious. Among lower animals without a fixed adult size, the period for which rapid growth can continue must often depend upon the inherited construction of the intestine. For instance, in flatworms, if the gut is a simple tube, increase of bulk rapidly brings down the relative surface, and the animal while still quite small can only eat enough to keep itself going, but not to grow; while if the gut is elaborately branched, growth will not be slowed down until a much larger bulk has been reached.

The same sort of arguments apply equally well to other processes, such as respiration and excretion, whose amount depends on amount of available surface. In small animals gills can be unbranched; in big ones they must be feathery. Large vertebrates like us could not breathe if their lungs were not partitioned off into millions of tiny sacs. The coiling and multiplication of kidney tubules in large animals are equally necessary. An embryo frog excretes by means of three pairs of kidney tubules. An adult frog would die from accumulation of waste substances if he possessed only six large tubes of equivalent proportions, even if their walls remained thin enough for secretion; what he needs is many thousands of small tubules.

When the animal is small, no transport system is necessary to get the food or water or oxygen to the cells from the original absorptive surface; all goes well by diffusion alone. But bulk brings difficulties here too. The flatness of the larger flatworms is partly due to the need for having every cell near enough to the surface to be able to get oxygen by diffusion. The elaborate branching of their intestines and all other internal organs is needed to ensure that no cell shall be more than a microscopic distance away from a source of digested food. Mahomet and the mountain meet halfway. With the biological invention of a blood-system, this need for branching disappears. The enormous area of surface which is needed is now furnished by the linings of innumerable tiny vessels, and the organs themselves can revert to a compact form. Finally, insects and spiders have developed a breathing system which supplies air direct to the tissues, providing a large surface for gas exchange in the tiny end branches of the air-tubes, which penetrate even into the individual cells.

In swimming and flying, too, surface comes into play. No large animal could move with sufficient rapidity by means of the microscopic 'hairs' we call cilia, since the size of a single cilium *can* never be more than microscopic, and their number depends on the extent of surface. The largest animals provided with cilia are new-hatched tadpoles, and all they can achieve is an exceedingly slow gliding.

When muscles are employed in swimming, their force

must be applied to the water through the intermediary of some surface—the body may be wriggled, or its motions communicated to an enlargement at the tail, or limbs developed as oars or paddles. When the animal is small, these swimming surfaces are relatively so big that little or no special adaptations are needed; but once it grows bulky, the swimming surface must be enlarged. The body itself is expanded sideways, as in leeches; or up and down, as in sea-snakes; a regular tail-fin is developed, as in most fish; or the limbs are expanded into flat plates, as in turtle or swimming-crab.

The necessary increase of surface in swimming limb or tail can at first be achieved by stiffening and multiplying hairs and spines; but as soon as the animal exceeds a few millimetres in length this ceases to be enough, and the organ itself must be expanded. The change is beautifully seen within the individual development of many crustaceans.

The same applies to wings. All flying animals more than a fraction of a gram in weight require a broad and continuous expanse to fly with, whether this be a sheet of skin, as in bats, a marvellous compound structure such as the wing of a bird, or the thin hinged flap of an insect's wing. But if they are much smaller, a double row of hairs on either side of a central rod will serve perfectly well. This is seen in some minute insects, such as the little thrips, which include several plant pests, and some tiny wasps which parasitize other insects' eggs. The lovely plume-moths are a little larger, and are intermediate in wing construction; their flight surface is made of hairs, but it is only rendered sufficient by a multiplication of the number of hair-fringed rods.

V

There are many other ways in which the big animal inevitably fails to be a mere scale enlargement of its smaller
relatives. The relative size of many organs decreases instead of increasing with total absolute bulk, so that in a big
animal they do not have to be proportionately so large as
in a small one. Relative wing-size is a case in point.

Then everyone knows the small-eyed look of an elephant or, still more, of a whale. To obtain a good image,
an eye has to be of a certain absolute size; this is because
the image even in our own eyes is really a mosaic, each
sensory cell in the retina behaving as a unit. The image
we see is built up out of unitary spots of colour, just as a
half-tone picture in a newspaper is built up out of combinations of single black and white dots. To give an image of
a reasonably large field, they must be numerous. Once a
certain absolute size of eye is reached, any advantage due
to further enlargement is more than counterbalanced by
the material used and the difficulties of construction, just
as very little advantage is to be gained in photography by
making a camera over full-plate size. Even in a giraffe,
which has an exceptionally large eye for a big animal, the
eye's relative weight is small compared with that of a rat.

Most sense-organs behave in a similar way. This is
especially true of the organs of touch and temperature in
the skin. It matters to a mouse to be able to deal with
things the size of breadcrumbs. But such trivialities do
not concern an elephant; the elephant accordingly can,
and does, have its skin sense-organs much more thinly
spread over its surface.

This in turn has an effect on the size of the nervous

system; for the fewer the sense-organs, the fewer sensory nerve-cells are needed, and the smaller the size of the ganglia on the spinal nerve-roots which are composed of sensory nerve-cells. Since the sense-organs of touch are distributed over the surface, we should only expect these ganglia to grow proportionately to surface, and not to bulk, even if the sense-organs were as thickly scattered over the skin of a big as of a small animal; but as they are more sparsely scattered in the big animal the weight of a ganglion does not even keep up with the size of the animal's surface, and its growth is actually only just more than proportional to the square root of the weight.

As a matter of fact, when the nervous system as a whole, or the brain by itself, is compared in a series of related mammals or birds of different size, it is found to increase only about as fast as the surface, instead of keeping pace with the weight; and the same is true of the heart. It would take us too far to go into the detailed reasons for this; but the fact that a large animal does not need a brain or heart of the same proportional size as a small model of the same type is important. It warns us not to be too hasty in drawing conclusions as to intelligence from *percentage* brain-weight, or as to the efficiency of circulation from *percentage* heart-weight. Size itself reduces the percentage weight; we must know the proper formula before we can tell whether an individual, a sex, or a species has a brain-weight *effectively* above or below that of another individual, sex, or species of different magnitude. In man, comparisons (often invidious) have frequently been made between the brain-size of men and women; but not until Dubois and Lapicque worked out the proper formulae for change of brain-proportion with size was it possible to say

144

whether the smaller brain of women meant anything save that the bodies of women were smaller.

Another such example, but of a rather different type. We marvel at the size of an ostrich's egg, which would provide a large party with breakfast, and is the equivalent by weight of about twenty hen's eggs. But we forget to marvel at the ostrich itself, which weighs as much as about forty or fifty hens. The size of birds' eggs, in fact, does not increase as fast as the size of the birds that lay them. A humming-bird lays an egg 15 per cent. of its own weight; that of a thrush is 9 per cent., that of a goose some 4 per cent., and that of an ostrich only 1·6 per cent. Two competing forces are here at work. It is advantageous to have large eggs, since they give the young bird a better start in life; but the purely physical fact that all the new material for the egg's enlargement must pass through the egg's surface will, as bulk grows, slow down egg-increase below body-increase. And, as a matter of fact, we find that in quite small birds, below the size of a goose or swan, egg-weight increases only a little faster than body-surface.

These figures apply to averages only. Adjustments can be made in response to special needs. In wading birds the young must run about immediately on being hatched; and accordingly their egg-size is well above that of equal-sized birds whose young are born naked and fed in the nest. The common cuckoo, to deceive its hosts, must have an egg not too unlike theirs in size; and accordingly its egg is uniquely small—appropriate to a bird one-third of its body-weight. The limitation of egg-size is prescribed by laws which apply to dead as well as to living matter; its regulation within these inexorable limits is the affair of the interplay of biological forces.

VI

We come back again to the advantages and disadvantages of size. At the outset, it is not until living units are quit of the frenzy of Brownian movement that they themselves become capable of accurately regulated locomotion. The first desirable step in size is to become so much bigger than ordinary molecules that you can forget about them.

But even then you are still microscopic, still wholly at the mercy of anything but the most imperceptible currents. Only by joining together tens or hundreds of thousands of cells can you begin to make headway against such brute forces. About the same level of size is necessary for any high degree of organization to be achieved. Size also brings speed and power, and this is of advantage in exploring more of the environment. But the effective range (apart from involuntary floating with the wind or the current) of any creature below about half a million cells and a hundredth of a gram is extremely limited. Ants with fixed nests make expeditions of several hundred yards, and mosquitoes migrate for a mile or so. When we get to whole grams, however, winged life at least has the world before it. Many migratory birds that regularly travel thousands of miles weigh less than ten grams. Swimming life soon follows suit; think of the migrations of tiny eels across the Atlantic, or of baby salmon down great rivers. Most land life lags a little; though driver ants are always on the move, and mice shift their quarters readily enough, controlled migration hardly begins in land animals till weight is reckoned by the pound.

If a certain size is needed for any degree of emancipation from passive slavery to the forces of environment, it is equally needed to achieve active control over them. Before anything worthy of the name of brain can be constructed, the animal must consist of tens of thousands of cells. The insects with best-developed instincts run from a milligram to a gram. But while a very efficient set of instincts can be built up with the aid of a few hundred or thousand brain-cells, rapid and varied power of learning demands a far greater number. For instincts are based on fixed and predetermined arrangements of nerve-paths, while efficient learning demands the possibility of almost innumerable arrangements. The facts are that no vertebrates of less than several grams weight (such as small birds) show any power of rapid learning, and none below several ounces weight (such as rats) are what we usually call intelligent, while even the smallest human dwarf has a body-weight to be reckoned in tens of pounds. We are far from knowing the precise size needed; but the intelligence of a rat would be impossible without brain-cells enough to outweigh the whole body of a bee, while the human level of intellect would be impossible without a brain composed of several hundred million cells, and therefore with a weight to be reckoned in ounces, outweighing the very great majority of existing whole animals. In any case, a very considerable size was a prerequisite to the evolution of the human mind.

Size too means a disregarding of obstacles: the rhinoceros crashes through the bush that halts and tangles man; the horse gallops over the grass that is a jungle to the ant. Size may help to intimidate or to escape from enemies, or may enable the carnivore to attack new and larger prey; and it usually goes with longevity.

Size thus holds out many advantages for life. But size

brings disadvantages as well as advantages, and so life finally comes up against a limit of size, where disadvantages and advantages balance.

The limits are different for different kinds of animals, for they depend upon the construction of the type, and upon the world which it inhabits. Single-celled animals, as we have seen, soon reach a limit on account of the surface-volume relation. Organisms that must swim and have only cilia to swim with come to a limit even earlier. Whether they be one- or many-celled, the limit is at about a milligram. Those which use cilia, not to swim, but to produce a food current, are not handicapped until much later; by folding the current-producing surface, and arranging neat exits and entrances for the current, many lamp-shells and bivalve molluscs reach several ounces; but as the current-producing cilia are confined to a surface, there comes a limit, which is attained when the soft parts reach a weight of a few pounds.

With most slow-moving sea animals, it is the food question which restricts size. It is usually more advantageous to the race to have a number of medium-sized animals utilizing the food available in a given area than to put all the biological eggs into the single basket of one big individual. Without some greater degree of motility than these possess, sea-urchins or sea-cucumbers as big as sheep would be inefficient at exploiting the food resources of the neighbourhood. The only such slow creatures above a few pounds weight of soft parts are jellyfish, the largest of which manage to obtain sufficient food in the crowded surface waters of cold seas by spreading prodigious nets of poisonous tentacles.

Insects and spiders have so low a limit of size because

of their air-tube method of breathing, which is inefficient
over large distances. Crustacea are limited by their habit
of moulting. A crab as big as a cow would have to spend
most of its life in retirement growing new armour-plate.
Land vertebrates are limited by their skeleton, which for
mechanical reasons must increase in bulk more rapidly
than the animal's total bulk, until it becomes unmanage-
able. And water animals are presumably limited by their
food-getting capacities.

VII

At last we come to the position of man, as a sizable object, within the universe. Eddington begins his fascinating *Stars and Atoms* by pointing out that man is almost precisely halfway in size between an atom and a star.

"The sun belongs to a system containing some 3000 million
stars. The stars are globes comparable in size with the sun, that
is to say, of the order of a million miles in diameter. The space
for their accommodation is on the most lavish scale. Imagine
thirty cricket balls roaming the whole interior of the earth; the
stars roaming the heavens are just as little crowded and run as
little risk of collision as the cricket balls. We marvel at the
grandeur of the stellar system. But this probably is not the
limit. Evidence is growing that the spiral nebulae are 'island
universes' outside our own stellar system. It may well be that
our survey covers only one unit of a vaster organization.

A drop of water contains several thousand million million
million atoms. Each atom is about one hundred-millionth of an
inch in diameter. Here we marvel at the minute delicacy of the
workmanship. But this is not the limit. Within the atom are
the much smaller electrons pursuing orbits, like planets round the
sun, in a space which relatively to their size is no less roomy than
the solar system.

Nearly midway in scale between the atom and the star there is

another structure no less marvellous—the human body. Man is
slightly nearer to the atom than to the star. About 10^{27} atoms
build his body; about 10^{28} human bodies constitute enough material to build a star."

We can pursue this train of thought a little further.
The size-range of living beings, the amount by which the
big tree is bigger than the filter-passer, is 10^{24}; in other
words, the biggest single organism is a quadrillion times
larger than the smallest. Among different phyla only one
has a range over half as great, and this is the unexpected
group of the Protozoa. Molluscs and coelenterates have
a range of 10^{11}, and vertebrates, arthropods, and worms
one of 10^{10}—ten thousand million. Echinoderms have
only a range of a million times, rotifers even less. As
proof of how soon the size of insects and of flying birds is
cut short, we find they have ranges of only a million and
ten thousand, respectively.

Man is a very large organism. During his individual
existence he multiplies his original weight a thousand
million, and comes to contain about a hundred million
million cells. He is a little more than halfway up the size-
scale of mammals, and nearly two-thirds up that of the
vertebrates.

Then we look at the range of life as a whole, and compare it with the size-ranges of not-living objects above and
below the limits of living things; here too there are sur-
prises. The sun is almost precisely as much heavier than
a big tree as the big tree is heavier than the filter-passer;
but the range from the filter-passer downward to the ultimate and smallest unit of world-stuff, the electron, is only
half this—only as much as from the big tree to such an
easily visible creature as the flea. It takes more tubercle

bacilli to weigh one man than there are electrons in a tubercle bacillus.

It is possible to calculate, on the Einstein hypothesis, a minimum weight for the whole universe, a minimum figure for the totality of matter. This is nearly 10^{24} times as much as the sun—in other words, the sun is halfway between the big tree and the whole universe of size.

Although the molecules of living matter are, for molecules, enormous, yet the smallest living organisms are far down on the world's size-scale. Once started, however, life has achieved a size-range which is two-fifths of that from electron to star, and probably well over a quarter of the whole range of size within the universe. Man is almost halfway between atom and star; he is nearly two-fifths up the cosmic scale from electron to the all-embracing weight of the universe. But so vast is that scale that to be halfway up he would have to be as big as a million big trees rolled into one. Even if we were to take the thousand million people who now inhabit the globe as constituting but one single organism, this would still be more than ten times too small. The individual man is all but halfway between atom and star; humanity entire stands in the same position between electron and universe.

THE ORIGINS OF SPECIES

Professor punnett once wrote that Darwin's great work had in point of fact been instrumental in deflecting attention away from the question of the origin of species and canalizing it into the broader problem of large-scale evolution. To-day, after eighty years, the species problem has come to the forefront of biological research. This is due partly to the progress of systematics itself, the amassing and analysis of detailed collections of animals and plants from every region, and partly to the rise of new branches of biology, such as genetics, cytology and ecology, which are illuminating the problem, often from unexpected angles.

If Darwin were alive to-day, the title of his book would have to be not the 'Origin,' but the 'Origins of Species.' For perhaps the most salient single fact that has emerged from recent studies is that species may arise in a number of quite distinct ways.

From another angle, we may say that the study of species is turning into the study of evolution in action. Large-scale evolution we can only deduce, or at best follow on its vast time-scale with the aid of fossils; but small-scale evolution is proceeding here and now, and lies open to analysis with the aid of the tools of modern research. We can hope for new facts and generalizations from its study, whereas it is unlikely that any further important principles concerning large-scale evolution remain to be brought to light.

Past students of the problem have pointed out with justice that the differentiation of new species depends on three factors—variation, selection, and isolation. Variation furnishes the raw material, the building-blocks of evolution; selection is the guiding and shaping agency; and isolation provides the barriers which allow forms to separate and diverge. But until recently these terms were largely covers for our ignorance. This was notably so in regard to variation, since until well into the present century little was known as to how organisms varied, and even as to what types of variation could be inherited. To-day, however, we would include under this head the nature of the hereditary mechanism and of its modes of change; and our new knowledge here has led to new results, some of them of great importance.

It is common knowledge now that the machinery of heredity is provided by the chromosomes of the cell nucleus. These exist in each species in a definite number, one half derived from the male parent, the other half from the female. Furthermore, each kind of chromosome has its own individuality, consisting of a large number of hereditary units or genes, arranged in a definite linear order. The genes, to use an old metaphor, are the cards with which the organism has to play the game of life; and normally each animal or plant has two complete packs of these genetic cards, one from its father and one from its mother.

The genes are alive in the sense that they are self-reproducing (or at least self-copying). Normally a gene persists in the same form from generation to generation. Occasionally, however, a change occurs in the gene—it mutates, as we say in technical parlance, and then it persists in its new altered form until a fresh mutation occurs. Thus each kind of card may exist in a number of sub-kinds, each sub-kind having a slightly different effect on its possessor: changing the colour of its eyes, reducing its fertility, increasing its resistance to cold, modifying the shape of its limbs, and so forth.

The sexual process shuffles and re-deals these cards so that every possible combination of the different types can be realized. This is one of the fundamental facts discovered by Mendel.

With this brief preamble, let us look at one or two aspects of recent work on the species problem. One of the most startling facts, which would have been regarded as impossible by earlier generations of biologists, is that new species may arise suddenly, at a single bound. This depends on another property of the hereditary machinery. Normally, when a cell divides, its chromosomes all split lengthwise and the halves separate, so that each daughter-cell receives a complete set. Occasionally, however, though the chromosomes split, the cell misses a division, so that it and its descendants have double the normal number of chromosomes.

Now consider what happens if two distinct species cross. Their offspring contain two packs of chromosomes; but these, even if of the same number in each pack, are in most cases so dissimilar that when the time comes to sort them out so that each reproductive cell contains a single pack, with one of each kind of chromosome instead of a pair, they are incapable of executing the very precise manœuvres needed to effect this properly. Accordingly, the reproductive cells receive too many of some chromosomes, too few of others, and the result is complete (or in some cases almost complete) sterility, either through the failure of the reproductive cells to form at all, or to function properly if formed, or to produce a normal individual if they should manage to unite.

But if the chromosomes have been doubled, then each can find a mate like itself; the microscopic manœuvres can take place according to the rules, and the organism is fertile. What is more, it is now largely or wholly sterile with either of its two parent species, as the offspring from such a cross will have three instead of two of each chromosome in one set, and this again upsets the manœuvres of sorting-out during the formation of the reproductive cells.

Quite a number of new species are now known which have originated in this way, some produced experimentally and some found in nature. They may even be more successful than their parents. This is the case with the rice-grass *Spartina townsendii* which is used by the Dutch to reclaim land from the sea: it resulted from a cross between a European species and an American one accidentally brought over by shipping.

So far, all the examples of such sudden species are from plants. It would probably be impossible for the process to occur in higher animals because of their special method of sex-determination, which would not work if the number of chromosomes were doubled.

Chromosome-doubling after crossing is a method of species-formation in which the isolation is not spatial but genetic—the barrier between the new form and the old is provided by a change in the microscopic machinery of inheritance, which prevents fertile crossing. Nor has selection played a part in modelling the new type. It arises suddenly and stands or falls on its intrinsic merits.

Other changes sometimes take place in the genetic machinery that may assist in isolating new types, though the isolation is not so complete. For instance, a considerable section of one chromosome may become inverted end-to-end, so that the genes it contains are now in reversed order. When this happens, the genes in the inverted section cannot be recombined freely with the corresponding genes in normal chromosomes. Thus this section of the germ-plasm of the species is effectively divided into two parts, which must remain isolated from each other in subsequent evolution, even if the species itself remains single. However, if there should subsequently arise mutations which reduce the fertility of crosses between the type with the inverted and that with the normal un-inverted section, the species may split into two.

Accordingly, such accidents to the chromosomes, while not immediately producing new or even incipient species, may pave the way for species-splitting later, in the same sort of way as is done by geographical isolation of a population on an island or a mountain-top.

Other similar rearrangements of the chromosome machinery may occur. For instance, a bit of one chromosome may become detached and then attached to a different kind of chromosome. Such accidents, each in their own special way, may provide partial isolation and pave the way for species-splitting. This sort of thing seems to occur in many animals. Certainly the little fruit-fly, *Drosophila*, which has yielded more information on heredity than probably all other organisms lumped together, is very prone to such happenings. The numerous different species of *Drosophila* are all characterized by such internal rearrangements of the chromosomes, and in many cases the rearrangements are both numerous and far-reaching.

Some species of *Drosophila* are so alike to look at that it was only their sterility on crossing which led to the discovery that they were separate species. In all such cases, accidents seem to have occurred to the chromosome machinery, providing some initial degree of genetic isolation to form a partial barrier between the two different stocks.

Another quite different type of barrier is that provided by ecological isolation, when groups are divided by differences in their habits or habitats. The best-analysed cases concern what are called 'biological races' of parasites adapted to different hosts, or of plant-eating insects adapted to different food-plants. At the outset, such groups seem to be held apart rather incompletely by accidental experience. The moth that has lived on a plant of kind A as a grub will generally prefer to deposit its eggs on a plant of the same kind instead of on a plant of kind B. Mutations crop up later and are incorporated into the animal's inheritance, giving it an instinctive preference for one or the other food-plant; still later other mutations give it an instinctive aversion to mating with an individual of the other race. The further the process goes, the more will selection encourage such mutations, for if each race is nicely adjusted to its particular food-plant, any mixture of the two races will be less closely adapted, and will therefore be at a disadvantage.

Once the isolation is fairly complete, other differences can and often will accumulate, so that the two types, after passing through a stage in which they are almost or quite indistinguishable by appearance, though they behave as good species do by exhibiting sterility when crossed, can be visibly separated as well.

Undoubtedly this sort of process, on a broader basis, has operated extensively in nature. For instance, in Lake Baikal the water-shrimps of the sandhopper family exist in numerous species unknown elsewhere in the world, some adapted to life in the open water and others to the depths, as well as to various more ordinary habitats; and there can be no question but that they have all diverged *in situ* from some one or two ancestral forms. The same sort of thing is often found on oceanic islands—as witness the mocking-birds of the Galapagos. Incipient stages in the process are also known, as with certain North American mice, where two distinct races are found in the same geographical region but in different habitats, one in woodland, the other in open country. Here the two forms are still merely subspecies, capable of fertile interbreeding if confined together, but kept apart in nature by the invisible barrier of their ecological preferences.

Finally, there remains the geographical type of isolation, in which the barrier between groups is provided by geographical features, like rivers, mountain ranges, or stretches of sea for land forms, stretches of land for water forms. The results of this sort of isolation have been the most thoroughly investigated, and are in many ways of great interest. One fact that has long struck systematists has been the much greater amount of divergence achieved on small islands as compared to large continental areas, even when the differences in environmental conditions are smaller. Thus there are almost as many different races of lizards in the Adriatic as there are islands, while on the neighbouring mainland the species is uniform over large stretches. Again, the common wren remains the same throughout Great Britain and all the mainland of western Europe. But on the islands off Scotland differentiation has set in. The Shetlands boast one quite distinct type, St Kilda a second, and the Faeroes yet another.

This excessive differentiation of isolated populations (the same thing happens in fish, as in the char of isolated lakes) has until recently remained as an empirical fact for which no adequate explanation was forthcoming. A few years ago, however, Professor Sewall Wright of Chicago showed that it was to be expected as a consequence of Mendelian inheritance. The mathematical reasoning involved is too complex to set forth here. But the results are simple enough. Briefly, if isolated populations are small enough in numbers, then mere chance will step in and largely override the effects of selection. New mutations or new recombinations of old genes will often become established even if they are not advantageous, and in some cases even if they are slightly disadvantageous. The result is to promote divergence which is non-adaptive and, biologically speaking, accidental and irrelevant. An analysis of the Adriatic lizards mentioned above has confirmed these deductions in a very pretty way. Other things being equal, their degree of difference from the mainland form is greater when the islands they inhabit are smaller. This is to be expected, since the effects of chance will increase as the size of the group goes down.

However, even on large continental masses some differentiation may take place, with mere distance and difference in climatic conditions as the isolating factors. The majority of widespread small birds and mammals, for instance, can be classified into distinctive subspecies, each with its own area of distribution. In many cases the process has gone further and split an originally single group into two or more 'good' species. An excellent example is that of the eastern and western European tree-creepers. While separated by the Ice Age, they diverged to such an extent that even though they now overlap in central Europe, they never interbreed.

Subspecies often interbreed freely where their areas touch, but the zones of mixture are almost always confined to narrow belts. This is at first sight puzzling. Why, if they meet and interbreed, is there not a continuous gradation from one extreme to the other, instead of two more or less stable subspecies separated by a narrow zone? Why is there not a smooth slope instead of a staircase of change? Here again genetics provides the probable answer. The two subspecific types are adaptive, not only in their relations to the outer world but in their internal constitutions. They differ in a considerable number of genes, and each set of genes forms a harmonious stabilized whole, adapted to give the maximum vigour and viability in the circumstances. When they meet, they can still interbreed. But as a result of their interbreeding, the harmonious constellations of genes are taken apart and recombined in all sorts of ways, which will almost invariably be less favourable than the two parent combinations. Thus, by adverse selection, the new combinations will be prevented from spreading and the mixed zone will be kept narrow.

Subspecies have often been stated to be species in the making. Undoubtedly many of them are. But, equally undoubtedly, many of them are not. Many widespread species are permanently divided into a number of these partially isolated subspecies, still exchanging a few genes with each other by interbreeding, but each relatively stable on the whole. And this condition, as Professor Wright has shown, is the most favourable one for rapid evolution.

It appears that there are two positions of relatively stable equilibrium in the process of evolutionary divergence. There is the stage of species or of complete biological discontinuity, and there is the stage of interbreeding subspecies or of partial biological discontinuity.

Finally, we must remember that in most cases, both subspecies and species are adaptive, in the sense that they are adjusted, often very closely, to their way of life or to the climatic conditions of their environment. Even when their visible characters do not seem adaptive, experiment shows that selection has been at work upon their invisible but much more important physiological characters, such as temperature-resistance, ductless glands, or metabolism.

We are now in a position to view the species problem in rather a new light. In the animal kingdom alone, about a million distinct species are already known, and the number is being increased every year by ten thousand or so new ones as the result of new exploration and discovery. Here is indeed an astonishing diversification of life. How is it related to the broad processes of long-range evolution? The answer seems to be that it is largely independent of them, or irrelevant.

Long-range evolution, guided by selection, produces divergent specialization of types over tens of millions of years: the placental mammals, for instance, gradually radiated out into carnivores and insectivores, bats and ungulates, rodents, cetaceans and primates. It leads to the widespread extinction of older types and their replacement by new types which radiate and specialize in their turn. It leads, in a few and ever-lessening number of lines, to true evolutionary progress.

Superposed on this, selection also sees to it that each type becomes adapted to different climates and to minor differences in habitat and environment. The garment of life in which the globe is clothed is thus adjusted in detail, as a suit of clothes is fitted by a tailor to the peculiarities of a client.

But on these processes of adjustment and progressive adaptation, major and minor, a series of discontinuities is superimposed. The cloth of life is divided up into a mass of snippets. Partly this discontinuity is imposed by accidents of the outer world. A mountain range or an arm of the sea produced by subsidence, an ice age or other geographical event, separates populations. Other groups are isolated by ecological accidents, in the shape of differences between habitats—woodland and open country, pond and swamp, high ground and low ground. But partly the discontinuity is imposed by accidents of the organism's internal constitution—by doubling of the whole chromosome-complement, by inversion or translocation of chromosome-sections, by the development of harmoniously stabilized gene-combinations which automatically restrict the spread of other combinations. And finally the two agencies may co-operate, as when geographical barriers isolate small populations, and then useless accidental characters automatically accumulate.

The result is that life finds its expression in the form of almost innumerable separate groups, some fully separate, like good species, some on the way to full separation, like geographically isolated subspecies, some at the halfway equilibrium point of partial separation, like continental subspecies still interbreeding at their margins.

It is quite irrelevant to the slow processes of long-range evolution whether the European tree-creepers should exist in the form of one or of many species. Owing to the accident of the Ice Age, they happen to exist as two species. It is equally irrelevant that the lizards of the Adriatic should have become divided into a large number of sub-species: they owe this to the geographical accident of the submergence of a mountainous coast with the resultant formation of many small islands.

Evolution in the broad sense consists of a few kinds of long-range trends. But these are cut up by isolation into species and subspecies, whose enormous numbers bear no relation to the major underlying trends. And even the adaptive nature of these small units is largely obscured by the frills and furbelows of non-adaptive accident which can lodge in these discontinuous group-units—mere di-versification abundantly but meaninglessly superposed on the adaptive meaning and slow advance of life.

VII

MICE AND MEN

EARLY in 1927 the newspapers contained accounts of
the havoc being wrought in California by field-mice.
These little creatures, increasing beyond all ordinary
bounds, had forced themselves by sheer quantity upon the
notice of man. In ordinary seasons they levy a modest
toll on the fruits of the earth, wild and cultivated—a toll
scarcely noticed by the farmer, still less by the community
at large. In this year and region, however, they had become a grave menace to agriculture, and the resources of
the state were being mobilized against them.

A similar plague occurred on the other side of the
Atlantic in 1892-93. In Scotland during that season vast
hordes of field-mice ravaged the farms and again became
such a serious pest that they were deemed worthy of a
Government investigation. In this Scottish plague the
mouse mainly responsible was the short-tailed field-mouse
or vole, *Microtus hirtus*. But other field-mice were abnormally abundant at the same time, such as the long-
tailed field-mouse and the bank-vole. This would indicate
at the outset that some general conditions in the season
were responsible for the sudden abundance, and not any
specific conditions favouring one kind of mouse only.

These plagues are accompanied by great gatherings of
birds which prey upon the mice. In 1892 large numbers
of kestrels and still larger numbers of short-eared owls
assembled at the feast, though by what means they received

intelligence of it is a mystery. So great was the supply of food that the owls prolonged their breeding season right into November, and even then produced broods much larger than the normal.

In a mouse plague which occurred in Nevada in 1907 three-quarters of the alfalfa acreage of the state was destroyed. The whole ground, for square mile after square mile, was riddled with mouse-holes till it was like a sieve. It was estimated that the several thousand mouse-eating birds and mammals busily gorging on mice in the affected district were killing over a million mice a month; and yet the numbers of the mice continued to increase in spite of this toll.

Why these sudden outbursts of generative energy on the part of rodents? That is a problem for animal ecology, the branch of biology which might be called scientific natural history—the study of animals in nature and their relations with their environment and with other animals and plants. The first thing the ecologist discovers is that the plagues are not such isolated phenomena as at first sight might appear. They are merely exaggerations of one part of a regular cycle. All small rodents (not at present to go beyond this group) appear to have the life of the species strung on a curve of numerical ups and downs, a cycle of alternating abundance and scarcity. Field-mice in England, for instance, have their ups every three or four years. There was a moderate degree of abundance in 1922, and again in 1926.

The best known of all such cases of cyclical abundance, however, is the lemming of Scandinavia, which has become almost mythical. In the sixteenth century, this animal was reported 'by reliable men of great probity' to fall down from the sky in huge numbers during storms of rain. The truth is not much less remarkable. The European lemmings live on the mountains in southern Scandinavia (and, farther north, at sea-level on the treeless tundra). Every few years they become enormously abundant in their mountain homes, and set off upon a strange migration. They move off in all directions downhill from the mountains, crossing roads and rivers and railways on their march. If they reach the seacoast they start to swim out to sea, and swim until they drown. After a lemming march the beach will be strewn with lemming corpses. But it is not only drowning and the accidents of the route which kill off the little creatures. Epidemics always seem to break out in years of abundance and slaughter thousands. The animals which migrate are almost exclusively young animals. The old ones stay at home, on their breeding-grounds; but there they too may succumb to the spread of the epidemic. These years of over-population occur with considerable regularity, and not only with regularity, but with the same rhythm as that which characterizes the rhythm of abundance in British field-mice. The average length of the cycle in both kinds of animals is close to three and a half years.

But the lemming introduces us to another fact of very great interest. Lemmings occur not only in Europe but also in Greenland and Canada. Here too there are years of abundance and of dearth, and the cycle appears to be the same or nearly so in both continents. Causes are at work which are simultaneously influencing the little rat-like animals on the Barren Grounds of Canada and in the mountains of southern Norway.

Before going further in our analysis it will be well to

remind ourselves that many other kinds of animals show the same sort of cyclical rise and fall in numbers. The year 1927 was of interest to English ornithologists because it witnessed a considerable irruption into England of that remarkable bird, the crossbill, with its mandibles crossed over each other for the purpose of feeding upon pine-cones. These irruptions come westward from the pine-forests of central Europe, and occur at more or less regular intervals. One, in the sixteenth century, brought prodigious numbers of the birds, which did great damage, since they discovered that their beaks were admirably adapted for slicing apples in half as well as for obtaining the seeds from pine-cones. The dates of crossbill irruptions, however, have not been quite so well recorded as those of two other kinds of birds, the Siberian nutcracker and the sand-grouse. The nutcracker is an inhabitant of the vast coniferous forests of Siberia. It has invaded western Europe at intervals of eleven years, with what would be extreme regularity if it were not for the fact that now and again one of the invasions is 'skipped.' Although observations on the spot in Siberia are not forthcoming, it appears almost certain that the migrations are due to over-population in the bird's natural home, coupled with a bad harvest of the pine-cones upon which they feed. Doubtless, when the failure of the pine crop is less extreme than usual, the pressure on population is not so great, and the wave of migration spends itself before reaching Europe.

Pallas' sand-grouse, on the other hand, is a bird of the steppes and deserts of Central Asia, where it lives upon the scanty vegetation of the salty soil. In every so many years the bird leaves its home in huge flocks, migrating both eastward into China, and westward into Europe, even as

far as the British Isles. Here again, a cycle of eleven years
is pretty closely adhered to, with the additional fact that
the alternate migrations are much bigger. As the records
go, we seem safe in prophesying the invasions at regular
intervals. The cause of the emigration again seems to
be relative over-population, or, what comes to the same
thing, food-shortage, owing to their food-plants being
covered by snow or heavy frosts.

The periodic migrations of locust and cricket swarms,
literally eating up the country in their advance, are well
known. Unfortunately a full analysis of them has not
yet been made. This is partly due to the fact that the
direction of insect-migration is entirely at the mercy of
the wind, and that a periodic increase of locusts in one
spot will cause emigration to various different countries
according to the accident of wind-direction. In addition,
insects, with their lack of a constant temperature, are more
likely than birds and mammals to show the effects of short
periods of very exceptional weather, less likely to sum up,
so to speak, the effect of moderate and irregular but long-
continued change. However, there seems little doubt
that investigation will reveal, in these and other insects,
such as the cockchafer, periodic cycles of abundance
similar to those found in birds and rodents.

However, the most remarkable facts on the problem of
periodic fluctuations in animal numbers are provided by
the books of the Hudson's Bay Company. This great
trading concern has kept records of the number of skins
of all the various kinds of fur-bearing animals brought in
each year by its trappers. The records show cycles of
abundance and scarcity in muskrat, Canadian rabbit or
varying hare, skunk, fisher, mink, wolverene, marten, lynx,

red fox, and arctic fox. The most spectacular changes, perhaps, are to be noted with the Canadian rabbit (*Lepus americanus*). One year these animals will be enormously abundant over vast areas of the continent. Next year an epidemic will set in, and in the succeeding season a rabbit will be a great rarity.

But more remarkable even than the change in abundance is the regularity of the cycle. The Hudson's Bay record goes back to 1825. The record for annual number of lynx skins, for example, when plotted as a graph, has the regularity of a temperature chart. At about every eleven years comes a peak, where the number of skins brought in averages about 50,000—always over 30,000, and sometimes 70,000. Halfway between these peaks are depressions, in which the average number of skins sinks to well below 5000, occasionally approaching zero. If records were available from single areas, the ups and downs would be even more marked, for the maxima and the sudden drops are not synchronous over the whole continent, although they do not vary in any one locality more than two or three seasons each way from the mean for the whole continent.

Both lynx and rabbit have a cycle of just over eleven years in length. The lynx eats the rabbit; and, accordingly, the lynx's maxima are one to two years later than the rabbit's.

Not merely are there more rabbits in existence at a period of maximum abundance, but they are reproducing faster. In bad years there will be only one brood in a season, and about three young in a brood; in very favourable years there will be two or three broods, and eight or ten young in each brood. The Indian trappers are said to prophesy the prospects of next season's rabbit crop by counting the number of embryos in this season's rabbits. The same sort of thing occurs in field-mice in England, as was first established by Mr C. S. Elton at Oxford; though the number of young per brood is not increased in favourable years, the number of months in the year during which breeding animals are to be found is markedly increased.

When the different records for all kinds of animals and birds from all over the temperate regions are analysed, it turns out that in most cases the average length of the cycle of abundance is either just about eleven years, or else one-third of this, namely about 3·7 years. But of course a periodically fluctuating curve of abundance might be due to two separate cycles interacting with each other. By mathematical analysis, however, when such is the case, the two components can be separated from each other. When such analysis is applied to the Hudson's Bay records, it is found that in fact the curves for the numbers of many animals are thus compound. Sometimes a curve which clearly has maxima every eleven years will be revealed as possessing in addition a minor rhythm of about three and a half years. This, for example, is the case with the red fox. On the other hand, the more northern arctic fox has an obvious period of about three and a half years; but when this is eliminated from the curve, lo and behold a minor, but none the less definite, eleven-year cycle remains. Is there any virtue in this period of eleven years? Every astronomer would at once exclaim 'sun-spots'; for the number of sun-spots visible on the sun's disc shows a well-marked fluctuation, and this cycle, too, has a period of just over eleven years. This cycle does, in fact, correspond with that of number in various animals, the sunspot minima about coinciding with the animals' maxima. What is more, the sun-spots do not always keep strictly to their eleven-year period, but may anticipate or delay matters by a year or so: and when this is so, the animals' curve of abundance is usually found correspondingly shifted.

II

There is little doubt that spots on the sun have an effect upon weather on the earth. They cause great magnetic storms; and, in addition, the amount of energy radiated by the sun appears to be greater at sun-spot maxima, less when sun-spots are few. One of the chief facts of terrestrial climate which seems to be definitely correlated with sun-spot number concerns the track of storms. If the tracks followed by heavy storms are plotted on a map, it will be found that, in North America for instance, there is in any one year a zone along which the majority of storms travel. Now this zone shifts up and down with considerable regularity from year to year, returning to the same position about every eleven years. Such a shift in the storm-tracks will obviously mean a slight shift of the margins of all the great climatic zones. It will mean that there will be cycles of rainfall, some areas getting more than the average every eleven years, while other zones in the same years will be getting less than the average; and this, according to the careful investigations of O. T. Walker, is what actually occurs. Such changes are likely to have the most noticeable effect upon plants and animals where conditions are difficult for life. For instance, a small change in rainfall in a semi-desert region will have much more effect than the same change in a well-watered country; and quite small temperature changes in the Arctic will have disproportionately large effects on the animals and plants which live there.

The three and one-half year period, on the other hand, has not so far been correlated with any meteorological facts. This, however, need not surprise us. What the meteorologist records are variations in single factors of climate such as temperature, rainfall, sunshine, and sometimes humidity. It is by no means likely that any one of these by itself is going to be the main factor responsible for the abundance or scarcity of a plant or animal. It is much more likely that what favours the growth of an organism beyond normal will be a particular combination of, say, temperature, moisture, and sunshine, probably no single one of the factors at work being either at its maximum or its minimum. Something of the sort can often be traced with life. For instance, the optimum geographical zone for white men is one of moderate temperature, moderate rainfall, moderate sunshine, and a good deal of changeable weather: no extremes are involved in it.

Though the sun-spots undoubtedly affect the weather, and so the growth of plants, the growth of small herbivorous animals, and this in its turn the abundance of their carnivorous enemies, the correlation of sun-spot cycles with cycles of animal abundance is not fully proved. The animal cycle may be an independent one, of slightly shorter period.

In any case, the abundance of rodents is an indicator for certain *combinations* of meteorological factors. The meteorologists themselves have not yet invented any instrument for recording these particular combinations of factors— indeed, they would not have suspected their existence but for the facts unearthed by the biologist. The lemming or the field-mouse or the Canadian rabbit is thus, from one point of view, a sensitive meteorological instrument for integrating and summating a number of different agencies which affect the weather, and transmuting a particular combination of them into an increase of numbers which catches the eye of observant man.

That important biological and meteorological effects are exerted by sun-spot cycles is rendered certain by corroborative evidence from other quarters. Professors Huntington and Douglass have examined the growth of the big trees (Sequoias) of California, as recorded in the thickness of their annual rings of wood. This biological record goes back over three thousand years; and in it they find a quite definite eleven-year cycle corresponding perfectly with the cycle in sun-spot numbers. Besides this, changes in the mean level of various large lakes, notably Victoria Nyanza, have been analysed and, as Brooks has shown, here too a correlation is apparent between rise and fall of water-level and increase and decrease of sun-spot number. It may be noted that lake-level will not be dependent on any single one of the factors usually measured by meteorologists, but will represent a balance between precipitation and evaporation, which latter in its turn will depend partly on temperature and partly on humidity. The lake thus integrates a number of weather components, as does an organism.

In passing, it should be observed that the short-period cycles, of three and one-half years, would be expected to affect only small animals which reach maturity in a year or less. Larger animals have lives which are too long to be upset by such small cycles. In precisely the same way, the choppy little waves which are so unpleasant to the inmates of a row-boat have no effect upon the bulk of a liner. Even the eleven-year cycles will have little effect upon animals like deer or wild asses. There are indications of fluctuations, however, in the larger herbivores, but these are of much longer range, a fact which in itself makes it more difficult to collect statistics on the subject.

It is of great interest to find that the beaver, almost alone among the smaller fur-bearing mammals of Canada, shows no periodicity in its numbers. This fact is doubtless to be correlated with its remarkable mode of life. It lives, not on short-lived herbs or grass, but on the bark of trees. It constructs dams by which it regulates its water-supply; and brings tree-trunks from considerable distances to serve as food-stores. When the local supply of trees is exhausted it migrates elsewhere. Since it lives in small, isolated colonies, it does not suffer from widespread epidemics. Here we seem to have a good proof that the fluctuations in numbers which affect other animals are not due to mysterious cyclical fluctuations in the animal's inherent reproductive capacities, but to a normal though indirect action of climatic influences via the animal's food, its parasitic enemies, and so forth.

A great deal has been heard recently of this theory of inherent or spontaneous changes in reproductive capacity, apropos of the fall in the human birthrate which has been so noticeable during the last half-century among most civilized peoples; and the upholders of this view attempt to support their conclusions concerning man by referring to the cycles obtaining in mice and lemmings. Far from lending them support, however, the biological facts tell in the opposite direction. We know of no single case of an animal changing its reproductive capacity, whether number of broods per year, or number of young per brood, so long as it is kept under really uniform conditions, while we know of a great many cases in which improved conditions of temperature, food, etc., do bring about an increase in reproductive output.

As Sir William Beveridge has ably pointed out, there is nothing in the fall of the human birthrate which cannot be accounted for by increased prudence coupled with increased practicability of contraceptive devices; nor is there anything, even in the most destructive plague of voles or rabbits, followed by the most spectacular disappearance of the marauders, which cannot be accounted for by causes simpler and more familiar than an otherwise unknown fluctuation in reproductive potency. Once conditions such as food begin to favour a small herbivorous mammal, the shortness of its life-span enables it to outrun the constable of its carnivorous enemies, which are handicapped through being of larger size, and so requiring longer to complete each generation. However, as the density of herbivore population increases, parasites will be able to spread more rapidly from one individual to another. Finally a density is reached at which some disease-germ can pass from mouse to mouse with great rapidity, with the result that a fulminating outbreak of disease occurs. This violent outbreak of epidemic disease has been reproduced experimentally with mice. The same bacillus, the same mice: but with one density of mouse population there are only isolated cases of disease, while with five times the density of population a devastating epidemic breaks out. The same appears to be true for animals kept under semi-artificial conditions for sporting purposes.

For instance, the Commission appointed to investigate grouse disease in Britain came to the conclusion that the mere fact of overstocking a moor would cause disease, by permitting a normally innocuous coccidian parasite to pass so rapidly and in such numbers from bird to bird that mass-infection and consequent disease resulted.

It appears to be a constant rule that the rapid increase consequent on outrunning larger, carnivorous enemies always has as consequence the running into new conditions more favourable to the invisible parasitic enemies of the species. As a result, an epidemic follows, and the numbers of the species are reduced below normal. This reduction may then be carried still further by unfavourable seasons.

This has one interesting consequence of general biological interest. The evolutionist normally assumes that the pressure of natural selection will be approximately equal, in natural conditions, over long periods of time. This may be so for animals like the beaver; but it will clearly not hold for those like lemmings or field-mice. In these, after a period of minimum numbers has been well passed, and the animal is filling the empty landscape once more under increasingly favourable conditions, natural selection will clearly be much less intense than normal, for there will be next to no competition due to population pressure, and weather and food conditions will be more favourable than normal. The shoe will pinch unusually hard twice in each cycle—once when weather and food conditions are most unfavourable, and once when the inevitable epidemic breaks out. Thus, as Elton puts it, the animals will be subjected in each cycle to two severe examinations of different type, while they will be hardly troubled by schoolmistress Nature during the rest of the time.

But when violent epidemics come, disease resistance will indeed be at a premium, since only one in a thousand or even one in a hundred thousand will survive, and from those scattered survivors the whole species will be reproduced. That is natural selection with a vengeance.

III

Important consequences of another type flow from the fact s. If lemmings and rabbits and mice are killed off in thousands by epidemics, may not rodent cycles bear some relation to human disease? The answer is not only that they may, but that they do. Most people know now that bubonic plague is spread to man from rats and other small rodents like gerbils by means of the animals' fleas. The years when the small rodents in Central Asia or South Africa show maxima in numbers the incidence of human plague increases.

After lemming migrations, visitations of disease are not uncommon among the human populations of the Norwegian valleys. The matter has not yet been properly investigated; but it is at least possible that some bacillus, acquiring new virulence by its rapid passage through its rodent victims, may produce this human disease. Hardly any work has been done on the causes of these natural epidemics of animals. The whole question would well repay investigation, both on account of its intrinsic interest, and because of its possible bearings on human health.

Immediate practical questions arise as to the means of coping with the periodic pests as they arise. All kinds of paradoxes here present themselves. The obvious course, and that naturally enough demanded by the suffering agriculturist, is the wholesale destruction of the voles or mice which are taking toll of his crops. Destruction, how-

M   177

ever, is often no easy matter. It is difficult to get at such small creatures which live in holes, swarm in myriads, and in a few weeks' time are grown up and ready to reproduce their kind. Both trapping and poison have their drawbacks and defects. Furthermore, killing the animals once they are so abundant that they are easy to kill is like locking the stable door after the horse has been stolen.

The bird-protectionist sees one step further. He reminds us that owls and many hawks prey upon small rodents, and would have us keep down the mice and voles by encouraging the predatory birds. But then steps in the ecologist and points out that both human destruction and avian enemies will have as their effect merely the slowing down of the geometrical increase of the mice (for certainly not even the dense hordes of owls and kestrels in 1892 served actually to decrease the numbers of the voles, and man's methods have hitherto proved a good deal less efficient than Nature's); and all that this can be expected to do is to delay the outbreak of the epidemic which alone can reduce the creatures to manageable numbers. The ecologist, on the contrary, would prefer to try some method which would actually encourage the multiplication of the rodents in the hope that the epidemic would come sooner, the agony would not be so prolonged, and the losses to agriculture consequently not so great. As alternatives he would suggest the effect of various bacterial cultures, which might provoke an artificial epidemic at an earlier stage of the cycle; or possibly some biological treatment such as that proposed by Rodier for rats, of trapping, killing all the females captured, but releasing all the males, in the hopes that the minority of females would be pestered out of successful breeding.

Common sense, however, may rightly ask one or two questions of the ecologist. It seems, for instance, to be a fact that epidemics set in among mice in all years of maximum abundance, whether the over-population becomes so intense as to constitute a real plague, or is so moderate as to be noticeable only by the professional naturalist on the lookout for such phenomena. How is it that the epidemic does not break out in the plague years as soon as the population intensity attained at the ordinary maximum has been reached? Clearly some other factor must come in—possibly a time factor, or, what comes to much the same thing, one involving the number of generations run through by one or all of the parasites of the rodent.

What is clear, however, is that no quite simple, straightforward methods will serve. The biological thinking of the man in the street—and of the professional biologist, too, for that matter—is much too much obsessed by military metaphor for him to be able yet to see quite straight on ecological problems. He is brought up to believe in a struggle for existence, which he envisages as a regular battle between an inoffensive herbivore and its enemies, or a sort of athletic competition between a carnivore and its prey. In both cases he thinks of the struggle as something in which victory is to be achieved, as in war or sport. As a matter of fact, it is nothing of the kind. A herbivorous animal without carnivorous enemies would tend to over-populate its territory, to be diseased and under-nourished, even to condemn itself to starvation by eating down its own food-supply; a carnivorous species which was restricted to one kind of prey, and a kind which it could too easily catch, would inevitably bring its own race to extinction by eating itself out of hearth and home. Both eventualities have, through the interference of man, been realized. When red deer were introduced into New Zealand they throve on the succulent forest and bush, and multiplied exceedingly owing to the absence of all carnivorous enemies. But after a few decades they had changed the face of the country where they were abundant, and to-day the fine heads and heavy beasts are found only on the outskirts of the deers' range, where they are still advancing into virgin country. Elsewhere the herds are full of stunted specimens and malformed antlers, and the authorities have been forced to play the part of natural enemy, and to adopt a rigorous policy of periodic thinning-out to save the stock.

As an example of the opposite effect, I may quote from Elton's *Animal Ecology* the curious case of Berlenga Island, off the coast of Portugal: 'This place supports a lighthouse and a lighthouse-keeper, who was in the habit of growing vegetables on the island, but was plagued by rabbits which had been introduced at some time or other. He also had the idea of introducing cats to cope with the situation— which they did so effectively that they ultimately ate up every single rabbit on the island. Having succeeded in this, the cats starved to death, since there were no other edible animals on the island.'

IV

We are often told that it is very important for children to select their parents wisely. It is becoming clear that a wise choice of enemies is an asset to an organism! One can hardly, perhaps, speak of an animal's enemies as part of its adaptations; but at least they are vital to its survival.

The fact is, of course, that in almost every case the word 'enemy' is only applicable when we are thinking in terms of individuals: as soon as we think of the species, the individual 'enemy' usually turns out to be a racial benefactor.

The two things needful are patience and research—patience in face of the popular demand for immediate action which is raised every time a plague of mice or a dearth of fish is experienced, and research to unravel the excessively complicated threads of the web of life.

The picture gained by research looks something like this, though we are not sure of the sun-spot influence on certain animal cycles:—The fluctuation in the number of sun-spots is probably connected with the distance of the great planet Jupiter from the sun's incandescent surface. The sun-spot fluctuations change the tracks of storms, brim and depress the waters of our lakes, alter our weather. The weather-changes make the giant trees put on more or less wood, promote the multiplication of rabbits, mice, and lemmings, cause an alternation of fat and lean years in the fur department of the Hudson's Bay Company, inflict periodic losses, through vole plagues, upon the world's agriculture. The multiplication of the rodents, besides reverberating upon fox and lynx, hawks and owls, affects our human health returns. Verily the dreams of astrology, even if they suffered from the defect of not being true, had at least the merit of simplicity in comparison with this web of cosmic influence spinning out from one corner of the solar system to another!

But the very complexity of what we do know, or can reasonably surmise, bids us take an infinity of pains to unearth the still greater complexities that are still hidden from us, if we are to control nature efficiently. Modern agriculture, with its massing of huge numbers of individuals of one species of plant or animal, is a deliberate invitation to parasites and pests to revel in the unaccustomed profusion. And when we come to tropical agriculture, we must remember that the tropical heat raises the insect to be the equal in activity of the warm-blooded mammal, including our own species. The mechanical and chemical triumphs of the last hundred years must give place in this century to biological triumphs of equal magnitude if man is to retain his dominant position on the earth.

Until synthetic chemistry has progressed a great deal further, the control of the plant kingdom is man's only means of supplying himself with the bulk of the food and the raw materials which he needs. The success of this control, as more and more of the earth's surface is given over to such vegetable exploitation, will come to depend more and more upon detailed knowledge about the animal and plant enemies, actual or potential, of the crops. We talk a great deal about safeguarding the food supply of the country in time of war. In fifty years' time we are much more likely to be talking about safeguarding the world's food supply in time of peace. And we shall not be looking to machinery for our safeguards, nor even to light cruisers or other forms of naval strength, but to the laboratories of entomology, mycology, and all the other branches of pure and applied ecology.

VIII

THE WAY OF THE DODO

I n 1938, the British Sporting Exhibition was held at the Imperial Institute. It is apposite to consider its subject-matter biologically in the twofold aspect of destruction and conservation. Speculative minds may wonder whether by the year 2038—or perhaps 3038 (a thousand years is of little account in the flow of biological time)—any such exhibition would be possible save as a museum record of the past. For the wild life of the world, including its game, big and small, has been diminishing with alarming speed all through recorded history. Some species have gone for ever; such are the dodo and the solitaire, the quagga, the aurochs, the blauwbok, the moa, the passenger pigeon, and the great auk. They are total losses: man can destroy a species, but he cannot restore it.

Perhaps one should say he cannot in most cases restore it; for the Germans have in the last decade produced a 'synthetic' aurochs, a form reconstituted by crossing the most primitive breeds of domestic cattle and selecting those types whose conformation most nearly resembles that of the original wild species. These resuscitated aurochs are said to be almost as ferocious as their prototypes. Such re-synthesis, however, is possible only with a wild species which has left domestic descendants: it would be a bold biologist who would undertake to produce a new dodo from a pigeon or to revive the quagga from the horse and zebra stock.

183

Other species now exist only in captivity. Such are the beautiful and fantastic white-tailed gnus (to be seen disporting themselves at Whipsnade), or the wild horse *Equus przevalskii*, identical with the horses depicted (and eaten) by Solutrean man, the last remnants of which in a wild state were killed off by bandits and deserters in Central Asia after the war. Camels may perhaps be included here—they exist only in domestication or as escapes from it. Then there are the numerous creatures which would have become extinct but for rigorous protection, and in most cases exist only in special reserves—such as the American and the European bison, the white rhinoceros, the Tuatara 'lizard' or *Sphenodon*, sole survivor of a whole order of reptiles, the kiwi, the platypus, the pronghorn, the Alaska fur-seal, or the giant tortoises of the Galapagos. The gorilla, the orang-utang, the Komodo dragon, and other creatures are on the margin of this category. Sometimes, even in spite of rigorous protection, the fate of species is still in the balance; this applies to the delightful koala of Australia.

Many other species are in danger of extermination owing to insufficient protection. The great whales are the outstanding example. The concern of the British Government over the problem has been shown by their arranging for the series of valuable investigations carried out by the research ship 'Discovery.' With the advent of pelagic whaling it seemed certain that, unless international regulation of the industry were achieved, whales would certainly become exceedingly scarce, and some species might be wiped out. It is therefore encouraging to know that an international convention on the subject has just been concluded, though our satisfaction is tempered by the war

Again, the sea-otter has been so persecuted for its beautiful pelt that it is on the verge of extinction, though a thriving colony has just been discovered in California.

In certain ways more serious than the loss of a few species, however beautiful or strange, is the general decrease of wild life all over the globe. Partly this is a mere quantitative decrease in numbers. The game in South Africa a century ago was more abundant than in the most famous reserves of Central Africa to-day. Early settlers in America found an abundance of bison, deer, duck, and wild mammals and birds of every kind, which does not exist to-day in any part of the United States, even in reserves or national parks. The stories of the pioneers read like fairy-tales or accounts of the Garden of Eden. Even in the last fifty years the numbers of wild ducks and geese and other migratory game-birds have declined so rapidly as to give real cause for alarm.

Partly the decrease is a decrease of range due to local extermination. Britain originally harboured as breeding species bears, wolves, beavers, bustards, spoonbills, sea-eagles, ospreys, ruffs, avocets. The kite was the chief scavenger of medieval London; now there are less than a dozen specimens in Britain. The lion used to be found in parts of Europe and ranged all over the East. Now, apart from a small area in India, it is confined to Africa.

A certain number of species, many of them undesirable pests, have increased; but in general it is all too true that both the variety and the abundance of life, especially in its larger and more striking manifestations, have decreased enormously in the historic period, and that the decrease has shown an alarming acceleration during the last hundred years.

Can anything be done to stop this trend before it is too late? Must we reconcile ourselves to scenery robbed of one of its major components (think of deer on the shoulder of a Scottish mountain, antelopes and zebra in the savannas of Africa, water-birds in the Camargue or the Naardemeer, cliff-breeders in St Kilda or the Farnes, the circling birds of prey giving point to distance in India)? Must we confine our knowledge of animals to dead specimens in museums instead of making the world a living museum?

A certain number of achievements encourage hope. At one time fewer than 1000 bison existed wild on the American continent: to-day there are several flourishing herds, reproducing so well that the surplus must be periodically killed. The beaver, thanks to protection, has reversed its alarming decline in eastern America, and is now becoming common; and the European beaver has been at least saved from extinction. The egrets of the United States, thanks to good laws and strong action, are on the increase. International agreement saved the Alaskan fur-seal.

In fact we can do a great deal. We have realized that the decline is almost wholly due to our own agency. Some of the destruction is direct, some indirect. Direct destruction may be for commercial gain, as with whales, egrets, or fur-bearers; or for sport, as of game; or in the interests of sport, as of so-called 'vermin' by gamekeepers; or for the protection of crops or other assets, as of bullfinches by fruit-growers, fish-eating creatures by fishermen, or elephants by the Governments of African colonies. Indirect destruction may occur as the result of the extension of agriculture, as with the great bustard in this country; by the draining of marshes for reclaiming land; by the extension of building; by the disturbances unwillingly caused by tourists and others bent on enjoying the countryside.

A final and frequent cause is the accidental or deliberate introduction of alien species. We in Britain suffer from the grey squirrel and have had to eradicate the muskrat. But other countries have much more serious problems. The unique marsupial fauna of Australia is in danger, almost in its entirety, as the result of the introduction of placental mammals, domestic, feral, and wild. The Galapagos giant tortoises are now threatened chiefly by the dogs, cats, and pigs introduced by man rather than by man's own destructiveness.

What can be done is manifold. Individuals can encourage birds around their homes and contribute to public opinion. They can multiply their contribution to the cause by joining one or other of the various societies concerned with conservation. The societies can set aside areas for sanctuaries, and can bring pressure to bear on local, national, and international authorities to secure the passing of proper legislation and the dedication of reserves and national parks.

Some societies, like our Royal Society for the Preservation of Birds, are concerned with the preservation of one type of animal in one limited region. They have done much in purchasing sanctuaries for rare birds and securing legislation for bird protection. Others, like the National Trust, are concerned with all aspects of nature, but again in a limited area. Apart from beautiful scenery and interesting buildings, they own fine bird reserves such as Blakeney Point and the Farne Islands. Then there are bodies such as the Fauna Society (or, to give it its full name, the Society for the Preservation of the Fauna of the

Empire) which deal with many types of animals over large regions; and bodies with general aims such as ULAWS (the University of London Animal Welfare Society); and finally those with the whole world for their province, such as the International Office for the Protection of Nature. This office operates through national committees, so that British subjects interested in world-wide fauna preservation will do best by joining the Fauna Society. In recent years this society has sent out special missions to survey and report on the situation in various parts of the Empire —Major Hingston to East Central Africa, Colonel Haywood to West Africa, Captain Caldwell to the West Indies, and Sir Thomas Comyns Platt to Malaya and Ceylon.

In a recent number of its *Journal* the Fauna Society exposes one of the numerous dangers to which big game is exposed—a 'safari service' organized primarily for the benefit of American 'sportsmen':—

> 'We can fix you up to a successful hunt—if you give us the chance, and then do your part, or allow us to do the necessary, in case you can't stand the gaff or become a rotten shot.' Bongo are 'difficult to get—but we get them.' Leopards—'in case of great urgency we can always get one with a trap-gun—if client demands it.'

Meanwhile the world's rhinos are being slaughtered because of the belief of Indians and Chinese in the aphrodisiac qualities of their horns; the whales are being dangerously reduced to make big profits for their slaughterers; seabirds are being battered and starved to death because vested interests stand in the way of the compulsory fitting of separators to oil-driven ships; fashionable women are still responsible for the death of some of the most beautiful winged creatures in the world; Australian 'opossums' are in danger of extermination for the value of their pelts; sportsmen will not agree to an adequate close season to keep up the numbers of wild-fowl; lizards and snakes are being killed out for shoes.

Two types of measure are of vital importance for the saving of the wild life of the world. One is the framing and ratification of international conventions for the protection of the fauna of large areas. That for Africa has already become operative; and it is hoped that later a further international conference will be held in London to discuss the possibility of extending the principles established by the African Convention to India and southern Asia. The other main measure is the establishment of national parks. National parks differ from sanctuaries in their size, and from game reserves in their permanence. They are places where Nature, not man's material interests, are paramount. Anyone who has seen Kruger Park in South Africa or the Parc National Albert in the Belgian Congo will take away with him an indelible impression of the wonder of wild life, and will wish to help in preserving more of it for future generations.

There are splendid national park systems in Canada and the U.S.A., and isolated parks in many countries, such as Switzerland, Italy, and Malaya. It is, however, urgent that many more be created in the British Empire, notably in Africa and in Britain itself. In Britain, apart from the need of preserving areas such as Snowdonia, the Lakes, or the Peak district for healthy recreation, the west coast of Scotland provides admirable opportunities for creating a national park for the preservation of the surviving remnants of our larger fauna.

IX

THE COURTSHIP OF ANIMALS

WE men like to see animals courting. It amuses us to see them thus imitating humanity, and throws something at once romantic and familiar into those dumb and hidden lives which they veil so closely from us. 'One touch of Nature makes the whole world kin,' we murmur, and find a new pleasure in the hackneyed words. They are really not quite apropos, however; for what we in our heart of hearts mean to say is one touch of *human* nature. Man is a vain organism, and likes to stand surrounded by mirrors—magnifying mirrors if it be possible, but at any rate mirrors. And so we read the ideas of our own mind into the animals, and confidently speak of 'suitors' and 'coy brides to be won' and 'jealous rivals' and what not, as if birds or even spiders or newts were miniature human beings, in fancy dress no doubt, but with the thoughts of a twentieth-century inhabitant of London or New York.

Some of the more reflective, perhaps, may wonder how far we are justified in our assumptions as to the motives and meaning of animal courtship; while others, with maybe some biological knowledge behind them, may try to look at it all from the other side of the gulf between man and beast, imagine how our own courtship would look to an external and dispassionate intelligence, wonder whether much of human behaviour had better not be interpreted from the animal side rather than the animal's from ours, and how much we are walled in by our biological heritage.

Animal courtship is an unfashionable topic among biologists at present; and I do not exaggerate when I say that it is also one on which both ignorance and prejudice prevail. My own real interest in the subject began when, one spring in Wales, I observed the beautiful courtship of the redshank, a common shore bird, and when I got back to libraries, could find no ordered account of it, or indeed of bird courtship in general. And now, after some twenty-five years of reading and thinking about the subject, interspersed with a number of pleasant if strenuous holidays in Britain, in Louisiana, in Holland, in Spitsbergen, trying to find out what really does happen with this or that common bird, I can confidently assert that Darwin's theory of sexual selection, though wrong in many details, yet was essentially right: that there is no other explanation for the bulk of the characters concerned with display, whether antics, song, colour, or special plumes or other structures, than that they have been evolved in relation to the mind of the opposite sex; that *mind* has thus been the sieve through which variations in courtship characters must pass if they are to survive.

Down at the base of the animal scale courtship of course does not exist. Jellyfish or sponges or sea-urchins simply shed their reproductive cells into the water and trust to luck for fertilization. It is only when male and female must actually co-operate for fertilization to be effected, that we can expect to find courtship; and even so it will not exist unless there is a fairly elaborate brain and nervous system.

Perhaps the first adumbration of courtship is seen in the

nuptial dances of certain marine bristle-worms (Poly-chaetes), in which at certain seasons of the year and phases of the moon the creatures swim up out of their crannies in the rocks and gather in groups, excited males wriggling round the females. It is possible that the presence of the dancing males in some way stimulates the females to lay their eggs, upon which the male elements are discharged in milky clouds. Snails too have a primitive courtship, which is complicated by the fact that they are bi-sexual and each in its rôle of male attempts to stimulate the other in its rôle of female.

But the first actions to which the name *courtship*, and not merely perhaps direct stimulus to fertilization, must be given are those of a few crabs and most spiders. Among the crustaceans, the fiddler-crab is characterized by the presence in the male of one enormously enlarged claw, which may weigh almost as much as the rest of the body, and is often brightly coloured. It used to be supposed that with this the males stopped their burrows, or fought other males, or seized and carried off the females. How-ever, the careful studies of Dr Pearce show that its main function is one of display. In the mating season, when a female comes past, the males throw themselves into a tip-toe attitude, with big claw rigidly held aloft. If the female takes no notice, the male runs again to where she can see him, and again strikes the statuesque pose: if she goes too far, he returns to his burrow. The observer summed up his impressions thus: 'One could only say that the males appeared to be displaying their maleness.'

There we have the clue to the origins of courtship in a nutshell. Once the brain reaches a certain complexity, it controls behaviour. A crab can react to various situations

—a food-situation, a hunger-situation, a fear-situation, a sex-situation; and the statuesque male with his uplifted claw is the sign and symbol of the sex-situation, just as the coming of a man or other large animal among the burrows constitutes an enemy-situation, with resultant scuttling. Doubtless even without such male advertisement, mating would eventually occur; but, as Darwin so clearly saw, the advantage may be to the male and not to the race—the male who did not display himself as such would not get mated and would leave no descendants.

In the spiders, we find a very interesting difference between the hunters and the web-spinners. Among the former, who catch their prey by sight and stalking, males perform strange dances before the females, and often have the parts they thus display brightly coloured. The latter are almost blind; and in them there are no dances, but the male comes up to the web of the female and vibrates one of the threads in a special manner, quite different from the vibrations made by trapped prey. In both cases it seems clear that the courtship's primary function is to indicate the existence of a 'sexual situation.' But here, to do so is a good deal more important than in the crab, for all the evidence goes to show that if this indication were not made, the female would simply treat the male like any other small living object, and eat him! In many species she actually does so after the act of mating (and this occurs too in the scorpions); and in some others she is definitely hostile at first, while the male, who is usually much smaller than she is, is always obviously very ready to run away during the early phases of courtship.

In one hunting spider the male offers the female a nice fly, neatly wrapped in silk. If put in a box by himself with a fly, he will eat it; but if with a fly and a female, he will wrap and offer it; and if in a box from which a female has recently been removed, and in which her odour still presumably lingers, he will still wrap it, and search, like Shelley with his bouquet, 'That he might there present it! —Oh, to whom?'

In the carnivorous flies of the family *Empidae*, strange developments of the love-gift have taken place. In some species the male offers an unadorned carcass to the female. In others, however, the prey is stuck in the front end of a glistening ' balloon,' made of bubbles of viscous liquid secreted by the male, larger than his own body, and carried in his legs as he flies to and fro; doubtless this makes the 'sexual situation' more conspicuous from afar. Finally, in a few species there has been a refinement. The balloon is there, but prey is no longer carried in it; instead, the males stick a leaf or flower-petal in it—and indeed they will dart down and pick up any small conspicuous objects, such as fragments of paper, that you may choose to sprinkle on the surface of the water over which they hover. Here, in quite a different evolutionary line from our own, we find quite definitely the employment of a non-utilitarian 'present' as gift from male to female.

When we come to the vertebrates, matters become even more interesting, for it is among them, especially in the birds, that courtship and display reach their highest elaboration. Only in a few fish is there much of a courtship, as would be expected from the fact that most species produce large numbers of eggs which are only fertilized after laying. The frogs and toads that make night pulse with sound in the warm regions of the earth use their voices, as do the grasshoppers their legs or wings, in the interests of reproduction; and if the grasshoppers were life's first instrumentalists, the frogs were the first vocalists.

The male frog, however, merely broadcasts an advertisement of his presence; it is among the tailed amphibians that true display is found. Our common newts in the breeding season take to the water and develop a high fin all along the back and tail. This is much larger in the males, who in addition change their winter livery for one of brighter colours. They may also be seen performing their courtship—actively moving in front of the females, often scraping up against them, all the time vibrating the bent tail. The strange fact about this procedure, however, is that they do not begin their display until after they have emitted their fertilizing elements. These are deposited on the bottom of the pond or aquarium inside a special packet or spermatophore, which the female must pick up for fertilization to occur; and courtship begins when this deposition is completed.

Here we see that display may have a racial function, adjuvant to successful fertilization, and not an affair between rival males. For even the most hardened Darwinian would hardly maintain that a female, if two males simultaneously deposited spermatophores and then began their display before her, would be able to remember which male had deposited which spermatophore even were she to be better pleased or more stimulated by the display of one rather than of the other; and of course unless the approved male were also to be the father of the young, his pleasing of the female could have no evolutionary effect. No: it seems clear that here the function of display has

again to deal with the 'sexual situation'; with the difference that it is not merely to advertise the male's presence
and masculinity, but to generate a sexual situation in the
mind of the female. As a matter of fact, Finkler has by
experiment shown that in the absence of a male's display,
the female will not pick up spermatophores, so that this
conception of courtship's function being to facilitate fertilization via the mind, by stimulating the mental mechanism
into the right phase, seems justified.

There is one species of bird for which Darwin's original
theory has been definitely shown to hold good. That is
the well-known shore bird, the ruff (*Machetes*). In the
winter the sexes are only to be told apart by size, but in
the breeding season the males grow a magnificent ruff—
a tippet or collar—round the cheeks and neck, and two
fine ear-tufts above. What is more, it is hard to find two
males alike; not only do they develop different ground-
colours in their plumage, but the collar and ear-tufts may
either or both be of some special colour or marking, one
black, the other white; or chestnut, pepper and salt, buff,
sandy, grey, sepia, and what not. Arrived at their breeding places, the males assemble at a definite spot, usually
known as a 'hill,' though it may be but a dry area in the
marsh. The females visit the hill from time to time, but
the males never go near the nests out in the marshes, nor
take any share in brooding or the cares of the young. On
the hill each male usually keeps to a little private area of
his own. When no females are present, the male birds
will be dancing, whirring round like Dervishes, and spar-
ring and jousting with each other. On the arrival of a
female, the scene is changed. The males crouch down,
immobile, sometimes flat on the ground with spread wings.

The hen may simply stroll round and fly away again—on which the cock birds rise rather sheepishly from their prostrate posture, as if pretending that nothing had been going on. Or she may approach a male and nibble at his neck, on which mating is consummated.

Edmund Selous watched one particular ruff hill in Holland for weeks, arriving at his hide at or before dawn. Every male on the hill was distinguishable by his appearance; and so Selous was able to discover that some were more successful than others.

Here is Darwin's theory in practice, working itself out in every detail—the adornments developed only by the male in the breeding season, and used only in sexual combat and sexual display; the male with no power to enforce his desires, the female completely arbiter of her choice; and, finally, the evidence that choice is exercised. The only puzzling point is the extreme variability of the males. This may be explained by some later discoveries. Various biologists, as we shall see later, have found that display, combat, and threat have a direct physiological effect on birds of both sexes, actually helping to ripen the reproductive organs. And Fraser Darling and others have recently shown that this effect is cumulative, some stimulus resulting from the sight of other birds courting or fighting. This at once explains the frequent occurrence of communal display-grounds: they are arrangements for heightening reproductive efficiency. But it also explains the ruff's variability. If, as seems reasonable, the unfamiliar is more exciting than the familiar, variety will have a greater mass-stimulating effect than uniformity. So, granted a tendency to marked variation, variety will be encouraged and preserved.

This clear-cut case is of importance, because it enables us to draw pretty definite conclusions in other similar cases. In the blackcock, for instance, a handsome member of the grouse tribe, there are similar assembly-places for mating—veritable temples of Venus. Here the individual males cannot be distinguished, but each again appears to have his own definite pitch or stand, and, both from direct watching and by analogy with the ruff, it seems that here, too, there is true selection. Finally, in some birds of paradise there are also mating-places, but in the trees, where the males dance and display their gorgeous plumes.

It is interesting to note that the evolution of such special mating-places with assemblies of males and visits by females has taken place at least three separate times in birds —in the waders, the game-birds, and the birds of paradise. The influence of mode of life on type of courtship is another problem that can be followed out in birds. Where there is polygamy and where the female alone broods the eggs and cares for the young, there we find the greatest disparity in colour and courtship-behaviour between the sexes. The female is generally drab, protectively coloured; the male, *per contra*, brilliant, and alone participating in display. Since there is polygamy (or promiscuity), the successful male will imprint his characters on a larger number of descendants—and so display-brilliance will be at a premium; while, since he plays no biologically useful rôle after fertilization is once effected, there is less need for protective colour, since it does not much matter whether he be killed or no.

Most birds are monogamous, however, at least for the season (or sometimes only for a single brood—like the American wren, which as bird-banding experiments have shown, usually changes partners between the first and second broods of a single year). Most of the largest group of monogamous birds, the song-birds proper, have their whole sex-life hinge on what we may call the territorial system. They have their young hatched naked and helpless, needing abundant food for their growth, and liable to die of cold if left too long unbrooded. Hence it is necessary, first, for both parent birds to feed the young; second, for the presence round the nest of an area sufficiently large to supply the young's needs, and not trespassed upon by other food-seeking parents of the same species. This is ensured through an extension of the instinct, nearly universal among birds, to resent intrusion into the area round the actual or future nest-site.

Even in colonial nesters, like egrets or guillemots, the defended area exists, though it may be only a couple of feet across. In what we may call the true territorial birds, or birds with feeding as well as nesting territory, the course of events is as follows (I follow in this particular Eliot Howard's admirable description of the course of events in the European warblers or *Sylviidae*). The males are first on the breeding-grounds. If the species be a spring migrant, the males generally migrate north a week or so ahead of the females. Arrived, they take possession of an area—a territory—sometimes without dispute, sometimes after a fight with a simultaneous arrival or a bird already in possession. Then they begin their singing. Contrary to usual belief, the song of most song-birds is at its best before the mate has even arrived. As Howard has, I think, convincingly shown, the prime function of song is an advertisement. It is an advertisement of eligibly-occupied territory, which serves the double purpose of attracting females and warning off other males. Similarly, many of the special display-characters of males are used in threat-display against other males as well as in courtship-display to females.

When the females arrive on the scene, no immediate courtship on the part of the males is to be observed. If the female is alone, she simply takes her place in the territory, and the two are a pair for the season. Nature abhors a vacuum, and this particular vacuum, the absence of the female from a territory, is filled with the least possible fuss. If two rival females arrive together, it is they who fight for the possession of territory-plus-male, while he hovers about, an interested and even excited spectator, but without participating. Then follows the strange fact, which at first sight seems to upset the whole Darwinian apple-cart, namely that courtship and display now begin vigorously —only now, after the two birds are mated for the season. The male vibrates his wings, spreads his tail, puffs his feathers, bows and scrapes, runs before his mate, often with a leaf or twig or other piece of nest material in his beak, and his antics may be so extravagant as to testify to the most ardent excitement within. How can this be fitted in with Darwin's view that these antics and displays have been evolved in large measure through the female's selection? To this, what we have learned from the lowly newt provides the answer. Courtship and display need not always have as their chief result the choosing of a mate. They may be, and indeed normally appear to be, accessory to the act of pairing and fertilization itself. The mind of a bird is a complex thing, and so is its life; the bird cannot always be tuned to a sexual situation. The simplest way, it would appear, of ensuring that it is not always so tuned (with consequent excessive pairing), and yet of ensuring that both sexes shall be simultaneously ready to mate often enough, is that one sex—the male—shall be more constantly in the phase of sexual preparedness, and by his display shall both advertise the fact and also help to stimulate the female to the proper emotional level.

Finally, as we have mentioned, there is a more direct biological advantage in display. It appears that in seasons which have been inclement just before and during egg-laying, the number of eggs is often reduced and the percentage of infertility raised. It is also known that all the reproductive processes of birds are very much under the control of the higher, emotional centres of the brain. For instance, a female dove brought up in isolation from infancy will usually lay no eggs; but the presence of a male bird in a near-by cage, or even the caressing of her neck with a human finger in a way reminiscent of the caresses of the male's nibbling beak, will almost always cause an egg to be laid. It has now been demonstrated that display and threat promote the ripening of the reproductive organs; this will be of advantage, especially in bad seasons, since birds' emotions are very much at the mercy of the weather.

Before leaving this group, mention should be made of the curious fact that in all-the-year residents who are also territory-birds, there is an 'engagement' period in the spring. For some weeks after the pair are in possession of a territory, fertilization is not effected. The biological reason for this is plain—it is advantageous for a bird to be on its territory early, or it may not find one; but it must not breed before a date which will give the probability of there being plenty of food for the young. The physiological machinery by which it is effected resides in the female; it is only at a certain season (probably depending on a certain mean temperature) that the eggs in her ovary start to grow rapidly, and only then that her full sex-instincts arise.

Finally, we come to the large group of birds in which both male and female not only help look after the young, but also share in incubation and in the building of the nest. Such are the herons, the pelicans, the grebes, the divers, and many others. In them, neither parent is biologically the more precious; so that if protective colour is needed, it is needed by both. Furthermore, their instincts have to be so similar in regard to nest, eggs, and young that the similarity, it appears, has spread to their courtship habits, too. For it is at any rate a fact that in a large number of this group of birds, and nowhere else, we find what we must call mutual courtship—both sexes developing bright colours and special structures for the breeding season, and both using them simultaneously in a mutual display (which, as with other monogamists among birds, begins only after pairing-up).

Anyone who, like myself, has watched such birds by the hour day after day, must be struck by the fact of their enjoyment of the courtship ceremonies for their own sake, and the further fact that the ceremonies are often what we may call biologically self-exhausting, in that the birds' emotional tension is often liberated through them, instead of being stimulated and leading on to actual pairing. It would seem as if these strange and romantic displays—head-shaking, or diving for weed, or aquatic dances breast to breast, or relieving guard on the nest with ceremonies of parade, or presentation of a twig with wings and crest a-quiver,—as if they constituted a bond between the two birds of the pair, binding them together so long as the breeding season lasted by emotional links. And after all, why not? Does not something similar obtain in human society? And does it not there play a valuable rôle, in cementing with love and joy the racially important edifice of the family? And if it has this value in man, why not in these birds, for whom too the co-operation of both parents for the good of the family is essential?

Here then we see display pressed, not merely into the service of one male against the rest, not merely facilitating fertilization, but into that of the super-individual unit, the family. And it is interesting that the family life of birds attains its highest development in these forms which have, we may say, equal sex rights and duties.

In yet other cases we see display becoming social, and courtship tending (as again sometimes in man) to be again diverted from its original character of individual wooing, this time toward the publicity of the dance. Among birds I myself have investigated, this is best seen in the oyster-catcher, the bold black-and-white shore bird, with red bill, sometimes known as sea-pie. Gatherings of eight or ten birds of this species may be seen in spring, all careering around together in their stiff courtship attitude with neck out-thrust and long bill pointing vertically downwards, and a piercing noise of trilled piping issuing from their throats. Observation revealed that this is not only the commonest form of display, but the only one used while on the ground; that it may be employed by the male alone, or mutually by male and female together; and that, in addition to its courtship function, it expresses jealous hostility of other trespassing birds, whether trespassing on territorial or sexual rights. When, in a flock in early spring, courtship begins, other birds may join in the excitement; hostility re-enforces love, and soon the whole number are careering round in frenzied excitement which is, it seems, neither sexual nor hostile, but social. Here the social dance appears to have little or no special function, but is rather a biological accident.

Psychologically, one of the most interesting things about bird courtship is the frequency with which in display the birds will carry in their beaks a piece of the material of which their nest is built. This holds good even for the Adélie penguins, charmingly described by Dr Levick. Here the nest is nothing but a rim of stones round a depression; and accordingly the male presents stones to his mate as part of his courtship. Interestingly enough, this action sometimes becomes diverted to serve other instincts and emotions, such as wonder—the birds will present stones to dogs and to men; and Dr Levick confesses to having felt quite embarrassed the first time he was the recipient! Still another tale hangs by these stones. The sitting birds are all the time stealing stones from each other's nests. Levick painted a number of stones different colours, and placed them at one margin of the nesting area. After this he could mark the rate of their progress (all by theft!) across the colony; and found that the red stones travelled much quicker than the rest. This is of great theoretical interest, for red is a colour which is to all intents and purposes absent in the penguin's environment —and yet they prefer it above all others. If a male penguin could grow a red patch he would probably be very quick to gain a mate.

Such an example also shows in what sort of way the

extraordinary bowers of the bower-bird can have developed. These are a blend between art gallery and museum, usually a tunnel of twigs with a collection of shells, bones, berries, and flowers at one end. In one species a space of ground is cleared, and large leaves laid upon it, their silvery under-surface upwards. As they wither, they are replaced; if they are blown over, the silver side is turned up once more.

Among the mammals, there is on the whole little courtship or display by the males, but correspondingly more fighting. This probably depends on the fact that the reproductive instincts of the female mammal are more rigidly under a definite physiological control, less under the fluid control of higher, emotional centres; the male deer or elephant-seal has but to guard his harem, and they will automatically accept him in due time. There is, however, a great deal still to be discovered of the courtships of monogamous mammals—a difficult subject, because so many are nocturnal or burrowers, but one that would well repay study. Among some intelligent quadrupeds, however, such as the elephant, a pleasant mutual courtship, of trunk-caresses, has been described; and when we move up toward *Homo sapiens* and reach the monkeys and apes, we find a number of display and threat characters among the males. Some are to us repulsive, like the naked scarlet and azure cheeks of the Mandril, or the blue of Stevenson's

> . . . blue-behinded ape that skips
> about the trees of Paradise.

But others, like the orang or some of the marmosets with their mustachios, or the Satan monkey with his fine beard,

are curiously reminiscent of ourselves, and we are reminded of Mr Hilaire Belloc's baboon—

> The Big Baboon who lives upon
> The plains of Caribou,
> He goes about with nothing on
> —A shocking thing to do.
>
> But if he dressed respectably
> And let his whiskers grow,
> How like that Big Baboon would be
> To Mister—So-and-So!

*　　　*　　　*　　　*

Courtship in animals is the outcome of four major
steps in evolution. First, the development of sexuality;
secondly, the separation of the sexes; thirdly, internal
fertilization, or at least the approximation of males and
females; and finally, the development of efficient sense-
organs and brains. Without any one of these, there would
never have existed that host of strange and lovely features
of life, summed up under the head of courtship, which
beautify the appearance and variegate the existence of so
many of the higher animals, including our own species.

X

THE INTELLIGENCE OF BIRDS

A CENTURY and a half ago, it was generally accepted, even by professional naturalists, that nature represented a single scale, culminating in man. There existed, they supposed, a ladder of life, each rung of which was represented by a different type of animal, with humanity as the highest of all. And from this point of view, each kind of living creature represented merely a step on the way to man, its nature an incomplete realization of human nature.

But with further study, especially after it was illuminated by the theory of evolution, a wholly different and more interesting picture emerged. The various types of animals—insects, fish, crustaceans, birds and the rest—could not be thought of as the rungs of one ladder, the steps of a single staircase; they now appeared as the branches of a tree, the ever-growing tree of evolving life. And with this, they took on a new interest. It might still be that man was at the summit of the whole; but he was at the top of the tree only by being at the top of one particular branch. There existed many other branches, quite different in their nature, in which life was working out its ends in a different way from that she had adopted in the human branch. By looking at these branches we are able to see not merely our own natures in an incomplete state, but quite other expressions of life, quite other kinds of nature from our own. Life appears not as a single finished article, but as a whole series of diverse and fascinating experiments to deal with the problems of the world. We happen to be the most successful experiment, but we are not therefore the most beautiful or the most ingenious.

Of these various experiments, the two which are the most interesting are on the one hand the insects, with their bodies confined within the armour of their skeletons, their minds cramped within the strange rigidity of instinct, and on the other hand the birds.

It is with these latter that I am concerned here; and I shall try to picture some of the differences between their minds and our own. But first we need a little evolutionary background so as to grasp some of the main characters of this particular branch of life. Birds, then, branched off from reptiles somewhere about a hundred million years ago, a good long time after our own mammalian ancestry had taken its origin from another branch of the great reptilian stock. The birds' whole nature was of course re-modelled in connection with flight, so that their fore-limb was irrevocably converted into a wing, and no chance was left of remoulding it into a hand. They clung obstinately to one important character of their reptilian ancestry—the shelled egg, whereas their mammalian rivals came to specialize in the internal nourishment of the young inside the mother's body; and by this the birds debarred themselves from ever being born into the world at such an advanced state of development as is possible to man and other higher mammals. But in one thing at least they went further than any mammal; they not only developed a constant temperature, but kept it constant at a greater height. Birds and mammals are unique among living things in having evolved the self-regulating central-heating system that we call ' warm blood,' a system which is of the utmost importance, since it enables their activities of body and mind to continue on a more or less constant level instead of being slowed down by cold, speeded up by heat, as is the case with all other kinds of animals, and makes it possible for them to laugh at extremes of temperature which send insects or reptiles into the sleep of hibernation or aestivation. But birds have pushed the invention to its limits: they live at temperatures which would be the extremes of fever for us.

It is this extremely high temperature, 105 degrees or over, combined with the agility that comes of flight, which gives birds their fascinating quality of seeming always so intensely alive. But being intensely alive does not necessarily, as we know from human examples, mean being intensely intelligent. And in fact, in respect of their minds just as much as their bodies, birds have developed along other lines than mammals. Mammals have gradually perfected intelligence and the capacity for learning by experience, until this line has culminated in that conscious reason and in that deliberate reliance upon the accumulated experience of previous generations, which are unique properties of the human species. And with the gradual rise of intelligence, the power and fixity of the instincts has diminished. Birds, on the other hand, have kept instinct as the mainstay of their behaviour; they possess, like all other backboned animals, some intelligence and some power of profiting by experience, but these are subordinate, used merely to polish up the outfit of instincts which is provided by heredity without having to be paid for in terms of experience. Indeed, the anatomist could tell you as much by looking at the brains of bird and mammal, even if he had never studied the way the creatures behave. For whereas in mammals we can trace a steady increase in the size and elaboration of the cerebral hemispheres, the front part of the brain which we know to be the seat of intelligence and learning, this region is never highly developed in any bird, but remains relatively small, without convolutions on its surface; while other parts which are known to be the regulating machinery for complicated but more automatic and more emotional actions, are in birds relatively larger than in four-footed creatures.

But enough of this generalizing. What I wanted to show at the outset was the fact that in the lives of birds we are not merely studying the actions of creatures which, though small and feathered, had minds of the same type as ourselves, albeit on a lower level, but of a branch of the tree of life which, in mind as in body, has specialized along a line of its own, showing us mind of a different quality from ours. They have raised emotion to the highest pitch found in animals; the line of mammals has done the same thing for intelligence.

Perhaps the most obvious way in which birds differ from men in their behaviour is that they can do all that they have to do, including some quite complicated things, without ever being taught. Flying, to start with, is an activity which, for all its astonishing complexity of balance and aeronautical adjustment, comes untaught to birds. Young birds very frequently make their first flight when their parents are out of sight. Practice, of course, makes perfect and puts a polish on the somewhat awkward first performance; but there is no elaborate learning needed as with our learning of golf or tennis or figure-skating. Furthermore, the stories of old birds 'teaching' their young to fly seem all to be erroneous. Some kinds of birds, once their young are full-fledged, do try to lure them away from the nest. But this merely encourages them to take the plunge; there is no instruction by the old bird in the movements of flight, no conscious imitation by the young.

But flight, after all, is something very organic. What is much more extraordinary than that a bird should be able to fly untaught (though this demands a formidable complexity of self-regulating machinery provided ready-made by Nature in the form of muscles and skeleton, nerves and nerve centres, eyes and balance organs) is that it should be able to build its nest untaught. And of this there can be no manner of doubt. Young birds, mating for the first time, can make perfectly good nests, and nests of the usual type found among their particular species. Some people have suggested that this may be due to their having absorbed the necessary knowledge from contemplating the structure of the nest in which they were brought up. But even if we were to admit that this was possible—which is very unlikely, considering that the young of small birds are very stupid, only live a few days in the nest after their eyes are open, and are never given any lessons in nest-building by their parents—it is negatived by the facts. For instance, the celebrated mound-builders or brush-turkeys of the Australian region build large mounds of rubbish and decaying leaves and deposit their eggs at the end of tunnels in the mounds, leaving them to be hatched out by the heat of the fermenting vegetation. The young brush-turkey on hatching scrambles out of the tunnel; it can get no instruction from its parents, since they have long since gone about their own business; and not only does it not stay around the mound long enough to observe how it is constructed, but does not bestow on it so much as a look. None the less, when the time comes for it to mate, it will build a mound just as its ancestors have done.

Secondly, even young birds which have been brought up by hand in artificial nests—boxes lined by cotton wool or what not—will build the proper kind of nest for their species when the time comes for mating, and will not attempt to reproduce their own early homes. We are reminded of Dr Johnson's comment on the suggestion that the attraction which woman's bosom has for the male sex is due to its pleasurable association with food during infancy. He did not notice, he said, that those who had been hand-fed when babies evinced any passionate fondness for bottles. In fact, the impulse of sex attraction in the one case, the impulse to construct a nest of a certain type in the other, cannot be explained by any rationalistic arguments of this sort; the one and the other are based not upon reason, not upon association, but upon instinct. The finch, for instance, has the impulse, when its mating urge is upon it, to weave coarse material into a rough cup, and then to line this with some finer material; the tailor-bird has the impulse to take leaves and sew them together; the house-martin to collect mud or clay and construct a cup against the side of a cliff or a house.

In a not dissimilar way, the bird which is in the physiological state of broodiness will have the violent urge to sit on eggs, or, if no eggs are available, it will often take something else. Crows have been known to brood golf-balls, gulls to sit on tobacco-tins substituted for their eggs; and the majestic emperor penguin, if it loses its egg or chick, will even brood lumps of ice in its inhospitable Antarctic home.

This fobbing off of a natural urge with an unnatural substitute is doubtless unintelligent; but we may ask whether it is more unintelligent than the behaviour of elderly maiden ladies who spend their maternal impulses upon lapdogs or canaries, or that of disappointed old bachelors who turn their energies into a useless hobby.

In all probability, however, the bird's behaviour *is* more unintelligent; for undoubtedly it does not even rationalize as we do, or seek to find reasons for its behaviour. How un-humanly a bird regards the central facts of its life is seen in many of its relations to its offspring. Birds undoubtedly have a strong emotional concern over their eggs and young, but it is an instinctive, irrational concern, not an instinct entwined, as is the human parents' concern, with reason, memory, personal affection, and foresight. A pair of birds is robbed of their whole brood; the parental instinct finds itself frustrated, and they will show great agitation. But if one or more of the nestlings die before they are fledged—a frequent and in some species a normal occurrence—the old birds show no signs of sorrow or even agitation, but merely throw the corpse out of the nest as if it were a stick or a piece of dirt. And while a chick is, to our eyes, obviously failing, the old birds, far from making special efforts to restore it, as would human parents, definitely neglect it. The fact seems to be that the bird parent feels parental only when stimulated by some activity on the part of its children. When they gape and squawk, this is a stimulus to the parent to feed and tend them assiduously; when the stimulus fails, the parental feeling is no longer aroused, the bird is no longer impelled to parental actions.

This same incapacity to experience things as men and

women would experience them is shown by the fact that if you remove young birds from a nest, as Mr Kearton did with some starlings, and substitute some eggs, the mother, after a moment's apparent surprise, may accept the situation with equanimity, and respond to the new stimulus in the proper way, by sitting on the eggs. There was no trace of the distraction and grief which a human mother would have felt.

But perhaps the familiar cuckoo provides us with the completest proof, over the widest field, of the dissimilarity of birds' minds with our own. The young cuckoo, having been deposited as an egg in the nest of some quite other species of bird—a meadow-pipit, say, or a hedge-sparrow—and having hatched out in double-quick time, the rate of its embryonic development being adjusted to its parasitic habits, so that it shall not lag behind its foster-brothers, next proceeds to evict all the rest of the contents of the nest, be these eggs or young birds. It is provided with a flat and indeed slightly hollow back; and, hoisting its victim on to this, it crawls backwards up the side of the nest, to pitch the object outside. Thus it continues to do until the nest is empty.

What cruelty, you will say, and what unpleasant ingenuity! But you will be wrong. The nestling cuckoo is not cruel, nor does he know why he is murdering his fellow nest-mates. He acts blindly, because he is a machine constructed to act thus and not otherwise. Not only is his back slightly concave, but this concavity is highly irritable and over-sensitive; the touch of any object there drives him frantic, and if it is continued, it releases the impulse to walk upwards and backwards until he has reached the edge of whatever he is walking on, and then to tilt the object overboard. He will behave in just the same way to marbles or hazel-nuts or any other small object. Indeed, if you think of it, he *cannot* know what he is doing. For he will act thus immediately he is hatched, before his eyes are open; even if he could be taught, his parents have never been near him, and his foster-parents are hardly likely to instruct him in this particular! No, the whole train of actions is the outcome of a marvellous piece of machinery with which he is endowed by heredity, just as he is endowed with the equally marvellous adaptive mechanism of his feathers. The machinery consists in the shape of the back, its hyper-sensitiveness, and the intricate pattern of nervous connections in the brain and spinal cord which set the particular muscles into action. The act in fact is purely instinctive, just as instinctive and automatic as sneezing or coughing in ourselves. And, like coughing, it has been brought into being by the long unconscious processes of natural selection, not by any foresight or conscious will.

Once the foster-brothers are outside, we shall get another surprising peep into bird mind. When the foster-mother comes home, she does not seem in the least distressed by the absence of all but one of her brood, but at once sets about feeding the changeling. What is more, she pays no attention to her own offspring, even should some of these be dangling just outside the nest. As long as there is something in the nest which appeals to her parental instincts, it seems that young birds outside the nest, even if they be her own, are treated as so many foreign objects.

Then the young cuckoo begins to grow. It grows into a creature entirely different from its foster-parents, and eventually becomes several times bulkier thàn they, so that they have to perch on its head to drop food into its mouth! But they are not in the least disconcerted, as would human parents if their children began growing into giants, and giants of quite a different appearance from themselves. They are built to respond to the stimulus of appeals for food from any nestling that starts life in their nest, and they continue their response, whether the nestling is their own or a cuckoo.

At last the young cuckoo is ready to fly, leaves his foster-parents, and very soon must leave the country on migration. So far as we know, all the old cuckoos have before this time left the country for the south, so that it is again without any teaching or any knowledge that the young ones must obey the migration urge.

Some very interesting experiments by Professor Rowan of Alberta have thrown a good deal of light on this mysterious question of the impulse to migrate. In autumn, he caught a number of birds which usually leave the regions of an Alberta winter for the south (crows and the little finches called juncos were the kind he used), and kept them in unheated aviaries. So long as they were supplied with plenty of food, they remained perfectly healthy and happy, even with the temperature many degrees below zero. One lot were simply kept thus, as 'controls' for the experiment: but another lot, in place of being exposed to the natural shortening of the days in early winter, had their days artificially lengthened by electric light, a little more every evening. In midwinter, Rowan liberated a number of birds. The controls made no attempt to migrate southwards, but just hung about the place. The birds whose day had been lengthened, however, for the most part did move away—but apparently most of them moved north and not south!

Other birds were killed and examined: all the controls, as was expected, had their reproductive organs shrunken to the tiny size characteristic of birds in winter; but the long-day birds showed reproductive organs which were enlarging like those of ordinary wild birds in early spring about the time of northward migration.

The view held by Rowan—and though it cannot yet be regarded as completely proved, it certainly seems probable—is as follows. The extra length of day caused the birds to spend more of their time in activity, less in sleep; this, by some mechanism we do not yet understand, caused the reproductive organs to begin to grow instead of shrinking; and the secretions of the reproductive organs control the migratory urge. When they are shrinking in early autumn, the changed secretion in the blood impels the birds to move south. When they are tiny and inactive, as normally in the dead of winter, there is no impulse to migrate at all; and when they are growing again, the secretion impels to northward movement, even if the bird be already in the most wintry and inhospitable conditions.

Whatever the precise interpretation, it is at least clear that the impulse to migrate is a strange blind urge, controlled and set in motion by the chemical agency of the reproductive secretions, and wholly unrelated to reason, or to any consciously-envisaged destination.

Then again there is the well-known 'broken-wing trick' practised by so many birds when their young are threatened. Most writers of natural-history books set this down as a remarkable example of intelligence:—the bird, seeing its offspring in danger, deliberately invents a ruse, and acts its part with consummate skill to draw the intruder away. All the evidence, however, points to this too being merely instinctive, a trick not invented by the individual bird, but patented by the species. If it were the fruit of intelligent reflection, we should expect to find some individuals of a species practising it, others not, and great variations in the efficacy of the performance; but in species like the purple sandpiper or the arctic skua, every individual seems to be a good performer, and this without any previous training. The trick, in fact, is on a par with the purely automatic 'shamming dead' which many insects practise: it is the inevitable outcome of the animal's nervous machinery when this machinery is stimulated in a particular way.

Besides instinctive actions, we could multiply instances of unintelligent behaviour among birds. If a strange egg is put among a bird's own eggs, the mother may accept it through uncritical instinct, or may intelligently turn it out of the nest and continue to sit. But a quite common reaction is for it to turn the strange egg out, and *then* to desert its nest—a most decidedly illogical procedure! Again, Mr St Quentin had two hens and one cock of a kind of sand-grouse in his aviary. This is a bird in which the hens normally sit by day, the cock by night. One year, both the hens laid at the same time. The cock tried his best, sitting part of the night on one clutch, part on another, but of course the eggs came to nothing. If the birds had had any intelligence, they would have divided up the twenty-four hours so that the eggs were always brooded; but the day-brooding of the hens and the night-brooding of the cock are mechanical instincts, and intelligence neither enters into them in normal nor modifies them in abnormal circumstances.

But because birds are mainly instinctive and not intelligent in their actions, it does not follow that their minds are lacking in intensity or variety: so far as we can judge, they must be experiencing a wide range of powerful emotions.

A bird clearly finds an intense satisfaction in fulfilling its brooding impulse or the impulse to feed its young, even though the impulse may be, for want of intelligence, what we should call a strangely blind one: and when the young birds are threatened with danger, the parents clearly are suffering very real distress, just as birds suffer very real fear when cornered by an enemy. In song, too, the bird, besides expressing a certain general well-being, is giving vent to a deep current of feeling, even if it does not understand the feeling or reflect upon it, as would a human poet or musician. For the moment, they *are* that feeling. Some birds are so obsessed by their emotions during their courtship display that they become oblivious of danger. The males of that huge bird of the grouse tribe, the capercaillie, have an extraordinary courtship ceremony which they carry out at daybreak in the branches of a favourite tree. While they are in the ecstasy of this passionate performance a man can easily creep up within range; and it is by this method that in certain countries many are shot.

Again, birds seem as subject as men to the emotion of jealousy. Rival cocks may fight to the death. One remarkable case with captive parrakeets is quite human in its incidents. Two cocks and a hen were in one cage. After much squabbling, one night one of the cocks killed the other: upon which the hen, who had hitherto rather favoured this bird, turned upon him and might have killed him too if they had not been separated.

Then bird-mind has sufficient subtlety to indulge in play. Dr Gill of Cape Town records seeing a hooded crow fly up into the air, drop a small object it was carrying, swoop after it, croaking loudly, catch it in mid air, and repeat the performance over and over again with the greatest evidence of enjoyment. And tame ravens often display what seems a real sense of humour, though it must be admitted humour of rather a low order. A pair of them will combine to tease a cat or dog, one occupying its attention from the front, while the other steals round behind to tweak its tail and hop off with loud and delighted squawkings. They will play tricks on each other; in an aviary, one raven of a pair has been seen to slink up from behind when its mate was sitting on a low perch, and then reach up to knock the perching bird's foot from under it, with evident malicious enjoyment.

But in all these varied manifestations of emotion, birds still differ in a fundamental way from ourselves. Being without the power of conceptual thought, their emotion, while occupying their life with a completeness which is perhaps rarer with us, is not linked up with the future or the past as in a human mind. Their fear is just fear: it is not the fear of death, nor can it anticipate pain, nor become an ingredient of a lasting 'complex.' They cannot worry or torment themselves. When the fear-situation is past, the fear just disappears. So, as we have seen, with their maternal instincts. The bird mother is not concerned with the fate of an individual offspring, as a human mother would be concerned about Johnny's career or Tommy's poor health. She is concerned just to give vent to her instincts impersonally, as it were; and when the young grow up and her inner physiology changes, there is no intellectual framework making a continuing personal or individual interest possible.

That indeed is the greatest difference between the bird and ourselves. We, whether we want to or not, cannot help living within the framework of a continuing life. Our powers of thought and imagination bind up the present with the future and the past: the bird's life is almost wholly a patchwork, a series of self-sufficing moments.

XI

SCIENCE, NATURAL AND SOCIAL

I. Methods in Social Science

SCIENCE, in the more restricted sense in which it is normally employed in English-speaking countries, is that activity by which to-day we attain the great bulk of our knowledge of and control over the facts of nature. This activity, like other human activities, has developed and evolved, and by no means all the stages in its evolution have merited the title of scientific. In remote prehistoric times, our early ancestors worked by trial and error combined with simple, intuitive common-sense. This pre-scientific approach, however, was combined with the non-scientific methods of control that we call magic, and equally non-scientific rationalizations in the field of explanation.

Once agriculture had given the possibility of settled civilizations, with written record and specialized social classes, the hand-to-mouth methods of common-sense could be replaced by something much more scientific. Science was born—witness the astronomy and geometry of ancient Mesopotamia and Egypt. But science in this phase was still, to our modern view, unscientific in two major aspects—it was traditional and it was esoteric. Scientific knowledge was confined to a limited group among the priesthood and it was cast in a mould of tradition which rendered change and progress slow. Being associated with the priesthood, it was also intimately bound up with non-scientific practice and non-scientific interpretation—magic and theology.

The era of groping trial and error lasted from the first dawn of essentially human intelligence, as marked by true speech, to the beginnings of settled civilization—perhaps a million, perhaps half a million years. The next, or traditional-esoteric phase, lasted for thousands instead of hundreds of thousands of years. After some three or four millennia, the Greeks suddenly burst free of the prison of secrecy and traditionalism and proclaimed the freedom of intellectual inquiry. The 'birth of science' is usually fathered on them, but the assumption is only a half-truth. At best, their achievement was the acquisition of freedom and self-consciousness by the scientific spirit, not the emergence of a wholly new activity called science. And secondly, the type of science which it inaugurated differed radically from modern science in several respects. It was almost entirely divorced from industry and practical application; it was exceedingly speculative and did not lay the same stress on experimental verification as we do; and, correlated with this, it had not invented the modern methodology of publication of the data and methods used, as well as the conclusions reached.

A few centuries later, the combination of Greek intellect and ingenuity with the practical spirit of the Roman imperium made Alexandrian science something much more like modern science in outlook and methods of working. But this was swallowed up in the anti-scientific Christian flood and the general collapse of Roman civilization.

During the Dark Ages in the West, the Arabs kept the scientific spirit alive, and by means of their mathematical inventions paved the way for immense improvements in the technique of scientific research.

Natural science, in its modern form, can fairly be said to date back no further than the seventeenth century. With Bacon as its St John the Baptist, it developed its gospel and its ministry. Curiosity for its own sake, but also interest in industrial techniques and practical control; freedom of inquiry; experimental verification in place of authority; full publication and abundant discussion—with these a truly new phase was inaugurated.

To-day it seems that we are again in the process of launching a new phase of science—one in which social as well as natural phenomena are to be made amenable to scientific understanding and rational control.

As with natural science, social science too has had its earlier stages. It too passed through the stage of trial and error, in which social organization shaped itself under the influence of unconscious adjustment together with non-rational rules of conduct and non-scientific interpretations of human destiny. It also had its traditional phases, often tightly bound up with philosophical and theological interpretative principles, as, for example, in the climax of the Middle Ages. And it has had its birth of free speculative inquiry, parallel to the Greek phase of natural science—but two thousand years later, in the philosophers of the seventeenth and especially the eighteenth century.

Finally, its modern stage now dawning has had, like the modern stage of natural science, its scattered precursors, its Roger Bacons and Leonardos—and it has had its precursor in the restricted sense, its equivalent of Francis Bacon in the Renaissance. Many, I am sure, would put Herbert Spencer in this position; but I believe that the true John the Baptist of social science is Karl Marx. Herbert Spencer, for all his academic knowledge, or perhaps because of it, was more in the position of an Old Testament prophet. His work was essentially analogical. He demonstrated that social science was an inevitable development; but his notions of what form it would actually take and what methods it should employ were vague and essentially erroneous.

Marx, on the other hand, developed a system directly based on social facts and directly applicable to them. He did not just prophesy *a* Messiah; he indicated *the* Messiah. As natural scientists tend to undervalue Bacon because he himself did not make discoveries or work out experimental techniques, so social scientists tend to underrate Marx because his system is a dialectical one, ready-made and complete with answer to any problem, not sufficiently empirical and inductive for their scientific taste. But at least Marx, like Bacon, gave expression to a new outlook and a new method of attack, and helped materially to alter the intellectual climate so as to make it propitious for scientific work in his field.

The question immediately poses itself as to why the emergence of social science into large-scale and efficient operation has been so long delayed. The triumphs of natural science, both in discovering radically new knowledge and in applying it practically to satisfy human needs, have been so spectacular and so fruitful that it would seem natural and obvious to extend the same methods to the field of social phenomena.

The answer is a very simple one: the methods are *not* the same. The scientific spirit remains unaltered whether it is contemplating a nebula or a baby, a field of wheat or a trades union. But the methodology of social science is inevitably different from that of natural science. It is different and must be different for one basic reason—the investigator is inside instead of outside his material. Man cannot investigate man by the same methods by which he investigates external nature. He can use the methods of natural science to investigate certain aspects of man—the structure and working of his body, for instance, or the mode of his heredity; but that is because these are shared with other organisms and because they are partial aspects which can be readily externalized. But when he starts investigating human motive, his own motives are involved; when he studies human society, he is himself part of a social structure.

What consequences does this basic difference imply? In the first place, man must here be his own guinea-pig. But this is impossible in the strict sense, for he is unable to make fully controlled experiments. Even if an absolute despot were to subject a group of people to rigorous experimentation—by depriving them of alcohol, for instance, or by adopting a new form of education—the results would have only a limited application. The smallness of the group, the compulsion involved, the inevitable limitations on the contacts and full social activity of the group, would make it impossible to apply the results directly to an entire normal society, however regimented. And the difficulties are of course enormously greater in any free society.

A second, more technical difficulty is in a sense a consequence of the first. Causation in social science is never simple and single as in physics or biology, but always multiple and complex. It is of course true that one-to-one causation is an artificial affair, only to be unearthed by isolating phenomena from their total background. None the less, this method is the most powerful weapon in the armoury of natural science: it disentangles the chaotic field of influence and reduces it to a series of single causes, each of which can then be given due weight when the isolates are put back into their natural interrelatedness, or when they are deliberately combined into new complexes unknown in nature.

This method of analysis is impossible in social science. Multiple causation here is irreducible. The difficulty is a twofold one. In the first place, the human mind is always looking for single causes for phenomena. The very idea of multiple causation is not only difficult, but definitely antipathetic. And secondly, even when the social scientist has overcome this resistance, extreme practical difficulties remain. Somehow he must disentangle the single causes from the multiple field of which they form an inseparable part. And for this a new technique is necessary.

Next, and in many ways even more important than the first two together, comes the question of bias. Under this head I include anything appertaining to the investigator which may deflect his scientific judgment. It is the equivalent of experimental and observational error in natural science. In natural science, there are statistical methods for discounting both sampling error and personal error; the limits of accurate measurement are determined for different types of instrument; the procedure of controlled experimentation has been reduced to a fine art. The procedure of the discounting of error in natural science by these methods has proved difficult enough. But to discover how to discount bias in social science is proving very much harder.

Then there is the inherent genetic bias imposed by his own temperament. For certain purposes, investigators in social science are their own instruments to a very great extent, and in a way unknown in natural science—and the individual instruments differ in their very construction.

Next we have the bias introduced by the peculiar psychological development of human beings. They can only resolve their inevitable conflicts during childhood and adolescence by relegating a great deal to their unconscious, whether by the psychological mechanism of suppression or that of repression. Roughly speaking, the former introduces bias by leaving gaps in a person's knowledge and outlook, whereas in the latter the gaps are accompanied by strong emotional distortions and resistances. The scientific study of sex, for instance, has been much retarded by repressional bias—witness the reception originally given to Havelock Ellis's great work and the extraordinary resistance still offered to Freud's ideas.

Bias of this type has the additional danger that those who make an effort to discount it may readily swing into over-compensation—a bias of opposite sign. The investigator whose youth was tormented by intolerant religion is apt to discount the social importance of religion far too much; the convert to Freudian methods is liable, in discounting his own early sexual repressions, to underestimate the social value of repression in general.

Bias has also been encountered in natural science, but only when its findings come up against emotionally held convictions—only, that is, when it has had social entanglements. We may cite the prohibition of anatomical dissection, the proscription of Galileo's findings, the hostility to the Darwinian theory, the Nazi distortion of racial anthropology, the Soviet attack on modern genetics. The present course of general anti-scientific feeling, so noticeable during the past decade, has been due in part to a general feeling that scientific findings, by sapping the traditional view of man's place in the universe and in society, are undermining the basis of ordered society.

Finally, there comes the most fundamental difference of all. Values are deliberately excluded from the purview of natural science: values and all that they connote of motive, emotion, qualitative hierarchy and the rest constitute some of the most important data with which the social scientist must deal. But how can science deal with them? Science must aim at quantitative treatment: how can it deal with the irreducible absolutes of quality? Science must be morally neutral and dispassionate: how can the social scientist handle the ethical bases of morality, the motives of passion?

Let us be frank with ourselves. There is a sense in which, because of this qualitative difference between its data and those of natural science, social science can never become fully and rigorously scientific. To understand and describe a system involving values is impossible without some judgment of values, and still more impossible without such value-judgment is the other scientific function, that of control.

However, this is not quite so serious as at first sight appears. Even in natural science, regarded as pure knowledge, one value-judgment is implicit—*belief in the value of truth*. And where natural science passes into control, a whole scale of values is involved. The application of natural science is guided by considerations of utility—utility for profit, for war, for food-production, for health, for amusement, for education. The application of science through the instrument of *laisser-faire* economic systems

has brought us to a position at which we are being forcibly
reminded that these different utilities may conflict.

Put in another way, this is because natural science, by
the fact of being applied, becomes a social problem and so
a subject for social science. In social science, to set up a
new value-system is in certain ways analogous to advancing
a new hypothesis in natural science, and to demonstrate
that such a new system is desirable or necessary is to
discover and formulate some of the 'laws of nature' for
the coming phase of social evolution.

Thus, rather crudely, we may say that in respect of the
problem of values, social science in its aspect of knowledge
is faced by the same difficulties as is natural science in its
aspect of control. The difficulty is thus in a sense an artificial one. Its consideration has reminded us that natural
science is not such a pure disembodied activity as is often
assumed. Language is in part responsible for the assumption. There is no such thing as natural science *per se*.
The phrase is a shorthand description of those activities of
human beings which are concerned with understanding and
controlling their natural environment. And, just as simple
one-to-one causation is a fiction, only approximated to in
artificially isolated systems, so the emancipation of natural
science from considerations of value is a fiction, approximated to by the possibility of temporarily and artificially
isolating scientific activity from other human activities.

The essential differences between natural and social
science thus boil down to this—that the phenomena with
which the latter deals are less readily isolated, and that as
an activity it is more closely entangled with human values.
These differences, however, even if only qualitative, are
very real, and it remains true that social science must

develop its own methodology if it is to become an efficient instrument.

In regard to multiple causation, we may look forward to an extended use of techniques of mathematical correlation. These have already been developed to a high pitch for dealing with problems of multiple causation in physical science, and special methods have been worked out by Spearman and his school for dealing with psychological questions. The use of probability methods is also indicated. Here again, these have been developed to a high pitch for use in natural science. Mathematical methods also enter into another technique which is now being rapidly developed in social science, that of the questionnaire, and especially the set of questions asked by the trained interviewer. The questionnaire method is widely used, but the reluctance or inability of large sections of the public to fill up its elaborate forms restricts its sphere and impairs its sampling accuracy. The success of the method in this form depends chiefly on two things—the proper framing of the questions and the obtaining of a truly representative sample of the population to answer them.

Some questions do not admit of a significant answer, or any answer at all; others will defeat their own ends by influencing the form of the answer. In any case, the method of questioning a representative sample of a large population can only be applied to a restricted set of problems, though within limitations it may become extremely efficient. The modern scientific public opinion poll, indeed, is developing such uncanny accuracy that it is infringing upon practical politics. Some people are asking whether a properly conducted straw ballot could not be profitably substituted for the trouble and expense of a full election; while others feel that the announcement of a straw vote may itself influence the course of the subsequent election.

Psychologists are busy devising modifications of the questionnaire method so as to build up objective rating scales (objective, that is, for the population of which the questionees are a representative sample) for various value-judgments. In addition, they are essaying to assess the distribution among the population of various human qualities. Intelligence-testing has long been practised, and is now approaching full scientific validity. Attempts are also being made to assess temperament and even more elusive qualities. The method of Mass Observation constitutes an attempt to attain objective information on various aspects of public opinion and behaviour which elude the method of yes-and-no questioning. Inquiries may concern the reaction of the public to a particular place, like the Zoo or the National Gallery; to a particular event, like the Coronation; to a particular activity, such as smoking or the time of rising; or to a general situation, like that of war. In some cases, composite pictures which could have been obtained in no other way have resulted from the use of this method. But in general its technique, both as regards sampling and questioning, will have to be refined a good deal before it can claim to be scientifically dependable.

Another set of methods which are being developed to cope with the complexity of social problems are those of anonymous group working, repeated drafting, and circulation of the preliminary draft results for comment and criticism. A combination of all three seems to yield the best results when tackling large and many-sided problems, such as the structure of a national agency like a health service or a big industry like steel or agriculture, the organization of leisure, or international adjustments.

Joint work is on the increase in natural science, but here largely because of the quantitative burden of routine procedures in subjects like biochemistry or genetics. We may distinguish such work from true group work, using the term group in the sense of a body of people pooling their different knowledges and skills to cope with qualitatively differentiated problems. Group work in this sense is also to be found in natural science, as when geneticists, ecologists and statisticians make a united attack on some problem of micro-evolution. But it is far more necessary in social science, where various bodies, such as P.E.P., are studying how to perfect it as a research method. Anonymity is often desirable in group work to enable the participation of public servants or well-known men whose opinions might be distorted or discounted in advance. It may also be desirable, for an essentially opposite reason, to give the weight of a recognized study organization to the work of young and unknown men whose findings would otherwise tend to be disregarded. In both these ways anonymous group working, in addition to securing greater efficiency, helps to discount bias of one sort or another.

Provided that a good drafter is available, together with a chairman and a small core of members who will give regular attendance, group membership can be fluid, and specialists invited for one or a few meetings as required.

Repeated drafting is a substitute for experimentation in problems where the experimental attack is ruled out. As soon as a preliminary survey has been made of the problem in its entirety, a draft is circulated for discussion at the next meeting. The gaps and errors thus brought to light form the subject of the next period of work, when the process is repeated. Three, four, or even more complete drafts may be required before publishable conclusions are reached, just as new sets of experiments must be planned and executed to deal with tentative conclusions and new facts arising in a piece of research in natural science, before it can be written up.

Some or all of the successive drafts may also be circulated to a comparatively large number of outside experts for written criticism. The collation of such comments often brings to light new details and unexpected points of view which the group, in its preoccupation with its own trend of thought, has overlooked. It affords a method of enlarging the group without the time-consuming business of large-scale discussion.

In other cases, the actual investigator may be a single man, while the group element is provided by interviews and by circulation of drafts. This method is best adapted to problems which are of large geographical scale and local diversity, though it may also be used for those which are qualitatively diversified in themselves.

It may be expected that the working out of various techniques made necessary by the nature of the data of social science will have fruitful repercussions in certain fields of natural science, such as evolution and comparative biological study in general, where the present bias in favour of experimental work and specific results is leaving vast bodies of published data awaiting the synthetic treatment which only organized group attack can provide.

I have already mentioned certain substitutes for the

controlled experimentation of the natural sciences. But experimentation as a method is not ruled out in social science, though it must take different forms. Regional or group experimentation is the most obvious method. Two regions or groups are chosen which are as similar as possible, and certain measures are introduced in the one, while the other serves as control. The Carlisle experiment on liquor control in Britain was an early essay in this method, but unfortunately it has been allowed to drag on without any serious attempts to draw theoretical conclusions or to frame practical policies on the basis of its operation. The T.V.A. in America is perhaps the largest social experiment ever undertaken, at any rate in a non-totalitarian country. The area involved, however, is so large that strict controls are difficult to find.

As the spirit of scientific planning extends with government, we may expect to see regional experiments tried out in many fields. Medical and health services would afford another excellent field. The social results of cheap electric power could be made the subject of local experiments much more rigorous than that of the T.V.A. Different methods of developing backward tropical territories—by international or national chartered companies, by public works schemes under the local administration, by the establishment of co-operatives—could and should be made the subject of carefully planned regional experiments.

The fact that in social science man is his own guinea-pig has a number of methodological consequences, both for social science research and for its practical applications. The social scientist often requires true co-operation from his material in the sense of understanding of the reason for his work and voluntary participation in its course. Education as a social experiment can never succeed without properly equipped teachers, specially trained in pedagogy. The interview method will give entirely misleading results without interviewers skilled in the technique of their job.

In the field of application, propaganda and public relations may be of prime importance. A good example is the cancer campaign recently instituted in the United States. Cancer has been presented to the public in such a way as to create a real interest in it as a social problem, and the public is collaborating in the attack upon it. The vast problem of malnutrition will never be solved unless the public is made to take a similar interest in it. The British Medical Association has made a beginning in this field with its milk campaign; but it is a beginning only.

In general the whole technique of propaganda, persuasion, and public relations needs the most intensive study before the findings of science can be socially applied. When does propaganda defeat its own ends by setting up counter-resistance? What are the relative values of reiteration and of variety of appeal? Of the printed word, the poster, the cinema, or the radio? Of rational persuasion as against mere suggestibility? Of intellectual comprehension as against a sense of active participation? We simply do not know, and until we know, our progress towards efficient social structure and a fuller life will be fitful and slow. In many ways, the enlistment of public co-operation is to social science what the enlistment of capital investment is to natural science: it provides motive power for application.

There remains the question of bias. In this there is no ready method to hand. It took generations for natural science to work out the technique of discounting experimental and observational error; it will take generations for social science to work out that of discounting the errors due to bias. The first step is obviously to make the world aware of the existence of bias and of the need for its discounting. Where human affairs are still handled in a pre-scientific spirit, bias is apt to play a very large practical rôle, especially the bias in favour of one's own group, whether class, religion or race. Such bias produces powerful rationalizations, which are then used to justify policies of the merest self-interest. The enslavement of negroes was justified on the basis of the scriptural authority for the menial destiny of the sons of Ham; the brutalities of the Nazi Jew-baitings on that of the racial superiority of 'Aryans.' The group bias of the prosperous classes in early nineteenth-century England appeared in astonishing assertions about the inherent inferiority of 'the poor'; the same bias is evident in certain aspects of the eugenics movement to-day.

Another widespread and disastrous form of bias arises from psychological conflict and tension. Censoriousness in respect of moral taboos, the desire to see the infliction of vindictive punishment, the unconscious reluctance of many parents to see the harsh school discipline under which they suffered replaced by humaner methods, the emotional basis of militarism—all these and many other undesirable determiners of human conduct are the result of bias arising from repression or emotional conflict and the inflicting of lasting distortion on the psyche.

In these fields, bias is thus an urgent subject for investigation by social science, and the application here will lie in making its findings universally known and accepted by the public in general and by administrators in particular.

But even in scientific circles bias may play a surprisingly large part. A good example was the resistance of the great majority of medical men during the early part of the last war to admitting any cause for breakdown among soldiers save physical shell-shock and malingering. And the uncritical assumption, even among scrupulously careful persons, that differences in intelligence between social classes were genetic and not due to nutrition or other social factors, is another. Again, we have the thesis of anthropologists like Lévy-Bruhl, that savage mentality is in some way qualitatively different from and inferior to our own, whereas it is in fact essentially similar, but operating in different material and social conditions.

No golden rule can be laid down for the avoidance of such pitfalls, apart from the obvious step of realizing that they exist. Beyond that, special methods must be worked out in each field.

Voices are still raised proclaiming that social science is a contradiction in terms, that human affairs are not intrinsically amenable to the scientific method. Those who hold this opinion are, I believe, wrong. They are confusing the methods of natural science with scientific method in general. Social science differs inevitably from natural science in many important respects, notably in its lesser capacity for isolating problems, and more generally in its lesser degree of isolation from other aspects of human activity and its consequent greater entanglement with problems of value. It must therefore work out its own technique and its own methodology, just as natural science had to do after Bacon and the eager amateurs of the seventeenth century had glimpsed natural science as a new form of human activity.

Let us not forget that the working out of this technique and this methodology by natural science took a great deal of time and is indeed still progressing. During the growth of modern science, the amateur has been largely replaced by the professional; university laboratories have been supplemented by governmental and industrial institutions; whole-time research has become a new profession; the team has in many types of work replaced the individual; co-operative group work is beginning; and the large-scale planning of research is in the offing.

Finally, the enormous growth of applied science has had effects of the utmost importance on pure research. It has done so partly by providing new instruments which would otherwise have been unavailable; one need only instance the gifts of the wireless industry not only to pure physics but to such unexpected branches of science as nervous physiology. And partly by suggesting new lines of research, the needs of wireless have again revealed new facts concerning the upper atmosphere, while the study of plant pests and human diseases has brought to light new modes of evolution.

We need have no fear for the future of social science. It too will pass through similar phases from its present infancy. By the time that the profession of social science, pure and applied, includes as many men and women as are now engaged in natural science, it will have solved its major problems of new methods, and the results it has achieved will have altered the whole intellectual climate. As the barber-surgeon of the Middle Ages has given place to the medical man of to-day, with his elaborate scientific training, so the essentially amateur politician and administrator of to-day will have been replaced by a new type of professional man, with specialized training. Life will go on against a background of social science. Society will have begun to develop a brain.

II. THE BIOLOGICAL ANALOGY

Writers and philosophers have often attempted to illuminate human affairs by means of biological analogies. Shakespeare, in *Coriolanus*, drew the analogy between the human body and the body politic in Menenius' speech on the body and its members. Herbert Spencer's work is shot through with the premise that human biology is but an extension of biology *sensu stricto*, and that, accordingly, biological analogies will in general have validity. Various German philosophers during the latter half of the past century justified war on the basis of the Darwinian conception of the struggle for existence, and the apostles of *laisser-faire* in Britain found support for economic individualism in the same doctrine. Socialists, on the other hand, have pointed to the fact of mutual aid in nature, as set forth by Kropotkin. Analogies with the social organization of ants and bees have been used, according to taste and prejudice, to glorify or to attack the doctrines of human collectivism. The Marxist thesis of progress being achieved through a reconciliation of opposites, only to lead to a new antithesis, which in turn paves the way for a new synthesis, is customarily documented in the works of communist philosophers by examples from biological evolution.

It is interesting to ask ourselves precisely what validity resides in this method of extending biological principles by analogy into human affairs. At the outset, it is clear that analogy, unless applied with the greatest caution, is a dangerous tool. This is clear to the modern scientist, but it has not always been so. Indeed, to put too great a burden on the back of analogy is a fundamental temptation of the human mind, and is at the base of the most unscientific practices and beliefs, including almost all magical ritual and much of supernaturalist superstition. During the last millennium, moralists, theologians and scholastic philosophers have often regarded analogy, even of the most far-fetched kind, as the equivalent of proof.

Has analogy, then, no part to play in scientific thought? Far from it. Analogy is in the majority of cases the clue which guides the scientific explorer towards radically new discoveries, the light which serves as first indication of a distant region habitable by thought. The analogy with waves in water guided physics to the classical wave-theory of light. The analogy with human competition, after playing an important rôle in Darwinian theory (did not Darwin arrive at the theory of natural selection from his reading of Malthus?), was transferred by Wilhelm Roux to a smaller sphere, the struggle of the parts within the individual.

But analogy may very readily mislead. Weismann sought to apply this same analogy of intra-organismal struggle and selection to the units of heredity; but the analogy happens not to hold good. The analogy of a stream of particles misled Newton as to the nature of light.

Analogy thus provides clues, but they may easily be false clues; it provides light, but the light may be a will-of-the-wisp. However pretty, however seductive, analogy remains analogy and never constitutes proof. It throws out suggestions, which must be tested before we can speak of demonstration.

But if non-scientists often overrate the importance of analogy, scientists themselves tend to be over-cautious and to underrate its potential value. Its value is especially great when the analogy is one between closely related subjects. The analogy between the evolution of different groups of animals is often surprisingly close, for the simple reason that both the material and the conditions are essentially similar throughout. None the less, unpredictable results are not infrequent. The adaptive radiation of the marsupials in Australia was in its broad lines similar to that of the placentals in the rest of the world; but the placentals never developed large jumpers like the kangaroo, and, conversely, the marsupials produced no quick runners like horse or antelope, and no freshwater fish-eaters like the otter. Again, the parallelism in the social evolution of the quite unrelated ants and termites is truly astonishing; yet the termites have never produced grain-storers or slave-makers, while the ants have no system of second-grade queens in reserve.

One further caveat before we pursue the biological analysis of man's social existence. Human societies, though indubitably organic, are unlike any animal organism in the mode of their reproduction. Strictly speaking, they do not usually reproduce at all, but merely perpetuate themselves. They exhibit no process of fertilization between living gametes, no distinction between mortal body and immortal germ-plasm. They continue indefinitely by the aggregate reproduction of their component individuals. In their development, change of structural and functional pattern can be dissociated from growth in a way impossible to a developing animal, and social heredity operates via cultural transmission, not by the physical transmission of material potencies of development. On the other hand, the separation of phylogeny and ontogeny, the development of the race and the development of the individual, which is so evident in higher animals, is blurred in social development to such an extent that the two often coincide.

All analogies between the birth, development and death of civilizations or nations and of animal organisms must be very heavily discounted because of this fundamental difference in the mode of their reproduction and inheritance.

Now, with these facts in mind, let us look at some of the biological analogies that lie near to hand. In the first place, there is the analogy between the societies of insects and those of man. This, however obvious and however often applied, must be rejected out of hand. The two rest on different bases—those of ants, bees and termites on the fixity of instinct, those of man on the plasticity of intelligence. For this reason man cannot and will not ever develop specialized castes, with functions predetermined by heredity, nor will human society ever work with the machine-like smoothness of an ant-hill or a termitary. Furthermore, we must not expect that in man the altruistic instincts will ever become predominant: as Haldane has demonstrated, this can only occur when neuter castes of workers or soldiers exist. Altruism in man must be fostered by education and given fuller play by appropriate social machinery; it cannot be implanted once and for all by heredity.

The next analogy to be considered is that between the body of a higher animal and human society. This has taken two main forms. In the one, the analogy is drawn between the main classes of society and the main organ-systems of the body, or, going a little further into detail, between the specialized functions of various agencies of social existence—trade, government, war, education and so forth—and those of particular bodily organs. In the other, which has been attempted only since the discovery of the cell and the rise of the cell-theory, the cell within the body is compared to the individual within society. An extension of this second analogy bridges the gap between it and the first: instead of the individual cell, attention is concentrated on the different types of cells and the different resultant tissues of the body; and these, rather than the still more complex organs, each composed of numerous tissues, are compared with the various specialized trades and professions in human society.

In assessing the value and limitations of these analyses, we must begin by recalling the basic difference between the animal body and human society, namely, the far greater subordination of the parts to the whole in the former. This is especially important for the comparison between cells and human individuals. The difference here is the same basic one as that between the castes of a social insect society and the specialized aptitudes of human beings, but pushed to a much greater length. The cells of the body are irrevocably specialized during early development, and their divergent specialization is far greater than that between even a queen and a soldier termite. Without embryological study, no one could guess that a nerve-cell, with its long nerve-fibre and its branching dendrites, a sperm, with condensed head and motile tail, and a fat-cell, an inert lump crowded with globules of reserve fat-stores, were all modifications of a single common type. Altruism, in the sense of sacrifice of the unit for the good of the whole, has also been carried to a much higher pitch.

As with drone bees, only one out of many sperms can ever perform its fertilizing function; but the ratio is one to many tens of millions, instead of one to a few hundreds. The cells of the outer skin have no other function than to be converted into dead horny plates, constantly shed and as constantly renewed; the red blood-cells lose their nuclei before being capable of exerting their oxygen-carrying function, and have a life much more limited even than that of worker bees. Units may even be pooled. The giant nerve-fibres of cuttlefish are the joint product of numerous united nerve-cells; our own striped muscle-fibres are vast super-units, comparable with a permanently united tug-of-war team.

In terms of biologically higher and lower, there is thus a radical difference between cells and human beings. Both are biological individuals which form part of more complex individualities. Cells are first-order individuals, bodies second-order ones, and human societies (like hydroid colonies or bee-hives) third-order ones. But whereas the individuality of the body of a higher animal, be it cuttlefish, insect or vertebrate, is far more developed than that of its constituent cells, that of a human society is far less so than that of its individual units.

This fact, while it makes the analogy between cell and human individual almost worthless, is of great value itself as a biological analogy, since it immediately exposes the fallacy of all social theories, like those of Fascism and National Socialism, which exalt the State above the individual.

A book could be written on the subject of analogies between biological organisms and society. One with peculiar relevance to-day is the tendency, repeated over and over again in evolution, for types to specialize on the development of brute strength coupled with formidable offensive or defensive weapons, only to be superseded by .other types which had concentrated on efficiency of general organization, and especially on the efficiency of the brain. The outstanding example is the supersession of the formidable reptiles of the late Mesozoic by the apparently insignificant mammals of the period.

This phenomenon is often somewhat misinterpreted as the replacement of specialized by generalized types. There is an element of truth in this idea, but the fact is often lost sight of that the successful generalized type always owes its success to some improvement in basic organization. Such improvements in general organization are specializations, but they are all-round specializations, whereas what are usually called specializations are one-sided. This distinction contains the kernel of what is probably the most important of our biological analogies—the analogy concerning desirable and undesirable directions of change.

A detailed analysis of type of evolutionary change shows that some of them can legitimately be called progressive, in the sense that they constitute part of a steady advance on the part of living matter toward a greater control over and independence of its environment. Only a small and steadily diminishing fraction of life participates in progressive change.

Each step in progress is constituted by all-round specialization—an improvement in general organization; one-sided specialization always leads into an evolutionary blind alley.

Here I have only space to mention the two types of

change which have been most important in the later phases of evolutionary progress. One is the development of mechanisms for regulating the internal environment of an animal, and so making it more largely independent of changes in external environment or better able to pass from one type of activity to another. The other is the improvement of the mechanisms for obtaining and utilizing knowledge of the environment, which in its later stages, after the efficiency of sense-organs had reached its limit, has been brought about by improvement in brain mechanism.

The biological analogy from the former is obvious. It provides the most abundant justification for the abandonment of *laisser-faire* in favour of social and economic planning: but the planning must be designed to give society an internal environment which shall be both stable in essentials and flexible in detail, and to enable it to undertake the greatest diversity of functions with the least dislocation.

The biological analogy from brain evolution is, however, even more illuminating. As animal evolution continued, the avenues of progress were cut off one by one. Changes that had been progressive in their time were exploited to the full and reached the limit of their potentialities. Mere bulk of body had reached its limit in the dinosaurs during the Mesozoic, some sixty million years ago. Ten or twenty million years later, temperature-regulation in certain animal forms had been perfected. The exploitation of the insectan type of social life by ants was over about twenty-five million years back, and ants have not evolved since.

Similarly, the number of the groups which might share in progressive change steadily narrowed down. Groups like the echinoderms were soon eliminated owing to their headlessness; then the great phylum of molluscs, through defects in general organization; then the insects, through their limited size. Only the vertebrates remained. The cold-blooded forms were eliminated by the biological invention of temperature-regulation; the birds, by their over-specialization for flight; the marsupials, by their greatly inferior reproductive mechanism. Among the placentals, now sole repositories of potential advance, the majority of lines cut themselves off from progress by one-sided specialization. Only the arboreal primates escaped, since their mode of life left teeth and limbs unspecialized, while demanding greater efficiency in the highest sense of all, vision, and greater correlation between hand and eye. This correlation meant improvement in brain structure, which spilled over in the form of increased educability and awareness. Finally, all the primate lines but one wandered into blind alleys, becoming over-specialized for tree life. Only the one stock which early redescended to the ground and concentrated on all-round adaptability remained potentially progressive—man. The human species has now become the only branch of life in which and by which further substantial evolutionary progress can possibly be realized. And it has achieved this enviable, but at the same time intensely responsible, position solely by concentrating on brain as against other organs as its line of specialization.

This evolution of brain, as the one inexhaustible or at least unexhausted source of progress, thus demands our closest attention as a biological analogy for social affairs. With some simplification, the process of brain evolution in vertebrates is resolvable into two main steps—first, the addition of two centres of correlation in different parts of the brain, one for the correlation of sensory knowledge, the other for the correlation of action, and of course with the two centres united by communicating cables. This is the stage arrived at in fish. The next step was the provision of a further quite new centre of correlation, superimposed on the previous mechanism. This organ of ultimate adjustment and control consists of the cerebral hemispheres, which are wholly unrepresented in the lowest vertebrates. Its essential exchange mechanism consists of the cerebral cortex. So far as we know, the cortex, in spite of all localizations and functional specializations within it, always acts as a whole, in the sense that its activity can be thought of as a complex field which is altered in its total functioning by any alteration in any of its parts.

The final step between ape and man is marked by the great enlargement of those areas of the brain which have the least specialized function—the so-called association areas, which lie between the regions wherein are localized the reception of relayed sensory information and the emission of executive messages for action. It is this, it seems, which has made possible self-consciousness and true conceptual thought.

During the course of their evolution, the cerebral hemispheres increased from zero to a mass which exceeds that of all the rest of the central nervous system taken together, and became one of the larger organs of the body.

Our brain analogy undoubtedly illuminates the social problem in an extremely valuable way. In the first place, the highest stage of evolution in this respect which has as yet been reached by any society is, by biological standards, extremely primitive. It corresponds with a quite early stage in the development of cerebral hemispheres and cor-

tex: higher than that of a fish, but certainly not beyond
that found in reptiles. Before humanity can obtain on the
collective level that degree of foresight, control, and flexibility which on the biological level is at the disposal of
human individuals, it must multiply at least tenfold, perhaps fiftyfold, the proportion of individuals and organizations devoted to obtaining information, to planning, correlation, and the flexible control of execution. The chief
increases are needed in respect of correlation and planning
and of social self-consciousness. In these respects, wholly
new social organs must be evolved, whose nature we can
only envisage in the most general terms.

In respect of planning and correlation, we can dimly
perceive that some large single central organization must
be superposed on the more primitive system of separate
government departments and other single-function organizations; and that this, like the cerebral cortex, must be at
one and the same time unified and functionally specialized.
It will thus contain units concerned with particular social
and economic functions, but the bulk of its personnel will
be occupied in studying and effecting the interrelations
between these various functions.

As regards social self-consciousness, the course of evolution must be quite different. Newspapers and books,
radio, universal education—these and other points of
technological and social advance have given us, in primitive form, the mechanisms needed. At the moment, however, they are being, in the light of biological analogy,
largely misapplied. Education stops dead for most people
in early adolescence, and concerns itself mainly with providing specialized techniques, together with a froth of
obsolescent 'culture.' The cinema to-day is primarily an

escape mechanism. Newspapers distort the balance of truth in the service of political or financial interests, and are driven by competition for advertising into sensation-mongering. The radio is as yet essentially a collection of scraps, a functional patchwork. Art as a communal function is moribund and needs to be recreated on a new social basis. Religion is in a similar position, and much of the population no longer feels its influence.

The first need is to recognize that, in this increasingly complex world, a free country cannot exist, let alone find satisfaction, without being self-conscious, and all the agencies of public opinion must be moulded to this end. A self-conscious society would be one in which every individual comprehended the aims of society, his own part in the whole, the possibilities of intellectual, artistic and moral satisfaction open to him, his rôle in the collective knowledge and will. But for this, as for correlation or planned control, the most elaborate organization is required.

Meanwhile our social planners would undoubtedly benefit from a study of the evolution of individuality in animals, and still more from an intensive course in the comparative neurology of vertebrates.

XII

THE ANALYSIS OF FAME

(WRITTEN AS A REVIEW OF *WHO'S WHO*, 1935)

Who really is who? Who, indeed? *Who's Who* should provide the answer, at least so far as concerns society's collective Who in Britain. The trouble is that the answer is so collective, so formidably vast. The present edition runs to 3694 pages of entries, involving something like 30,000 miniature biographies.

Obviously there are numerous methods for approaching our problem of who really is who, and why. As a scientist, I feel that the quantitative method should first be given a chance. There are plenty of interesting questions to which it could provide an answer. For instance:—How many foreigners does the editor admit within the British precinct? In what proportion are the different professions and occupations represented in this Annual Hall of Fame? Are these proportions sensibly different for the British-born and the foreigners? What relation, if any, does length of entry bear to degree of eminence? What are the proportions of the sexes, both in bulk and detail?

I cannot claim to have penetrated very far along this road, but I have made a beginning. I have taken a random sample of over two hundred names, under a couple of letters of the alphabet, and present a few facts resulting from its preliminary analysis.

The Army, to my surprise, comes an easy first, with 34 entries out of 222. The mere fact of belonging to the

Aristocracy ties for second place with Religion—19 each. Literature also accounts for 19, but only when it is enlarged by journalism and publishing. Then come Foreign and Imperial administration, including the diplomatic and consular services (17); Finance and Business (16); Science and Engineering (15); representatives of academic learning in other fields than science (14); Home politics and administration (13); the Navy, surprisingly low, with 12; Medicine (10); the Fine Arts, Music, and Architecture (8); Education (8); Miscellaneous (7); Law (6); the Air Force and Aviation in general (3); and last the Drama, including both acting and management, with only 2. (The Miscellaneous, by the way, include a food expert, a girl-guide organizer, and a traveller.)

The male sex-ratio is very high. In fact, there are only 6 women in the sample, or less than 3 per cent., and 4 of these are in literature.

Non-Britishers are much more generously treated than mere females, there being 26 of them. Ten of these are from the United States, 9 are Hindus, 4 Europeans, 2 from the British Dominions, and one is a native African.

However, the selection of representatives of foreign countries is curiously haphazard. For instance, Hemingway is in, but not Faulkner; Sherwood Anderson, but not Stark Young; William Beebe, but not Thomas Barbour; Lindbergh, but not Professor Piccard; Frankie Buchman of the Oxford Groups, but not Aimée Semple MacPherson; Edith Wharton, but not Gertrude Stein; Charles Seltzer (author of *The Boss of the Lazy Y*, etc., etc.), but not Christopher Morley; Mary Garden, but not Lawrence Tibbett; General Smuts, but not General Botha; Ethel

Barrymore, but not Ruth Draper; the Abbé Dimnet, but not Ogden Nash. . . . It is all very mysterious.

This quantitative method of study is capable of almost indefinite extension. In fact, it might be good for the progress of science if for a year, say, our army of sociologists were to relinquish all other research, and make a vast co-operative study, intensive, extensive, and comparative, of the 'Who's Whos' of the world.

There is the question of Clubs, for instance. What sort of men are those without a single club, and those who belong to more than one? Is there as much correlation as is popularly supposed between clubs and professions—the Athenaeum and the upper ranges of an ecclesiastical career, for instance, or the Authors' and the practice of literature? There is further the question of recreation. What sort of men, on the average, are they who have no recreations, or at least do not record them? Of what type are the comparatively rare few who comply with editorial request and insert their motor-car numbers? What types of men and women omit to state their ages?

On all these and many other points of absorbing interest *Who's Who* could provide an answer if only sociological science would undertake the research. Unfortunately, the statistical labour involved is too great for an unaided worker, and I must pass on to the less precise but none the less absorbing facts to be gained by the merely qualitative methods of browsing and pouncing.

I cannot pretend, for example, to any precision of result on the question of length of entry. For a considerable time, I thought that the record was held by Nicholas Murray Butler—a proud position for a foreigner to hold among alien hosts! But he is exceeded, by another *Bu*,

curiously enough—Sir Ernest Wallis Budge, the archaeo-
logist, who runs to 165 lines against N. M. B.'s 135 (and
this in spite of the list of the latter's foreign orders running
to 20 lines).

However, it is true that the United States entries tend
to be on the long side. Professor Rice of the Peabody
Museum gets (or perhaps one should say takes) 108 lines:
by the way, he achieves what appears to be a record in the
matter of club memberships, listing 22 (as against the
mere 16 of Will Hays). Harry Elmer Barnes has 106;
Irving Fisher 89 (as against H. A. L. Fisher's humble 42).
That is three American 'centenarians': among other
nationals I can find but one—Monsieur Bouchor, French
artist (102); and in the ranks of the far more numerous
British I can only trace seven.

By way of contrast with these long entries we find that
even Mr H. G. Wells's formidable list of publications (he
does not, however, cite his articles) only gives him 84 lines,
while Shaw has 65; Mussolini and General Smuts are
content with 32, the Rockefellers, Sen. and Jun., with 29
and 18 respectively, Lloyd George with 21, Franklin
Roosevelt with 18. However, for real restraint give me
Stalin. Let me quote his entry in full:

> STALIN, Joseph Vissarionovich Djugashirli [surely, by the
> way, this is one of *Who's Who's* rare misprints: should it not be
> Djugashvili?], b. Gori, Tiflis Province, 1879; m. Nadejda
> Sergeyevna Alleluya (d. 1932); two c. Address: The Kremlin,
> Moscow, Russia.

I suppose, however, this entry is an editorial production. For personal modesty give me Professor Griquard,
who, though he once divided the Nobel Prize for Chemistry,
takes up but 5 lines. I like too his publication:—'Traité

de Chimie Organique (10 vols.), commencera à paraître
en 1934.'

No, the correspondence between length of entry and
degree of eminence is not high. I⁺ is, however, doubtless
positive: I should put the coefficient of correlation at
about 0·2, perhaps 0·3.

One curious point is the stern, almost puritanical, atti-
tude taken up by the Editors to the theatre and the screen.
Charlie Chaplin and Douglas Fairbanks get reasonable
entries. The only producers I can find are Alexander
Korda and Jesse Lasky. Mary Pickford and George
Arliss receive 8 lines each, and the Garbo 5; but Marlene
Dietrich, Norma Shearer, Marion Davies, Jean Harlow,
Katharine Hepburn, and even Mae West are absent, as
are Clark Gable, Gilbert, Cagney, and all four of the Marx
Brothers. Even on the stage, and the British stage at that,
there are curious gaps: for instance, I can't find Leslie
Howard, Diana Wynyard, or Elsa Lanchester.

This is the only general criticism I have of this very
great work. No one can, or at least ought to, deny that
Norma Shearer, Cecil de Mille, or Harpo Marx are most
definitely WHO, much more so than professors and
second-rate novelists, or the hordes of Brigadier-Generals
and Archdeacons.

Another gap concerns royalty. There is a sort of proem
concerning the British Royal Family, but nothing whatever concerning other monarchs, which seems a pity, and
also illogical. Even ex-kings, however much in the public
eye, are omitted. The only exceptions to the rule are subject kings, like the King of Buganda.

Of course, the most obvious source of interest for the
reviewer is to be found under *Recreations*. For years

George Bernard Shaw's 'anything except sport' has been a classic *mot*. The Sitwells live up to their reputation for demanding public notice. Osbert recreates himself by 'entertaining the rich and charity generally'; Sacheverell by 'model aeroplanes, plats régionaux, improvisation, the bull-ring.' Edith has no specific recreation, but she makes up for this by giving her antipathies: 'in early youth took an intense dislike to simplicity, morris-dancing, a sense of humour, and every kind of sport except reviewer-baiting, and has continued these distastes ever since.'

The Sitwellian sense of satire is further illuminated by such entries as this of Sacheverell's, '*educ*. Eton Coll.; Balliol College, Oxford. Left latter owing to continued success of Gilbert and Sullivan season at Oxford; mainly self-educated.' Or, even more, by Osbert's '*educ*. during the holidays from Eton . . . was put down for M.C.C. on day of birth by W. G. Grace, but has now abandoned all other athletic interests in order to urge the adoption of new sports such as: Pelota, Kif-Kif, and the Pengo (especially the latter).' Considering the high cost of composition, ought not the editors to undertake some cutting in cases such as this?

Among the recreations of the great are these:—Naomi Mitchison, 'hitting back'; E. S. P. Haynes, 'divorce law reform'; Sir Denison Ross, 'languages' (such busmen's holidays are frequent); Evelyn Underhill, the writer on mysticism, 'talking to cats'; Benito Mussolini, 'violino, equitazione, scherma, automobilismo, aviazione'; A. M. Low, the writer on popular science, 'the encouragement of scientific research'; Sir William Bowden, the newspaper proprietor, 'lecturing for charitable and educational purposes' (golly! but this is not unique—Professor

Henderson of the University of North Carolina, lists simply 'public lecturing'); Senator Gogarty of the Irish Free State, 'archery and aviation'—delightful combination; the Rev. Hon. E. Lyttelton, late Headmaster of Eton, 'scenery' (this is curiously rare; perhaps many people include it under *travel*); Sean O'Casey, sweepingly and, it seems to me, rather rashly, 'everything except work'; M. E. G. Sebastian, D.S.O., British Consular Service, 'needlework'; Athene Seyler, 'walking, talking.' It is an interesting commentary on the social conventions that whereas music is set down quite commonly, and at least Ernest Hemingway has had the courage to include *drinking*, nowhere can I find either *gambling* or *women* as a recreation.

Often the biographies include fascinating facts. A hint that Epstein may possess an inferiority complex is given by the remark that his work on the British Medical Association, though 'attacked by newspapers, religious bodies, etc., was defended by *Times*.' It is pleasant to know that J. D. Rockefeller senior has given away more than $500,000,000 in charity. It is also pleasant that in these days of specialization such a paragon of versatility can exist as Dr Satischandra Bagchi, Principal of the University Law College at Calcutta, who, in addition to numerous legal works, notably on the 'Juristic Personality of Hindu Deities,' has written books on 'The Mathematics of Transformation and Quantum Theory'; 'Rabelais'; and 'Morality in Art,' besides translating French stories into Bengali.

It is tempting to browse on. Almost every page has its rewards. The clergyman whose recreations are caricature and philately; the fact that Marie Stopes mentions her marriage to her first husband, but that he does not mention the fact of his marriage to Marie Stopes; the omission by H. G. Wells of any mention of the first marriage for which in his autobiography he finds so much space; the fact that neither Sir Charles Sherrington nor Miss Ethel M. Dell give their ages. . . . But I must refrain.

Who's Who is a great work. It is not only so useful as to be all but indispensable; not only, as I have tried to point out, one of the world's most valuable source-books in sociology; but also contains more interesting specimens of what are usually known as 'human documents' than any other work in existence. And if you think the price is high, reflect that it works out at less than a farthing per closely printed page—far cheaper than a novel.

XIII

SCIENTIFIC HUMANISM

W HAT are the aims before humanism? One phrase, to my mind, really contains them all: to have life and to have it more abundantly. Although, like all one-phrase programmes, this needs amplification and definition, it proclaims at the outset the humanist's main creed: that the sole source of values which we know of in the universe is the commerce between mind and matter that we call human life, for it generates not only our standard of values but the experiences, objects, and ideas which are of highest concrete value in themselves; that life as a whole is more important than any single part or product of life; and that since life, however complex, is essentially one, it is false to give absolute predominance to any system of ideas or conduct, to any one aspect of life.

A humanism that is also scientific sees man endowed with infinite powers of control should he care to exercise them. More importantly, in the perspective of scientific knowledge it sees man against his true background— a background of the irresponsible matter and energy of which he is himself composed, of the long and blind evolution of which he is himself a product. Humanity thus appears as a very peculiar phenomenon—a fraction of the universal world-stuff which, as result of long processes of change and strife, has been made conscious of itself and of its relations with the rest of the world-stuff, capable of desiring, feeling, judging, and planning. It is an experiment of the universe in rational self-consciousness. (So far as we are yet aware, it is the only such experiment; but that is a matter of secondary importance.) Any value which it has apart from its selfish value to itself resides in this fact.

The apprehension of values depends upon a balancing of motives and ideas; a standard of values demands conceptual thought. Even the highest animals have only the barest rudiment of such possibilities. But once man, by the aid of language, could think abstract thoughts, a new framework was generated, a framework as important to mental life as the skeletal framework to bodily life—the framework of universals and ideals. This is an immediate by-product of language and logic. It is impossible to pronounce the simplest judgment—'this is true,' or 'that is not true'—without implicitly setting up a category of abstract truth. Once you can argue whether an action is right or wrong, you presuppose an ideal of rightness. You may not consciously envisage such ideals, but your own or others' logic will sooner or later lead you to them. The humanist sees no other absolute quality in truth or goodness than this.

The actual way in which these abstract ideas are applied as standards of value is subject to change. The ideas about truth held by a believer in verbal inspiration must be different from those of one trained in the methods of philosophy or of mathematical physics. Just as the bodily skeleton was moulded and improved during the course of its evolution, so this spiritual framework grows and is modified.

The different emphasis laid upon this world and the next, for instance, has produced very different measuring rods for goodness in the minds of the medieval theologian and the modern social worker. Again, many religious minds have found acceptance of a fixed creed the highest good, because they believe it the only avenue to salvation. To the evolutionist, who knows the variety but incompleteness of life, and the necessity for change, this good turns to bad. These universals are but frameworks. To revert to our metaphor, they resemble the archetypal plans of construction of this or that animal organ which have no concrete existence (save in the pages of zoological textbooks), but yet underlie and in part determine the construction of every actual organ. The archetypal plan of vertebrate skeleton could be pinched and pulled to support a flying or a swimming or a running creature. The framework of our abstract and universal ideas can be practically moulded in a not dissimilar adaptive way.

In the course of its evolution, human life comes to generate new experiences, new ways of living and of expression, which are concretely of value in themselves; in this way new qualities and also new heights of value are attained. Stoicism was the means of giving the world a new type of character. Dante's 'Vita Nuova' was the expression of a new way of love between man and woman which in previous ages had not been possible. The transference of the sense of supreme sacredness from fear to love, accomplished by Jesus, led man to wholly new levels of religious value. Pure knowledge has absolute value: and in the intellectual comprehension of the world about us given by Newton, by Darwin, or by the latest discoveries in astrophysics, science has produced something new and valuable. Beethoven in his posthumous quartets and other late works produced something wholly new in the world; it is not new knowledge of the external world but knowledge of new capabilities of the human spirit—new experience. In all such cases, of course, others may not be capable of appreciating the new-found value, may not wish to employ it. But the value has been created; it is there, waiting to be used.

One of the functions of humanity in its evolutionary experiment is thus, it seems, the creating of new experiences of value, in any and every realm, from character to pure intellect, from religion to art.

As a matter of history, the course of events in this progressive change of framework and progressive realization of new value has so far been rather a curious one. At the risk of over-simplification, I may put it thus. In primitive man, and in many of the uneducated to-day, different values are not much thought about or analysed, but just accepted. Each separate activity, as it happens to come along, is instinctively valued for its immediate satisfaction. Further, since the value of many later and complex human experiences cannot be felt by a mind which is not trained or not set in a certain direction (I do not suppose you could ever get a Masai warrior to see that there was 'anything in' the Vita Nuova, any more than a wholly untrained mind could be thrilled by reading the latest cosmogony by Jeans or Eddington), the experiences regarded as valuable are themselves more primitive.

A large part of early man's values must have been concerned with physiological satisfaction, his life a series of activities only very partially related in thought, his various mental activities existing in more or less 'thought-tight' compartments. But just because he was not too logical, and because he was endowed with a variety of instinctive impulses, his life, though on a low level, was full and varied.

Man's intellectual faculties, hovering protectively over his naked feelings and desires, have doubtless always done something to cloak them with the respectability of reason —or at least of reasons. But in the beginnings of society this rationalizing power must have been very incomplete and unco-ordinated. With settled civilization, the reflective mind had new leisure and new opportunities. The result was apparent in the various theological and philosophical schemes, aiming at some degree of logic and completeness, which have characterized the last three or four thousand years.

It was as if the human spirit, growing more fully conscious of itself, ..s needs and its defects, its strange isolation in an incomprehensible and often hostile world, felt the imperative need of some support, some framework of authority outside the individual and, if possible, outside the species, some relief from vague fears and speculations by means of clear-cut explanations.

The support may have been needful; but it was in danger of becoming a prison. Abstract thought can be so devastating just because it is general, because of its apparent absoluteness. There is no gainsaying logic. Once you cease to have the saving grace of humility, and believe that you possess any final or definitive knowledge of the nature of things, whether off your own bat, or conferred by external grace of revelation, you are doomed if you make the appeal to logic. Your premises are bound to be incomplete; and the inaccuracy, multiplied by the chain of levers which logic provides from particular to general, at the last assumes portentous proportions.

If men really believed the medieval Christian scheme, they were bound to be intolerant, bound to persecute and establish inquisitions. If you really believe that kingship or marriage or the decalogue was divinely ordained, you cannot help drawing certain practical conclusions which will in time put you in violent opposition to the humanist view on such subjects.

The period of human evolution which we may call the period of the great theological religions was from this point of view one in which perplexed human beings, in their struggle with the outer world, with other human beings, and most of all with the tortuous inconsistencies and treacheries of the human spirit, found much-needed help in the fixity of generalized schemes of thought. They discovered that they could gain support from abstract ideas such as of reason or justice; from unattainable but absolute ideals, as of goodness or truth; from the unassailable logic of complete schemes of creation and salvation. The externalizing of the compulsive but changeable inner voice of impulse and conscience in outer authority and codes of divine revelation was another method of finding support, and the psychological trickery involved in this projection of inner feeling into outer sanction was so simple and natural to untutored thinking that it passed unnoticed.

But the method had its inevitable defects. Grateful support could become imperceptibly converted into cramping rigidity. The inevitable slight pre-eminence given to this or that quality in the original scheme of thought could become magnified by logic into an entire one-sidedness. The general and abstract could be taken for the absolute and complete, and so the way barred to novelty or fresh achievements.

In the last half-millennium there has been a change. Thought has not only attacked the rigidity of the old schemes but has also devoted itself to new creation. The absoluteness and externality of the old frameworks are gone. Scientific law, for instance, is no longer regarded as the transcription of some prodigious code laid up in heaven, but as the most convenient way in which our human intellect can sum up the controllable aspects of phenomena.

The new attack has at last invaded the citadel itself. No longer can we set matter against life; or life against mind; or mind against spirit, as two essentially different realms.

The time is beginning to ripen in which we can attempt to recover a greater elasticity of our framework by going back to the beginning, to the nature of things and the nature of man as seen in the light of new knowledge, and by building up our scheme anew. This new humanism, if we attempt it, must in the first place try to do justice to the variety of human nature and refrain from giving pre-eminence to any one aspect—a task which demands a difficult combination of altruism and tolerance. It must attempt to do justice to our incompleteness, and to the constant change in knowledge and outlook which we must hope for. This demands a sacrifice almost intolerable to certain minds—the sacrifice of certitude. It must finally attempt to provide some real and strong framework of support, and so prevent the exaggerated individualism, the social disintegration, and the tolerance that turns to indifferentism, which have characterized other humanistic periods such as the early Roman Empire or the Renaissance.

But humanism, with the aid of the picture given by

science, *can* achieve a framework strong enough for support. In the light of evolution, it can see an unlimited possibility of human betterment. And it can see that possibility as a continuation of the long process of biological betterment that went before the appearance of man. If humanism cannot have the fixed certitude of dogma, it can at least have a certitude of direction and aim. The altruistic forces of human nature need not be restricted to isolated acts of doing good. They can harness themselves for the task, inspiring because of its very size, of slowly moving mankind along the upward evolutionary path.

The other certitude it can lay claim to is the certitude of its own values. They cannot be disputed—they are simply experienced. Anyone who has experienced the illumination of new knowledge, or the ecstasy of poetry or music, or the deliberate subordination of self to something greater, or the self-abandonment of falling in love, or complete physical well-being, or the intense satisfaction of a difficult task achieved, or has had a mystical experience, knows that they are in some way valuable for their own sakes beyond ordinary everyday satisfactions, such as being just moderately fit, earning one's own living, or filling one's belly. We must see to it that our pursuit of these experiences does not conflict with other sides of our nature, or with other human beings; here again what is absolute in its own right is purely relative within the general scheme. But the values are there and are real, and there is some general consensus as to their scale of grading. The difficulty for many minds is that these values are of our own generating, not in any way endowed with external authority. But in the religious sphere was it not Jesus who laid down once and for all that the kingdom of heaven is within us? And if we abandon the idea of external certitude in regard to scientific law, we need not worry about doing so for our scheme of values.

At the present moment we have no policy of values such as, at least in theory, the Middle Ages possessed. The world is but limited in size; yet we permit this or that incomplete idea to go spreading patchily over its surface, almost without reference to what else it may make impossible. If there is one thing which is obvious, it surely is that economic aims are not a final end in themselves. To be prosperous is a prerequisite to innumerable other activities; but prosperity is not the chief measure by which we should judge success. The same applies to the quantitative mania for which American cities have been famous, but from which no nation is really exempt—the mania which assumes that what matters is the number of people in a town irrespective of their qualities or what they are doing, the amount of money spent on a building irrespective of its beauty, and so on.

Without any general scheme of values, we take a whole series of human needs and aims in turn, pretend that each is somehow absolute, try to push it to its logical conclusion, and then let them all fight it out. In the resultant chaos, of course, many other subtler values languish.

Let us take population. The value of human life becomes so absolute that it is murder to put away a deformed monster at birth, and criminal to suggest euthanasia; and we push on with our reduction of infant mortality until we save an excess of cripples and defectives from which to breed. The enhanced control that is in our hands and the fact that much of the world is actually filling up are at last giving us pause. The Indian mortality rate could doubtless be reduced by half—but what would you do with the increased population? Even if you bring huge areas of arid Indian land under irrigation and cultivation, it is only a matter of a generation or so before the new vacant space will be overrun by new population on the same low level of prosperity, health, and education as the old. Have you done any good by causing more babies to live and so creating greater population-pressure, or by opening up new land to be filled at once by the human flood? Might it not have been better to have left the death side of nature's population-control to itself until we had some future policy for dealing simultaneously with birth? or to have kept some open spaces in reserve until there was some better reason for filling them? At the moment, most people do not even put such questions, much less try to answer them.

In England the tiny size of the country has at last forced us to ask ourselves questions of this kind. Here again, we have let each partial aim be carried out without reference to a general policy and are suddenly awaking to the fact that they are all cutting each other's throats. At last we have begun to ask what we want to live for, and to realize that the intangible values must be planned and worked for as much as the tangible ones, that there are people to whom solitude and wild nature provide some of the highest values in their lives, as there are others to whom social intercourse is the greatest pleasure.

Humanism thus would try to plan its limited physical environment so that within it different values are balanced and do not conflict too disastrously. This is a fairly obvious step to take. But a subtler reaction of the humanist point of view will be its influence upon our equally limited individual lives. With the decay of rigid codes, rigid schemes of valuation, rigid ideas of externally imposed law, we need be much less the victims of consistency.

There is value in logical thought; so there is in mystical experience. Because for the moment we cannot intellectually grasp why the mystical experience is of value, we need not reject it, any more than we need reject the value of logical thought because it does not give the peace or sense of completion produced by the mystical experience.

Self-sacrifice and asceticism can be experienced as of the utmost value; so can self-expression or the fullest satisfaction of bodily needs. It is very difficult, however, for some people to think that they or anyone else can be genuine in deliberately practising what are loosely called self-denial and self-indulgence at different times. Yet so long as the impulse to either is genuine, both can be of value, and it is often only the demon of consistency which prevents us from achieving the needed genuineness of impulse. Both purge the soul and nourish it, though in different ways, and we have to accept that as fact instead of trying to explain it away by logic. Even should we eventually choose one way or one activity as having supreme value for us, we must not deny the right of others to choose differently. And also we are not likely to practise our choice well unless we have had experience of other activities. It is no coincidence that many saints, like Augustine or Francis, began by tasting the variety of life's ordinary joys to the full.

Do not let it be supposed that I am preaching hedonism, even a spiritualized hedonism. Hedonism, like utilitarianism, is another of those paper schemes, beautifully logical, that just are not true. The humanist, looking into human nature, must acknowledge that effort is often its own reward, that pain may be essential to development, that limitation is frequently a prerequisite to achievement. He finds the desire for sacrifice and self-mortification just as natural and almost as widespread as the desire for achievement and self-assertion—and sees that the one tendency is just as dangerous and unpleasant as the other if indulged in the wrong way.

And he sees, looking beyond man by the light of science, that all these qualities have their counterpart in biological evolution, and all seem necessary for the advancement of the evolutionary experiment. Sacrifice and self-assertion are both biological necessities in their place and time; without effort there could be no survival, without pain no surmounting of harm, without limitation of possibility no realization of actual biological success.

The difference between human and biological affairs is that man, through his new powers of mind, has reached a new stage. From the purely biological standpoint, the main criteria are survival and reproduction. Man has entered a realm where things and experiences can have a supreme value in themselves even without subserving any purely biological needs. The love immortalized in the 'Vita Nuova' has been spiritualized away from its original connection with reproduction. A life devoted to pure music or pure mathematics has no counterpart whatever among lower organisms. Up till now, most of the energies of the human race have been devoted to the biological needs of individual and racial survival. But now we are at least able to envisage a future in which the control of environment provided by science will be so effective that only a small fraction of human energy need be devoted to merely biological ends. The rest will be free to satisfy itself as it wishes. One of the problems of the past has been to keep the sense of values unimpaired by disease, misery, and grinding poverty. A serious problem of the future will be how to keep values unimpaired by super-abundance of leisure.

At the moment there are vast possibilities of values running to waste because they are not harnessed, or because they are not even realized. The number of subtle and individual minds that find themselves unable to join whole-heartedly in any corporate organization is increasing; they find themselves over-individualized, incapable of experiencing many of the values which come from losing self. The organizations in which the individual can lose himself and taste self-sacrifice and corporate enhancement, are for the most part blatantly irrational like political parties, or committed to out-of-date or one-sided ideas like most of the churches; or, like public schools, they encourage crude and juvenile loyalties; or, as in the team-work of sport, they satisfy only a limited part of human nature.

One real task for humanism as I see it is to develop organizations which shall satisfy the need for corporate action and loyalty—the desire we all have to feel of use—and shall provide an outlet for self-sacrifice as well as for intellectual aspirations. Mr Wells once sketched out such an organization in his 'New Samurai.' The success they might have is foreshadowed by the success already attending such imperfect adumbrations of the idea as the Boy Scouts or the various Youth Movements in Central Europe. I do not think it would be impossible to build up a scheme of the sort in connection with education, though at present most people not already committed to organizations are too much ashamed of showing enthusiasm in unfashionable ways to begin planning along the proper lines and on the proper scale.

The fact is that no community has ever yet set itself seriously to the task of scientific humanism. No nation has really attempted to think out what are the valuable things in life and the relations between them, or to work out the best means of realizing these values in fullest intensity and proper relative dosage. A few individual thinkers have tried their hands, but until society as a whole gets busy with the problem, individual attempts will have little effect.

Is it possible to plan a body which shall engender enthusiasm and canalize devotion after the fashion of a young religious order, but which shall not fall into the dangers of religious dogmatism and shall not by defects in its organization slip into the conservatism or worldliness which is the usual fate of so many orders?

Is it possible to organize a body of opinion which shall combine the enthusiasm of a political party with the suspension of judgment of the scientific investigator? Is it possible during education to give the average boy and girl such a taste for various values—beauty in art, say, or beauty in nature—that they will cherish them throughout life? At present we for the most part stuff them with facts so as quite to ruin their taste for knowledge, and we leave other values to look after themselves. It is the custom to say that modern psychology delights in revealing the most unsavoury motives to our most respectable actions. It was Freud himself, however, who said that if the average man is in some ways much more immoral than he suspects, he is in others much more moral. There is, in fact, a reserve of the angelic in ordinary people which is unused and even unsuspected because it does not fit in with everyday ideas, because we most of us are subconsciously rather apologetic about such impractical and inconvenient idealisms. Is there a way of tapping this reserve of moral power without letting it loose in the form of irrational prejudice or wild fanaticism, moral, religious, or patriotic? On these and hundreds of similar questions we are blankly ignorant. We build laboratories to test out how we can harness and concentrate electrical and chemical and mechanical forces; but the corresponding problem of harnessing and intensifying the latent powers and activities of human nature we have scarcely even begun to envisage.

Scientific humanism is a protest against supernaturalism: the human spirit, now in its individual, now in its corporate aspects, is the source of all values and the highest reality we know. It is a protest against one-sidedness and fixity: the human spirit has many sides and cannot be ruled by any single rule; nor can it be restrained from making new discoveries in the adventure of its evolution. It insists that the same scientific procedure can be applied to human life as has been applied with such success to lifeless matter and to animals and plants—scientific survey, study, and analysis, followed by increasing practical control. It insists on human values as the norms for our aims, but insists equally that they cannot adjust themselves in right perspective and emphasis except as part of the picture of the world provided by science. It realizes that human desires and aspirations are the motive power of life, but insists that no long-range or comprehensive aim of humanity can ever be realized except with the aid of the pedestrian and dispassionate methods, the systematic planning, the experimental testing which can be provided by science alone.

At the moment a particular task of scientific humanism is to clarify its own ideas as to the limitations of the various activities of the human mind. To take but three, science, religion, and art. Science is a way of collecting and handling experience of the controllable aspects of phenomena. Religion is a way of experiencing the impact of the outer universe on the personality as a whole; the universe and human personality being what they are, this way of experience will always involve some feeling of sacredness. Art is a way of expressing some felt experience in communicable form; and in a manner which always involves that most difficult of things to define, the aesthetic emotion. Each selects and correlates in its own special way out of the common flux of experience. Each tells you something about reality—science more about the external aspects of it which can be controlled either in thought or practice; religion more about the kingdom of heaven that is within us; art about the fusion of inner and outer in individual experiences of value in themselves. Each is limited in its scope and its bearings, but each can be universally applied.

In my term 'scientific humanism' I have chosen to emphasize science as against all the other human activities for a simple reason—that at the moment science is in danger of setting itself up as an external code or framework as did revealed religion in the past; and only by putting it in its rightful place in the humanist scheme shall we avoid this dangerous dualism. But if science must beware of trying to become a dictator, the other human activities must beware of the jealousy which would try to banish the upstart from their affairs. The only significance we can see attaching to man's place in nature is that he is willy-nilly engaged in a gigantic evolutionary experiment by which life may attain to new levels of achievement and experience. Without the impersonal guidance and the efficient control provided by science, civilization will either stagnate or collapse, and human nature cannot make progress toward realizing its possible evolutionary destiny.

XIV

RELIGION AS AN OBJECTIVE PROBLEM

R ELIGION, like any other subject, can be treated as an objective problem, and studied by the method of science. The first step is to make a list of the ideas and practices associated with different religions—gods and demons, sacrifice, prayer, belief in a future life, tabus and moral rules in this life. This, however, is but a first step. It is like making a collection of animals and plants, or a catalogue of minerals or other substances, with their properties and uses. Science always begins in this way, but it cannot stop at this level: it inevitably seeks to penetrate deeper and to make an analysis.

This analysis may take two directions. It may seek for a further understanding of religion as it now exists, or it may adopt the historical method and search for an explanation of the present in the past.

With regard to the historical approach, it is clear that religion, like other social activities, evolves. Further, its evolution is determined by two main kinds of factors. One is its own emotional and intellectual momentum, its inner logic: the other is the influence of the material and social conditions of the period. As an example of the first, take the tendency from polytheism towards monotheism: granted the theistic premise, this tendency seems almost inevitably to declare itself in the course of time. As examples of the second, we have the fact of propitiatory sacrifice related to helplessness in face of external nature.

The comparative evolutionary study of religion brings out two or three main points. For instance, we have the original prevalence of magical ideas, and their application first to the practical activities of communal existence such as food-getting and war, and only later to the problems of personal salvation: and these in their turn come gradually to be dominated more by moral ideas and less by magic. In the sphere of theology we have the early prevalence of rambling myth, and its gradual crystallization into a fully rationalized system. In this domain too we see an interesting evolution from an early stage in which certain objects, acts, and persons are supposed to be imbued with an impersonal sacred influence or *mana*, and a later stage at which this sacred influence is pushed back a stage and attributed to supernatural beings behind objects.

Finally, there is the important fact that religious beliefs and practices have a very strong time-lag—a high degree of hysteresis, if you prefer a physical metaphor.

We next have to ask ourselves what is the result of our other type of analysis of the nature of religion. In the most general terms, it is that religion is the product of a certain type of interaction between man and his environment. It always involves an emotional component—the sense of sacredness. It always involves a more than intellectual belief—a sense of compulsive rightness. It is always concerned with human destiny, and with a way of life. It always brings the human being into some sort of felt relation with powers or agencies outside his personal self. It always involves some sort of escape from inner conflict. These different components may be very unequally developed, but they are always present.

Pushing the analysis a stage further, religion is seen as

an attempt to come to terms with the irrational forces that affect man—some cosmic, some social, some personal. These terms may be terms of capitulation or of victory, of compromise or of escape. Here once more there is immense variety.

A very important further point is this—that there is no single function of religion. We may class religious functions by their external points of reference or by their internal origins. Externally, the first religious function is to place man in a satisfactory emotional relation with his non-human environment, regarded as outer destiny or fate. The second is to do the same for his social environment; the third, to do the same for his personal actions.

Looked at from the point of view of internal origin, the matter is much more complicated. One very important religious function is that of rationalization—giving coherent explanations in rational terms for acts and feelings which arise from instinctive and therefore irrational sources. Another is that which we have already mentioned, the desire for unity. These two between them provide the theological side of religions.

More fundamental—since they provide the raw materials on which the rationalizing and unifying urges act—are the purely emotional components. These fall under two main heads—the functions arising from conflict or reaction between the self and the outer world, and those arising from conflict or reaction between parts of the self.

Among the former we may mention the need to escape from frustration and limitations; and the need for enhancement of the actual, the gilding of the imperfect. At length we come to relations between parts of the self, which are the most potent of all in generating religious reactions. Here we must take account of several basic facts of human mind. First there is the inevitability of conflict—a necessary consequence of man's mental make-up. Then there is the illimitable nature of desire and aspiration. Analogous to this last, but in the intellectual instead of the emotional sphere, is man's concept-forming activity, which inevitably gives rise to abstract terms like justice, truth, and beauty. These, being abstract, are empty; but illimitable desire perennially fills them with its imaginations. Then there is the fact of childhood repression, with its consequences, only now beginning to be realized by the world, of a burden of (often unconscious) guilt. Closely linked with this is the obsession of certitude. The mechanism of repression is an all-or-none mechanism: and the conscious accompaniment of such a mechanism is a subjective sense of certitude.

Another very important function is to provide something which is felt as eternal and unchanging (even though in reality it may merely be long-range and slow-changing) over against the limitations and changes of ordinary existence.

But I must not spend too much time on mere analysis. The next question is whether the scientific approach can throw any light on the present crisis in religion and its possible future solution.

The particular situation that confronts the religion of western civilization is this. The concept of God has reached the limits of its usefulness: it cannot evolve further. Supernatural powers were created by man to carry the burden of religion. From diffuse magic *mana* to personal spirits; from spirits to gods; from gods to God— so crudely speaking, the evolution has gone. The particular phase of that evolution which concerns us is that of gods. In one period of our western civilization the gods were necessary fictions, useful hypotheses by which to live.

But the gods are only necessary or useful in a certain phase of evolution. For gods to be of value to man, three things are necessary. The disasters of the outer world must still be sufficiently uncomprehended and uncontrolled to be mysteriously alarming. Or else the beastliness and hopelessness of common life must be such as to preclude any pinning of faith to the improvement in this world: then God can, and social life cannot, provide the necessary escape-mechanism. The belief in magical power must still be current, even if it be in a refined or sublimated form. And the analytic exploration of his own mind by man must not be so advanced that he can no longer project and personify the unconscious forces of his Superego and his Id as beings external to himself.

The advance of natural science, logic, and psychology has brought us to a stage at which God is no longer a useful hypothesis. Natural science has pushed God into an ever greater remoteness, until his function as ruler and dictator disappears and he becomes a mere first cause or vague general principle. The realization that magic is a false principle, and that control is to be achieved by science and its application, has removed the meaning from sacrificial ritual and petitionary prayer. The analysis of the human mind, with the discovery of its powers of projection and wish-fulfilment, its hidden subconsciousness and unrealized repressions, makes it unnecessary to believe that conversion and the like are due to any external spiritual power and unscientific to ascribe inner certitude to guidance by God.

And theological logic, inevitably tending to unify and to universalize its ideas of the Divine, has resulted in a monotheism which is self-contradictory and incomprehensible, and in some respects of less practical value than the polytheism which it replaced.

If you grant theism of any sort, the logical outcome is monotheism. But why theism at all? Why a belief in supernatural beings who stand in some relation to human destiny and human aspirations? Theistic belief depends on man's projection of his own ideas and feelings into nature: it is a personification of non-personal phenomena. Personification is God's major premise. But it is a mere assumption, and one which, while serviceable enough in earlier times, is now seen not only to be unwarranted, but to raise more difficulties than it solves. Religion, to continue as an element of first-rate importance in the life of the community, must drop the idea of God or at least relegate it to a subordinate position, as has happened to the magical element in the past. God, equally with gods, angels, demons, spirits, and other small spiritual fry, is a human product, arising inevitably from a certain kind of ignorance and a certain degree of helplessness with regard to man's external environment.

With the substitution of knowledge for ignorance in his field, and the growth of control, both actually achieved and realized by thought as possible, God is simply fading away, as the Devil has faded before him, and the pantheons of the ancient world, and the nymphs and the local spirits.

> Peor and Baalim
> Forsake their temples dim . . .

Milton wrote of the fading of all the pagan gods; and

Milton's God too is joining them in limbo. God has become more remote and more incomprehensible, and, most important of all, of less practical use to men and women who want guidance and consolation in living their lives. A faint trace of God, half metaphysical and half magic, still broods over our world, like the smile of a cosmic Cheshire Cat. But the growth of psychological knowledge will rub even that from the universe.

However—and this is vital—the fading of God does not mean the end of religion. God's disappearance is in the strictest sense of the word a theological process: and while theologies change, the religious impulses which gave them birth persist.

The disappearance of God means a recasting of religion, and a recasting of a fundamental sort. It means the shouldering by man of ultimate responsibilities which he had previously pushed off on to God.

What are these responsibilities which man must now assume? First, responsibility for carrying on in face of the world's mystery and his own ignorance. In previous ages that burden was shifted on to divine inscrutability: 'God moves in a mysterious way.' . . . Now we lay it to the account of our own ignorance, and face the possibility that ignorance of ultimates may, through the limitations of our nature, be permanent.

Next, responsibility for the long-range control of destiny. That we can no longer shift on to God the Ruler. Much that theistic religion left to divine guidance remains out of our hands: but our knowledge gives us power of controlling our fate and that of the planet we inhabit, within wide limits. In a phrase, we are the trustees of the evolutionary process and, like all trustees, responsible for our trust.

Thirdly and most urgently, responsibility for the immediate health and happiness of the species, for the enhancement of life on this earth, now and in the immediate future. Poverty, slavery, ill-health, social misery, democracy, kingship, this or that economic or political system —they do not inhere inevitably in a divinely appointed order of things: they are phenomena to be understood and controlled in accordance with our desire, just as much as the phenomena of chemistry or electricity.

Finally, there is the question of the immediate future of religion. Can science make any prophecy or offer any guidance in regard to this? I think that within limits, it can. In the first place, by analysing the reasons for the breakdown of the traditional supernatural religious systems of the West, it can point out that, unless the trend of history is reversed, the breakdown is an irremediable one. For it is due to the increase of our knowledge and control, the decrease of our ignorance and fear, in relation to man's external environment—machinery, crop-production, physical and chemical invention, floods, disease-germs—and unless science and technology disappear in a new Dark Age, this will persist.

The collapse of supernaturalist theology has been accompanied by the collapse, first of supernatural moral sanctions, and then of any absolute basis for morals. This too must be regarded as a process which, in the event of the continuance of civilization, is irreversible.

We can, however, go further. We have seen that the breakdown of traditional religion has been brought about by the growth of man's knowledge and control over his environment. But biologists distinguish between the external and the internal environment. Our blood provides our tissues with an internal environment regulated to a nicety both as regards its temperature and its chemical constitution, whereas the blood of a sea-urchin affords no such constancy. The organization of an ants' nest provides for the species an internal environment of a social nature. And in contrast with the rapid increase of man's knowledge of and control over his external environment, there has been little or no corresponding progress as regards the internal environment of his species. This is equally true in regard to the structure of society which provides the social environment for the individual and the race, and for the complex of feelings and ideas which provide the psychological environment in which the personal life of the individual is bathed.

These two aspects of man's internal environment of course interact and at points indeed unite—witness the field of social psychology: but for the most part they can be best considered from two very different angles—on the one side from the angle of economics, politics, law and sociology, on the other from the angle of psychological science. Not only have we as yet no adequate scientific knowledge or control over these phenomena, but our absence of control is causing widespread bewilderment. The common man to-day is distressed not only over his own sufferings, but at the spectacle of the helplessness of those in responsible positions in face of the maladjustments of the world's economic and political machinery.

In this field the fear of the uncomprehended, banished elsewhere, has once more entered human life. The fear is all the more deadly because the forces feared are of man's own making. No longer can we blame the gods. The modern Prometheus has chained himself to the rock, and himself fostered the vulture which now gnaws his vitals: his last satisfaction, of defying the Olympian tyrant, is gone.

The distress and the bewilderment are experienced as yet mainly in the more tangible realm of social and economic organization: the mental stresses and distortions arising from the social maladjustment remain for the time being in the background of public consciousness.

With the aid of our analysis of the nature and functions of religion, we can accordingly make certain definite assertions as to its future. The prophecy of science about the future of religion is that the religious impulse will become progressively more concerned with the organization of society—which, in the immediate future, will mean the organization of society on the basis of the nation or the regional group of nations.

The process, of course, has already begun. Many observers have commented on the religious elements in Russian communism—the fanaticism, the insistence on orthodoxy, the violent 'theological' disputes, the 'worship' of Lenin, the spirit of self-dedication, the persecutions, the common enthusiasm, the puritan element, the mass-emotions, the censorship. A very similar set of events is to be seen in Nazi Germany. In that country, of especial interest to the scientist and the student of comparative religion are such phenomena as the falsification of history and anthropological theory in the interest of a theory of the State and of the Germanic race which serves as the necessary 'theological' rationalization of the emotions underlying the Nazi movement, and the dragooning of the Protestant churches to fit them into the Nazi scheme of things. The modern persecution of the Jews, which has its real basis in economic and social dislike, is justified on the basis of this new religiously-felt Germanism, just as the medieval persecution of the Jews, which equally sprang from economic and social dislike, was justified on the basis of Christianity.

These are the first gropings of the human mind after a social embodiment of the religious impulse. They are as crude and in some respects as nasty as its first gropings, millennia previously, after a theistic embodiment of religion. The beast-headed gods and goddesses of those earlier times, the human sacrifice, the loss of self-criticism in the flood of emotional certitude, the sinister power of a privileged hierarchy, the justification of self, and the vilification of critics and the violence toward opponents—these and other primitive phenomena of early God-religion have their counterparts in to-day's dawn of social religion. And the general unrest and the widespread preoccupation with emotionally-based group movements such as Fascism and Communism, is in many ways comparable with the religious unrest that swept the Mediterranean world in the centuries just before and after the beginning of the Christian Era.

To achieve some real understanding and control of the forces and processes operating in human societies is the next great task for science; and the applications of scientific discovery in this field will have as their goal what we may call the Socialized State. The religious impulse, itself one of the social forces to be more fully comprehended and controlled, will increasingly find its outlet in the promotion of the ideals of the Socialized State.

Exactly how all this will happen no one can say—

whether the religious impulse will again crystallize into a definite religious system with its own organization, or will find its outlets within the bounds of other organizations, as it does for instance in the Communist party in Russia. We can, however, on the basis of the past history of religion, make a further prophecy. We can be reasonably sure that the inner momentum of logic and moral feelings, combined with the outer momentum derived from increasing comprehension and control, will lead to an improvement in the expression of this socialized religion comparable to the progress of theistic religion from its crude beginnings toward developed monotheism.

Accordingly, we can prophesy that in the long run the nationalistic element in socialized religion will be subordinated or adjusted to the internationalist: that the persecution of minorities will give place to toleration; that the subtler intellectual and moral virtues will find a place and will gradually oust the cruder from their present pre-eminence in the religiously-conceived social organism.

We can also assert with fair assurance that this process of improvement will be a slow one, and accompanied by much violence and suffering.

Finally, we can make the prophecy that part of this process will come about through interaction between two expressions of the religious spirit—one which strives to identify itself with the Socialized State, the other which reacts against the limitations thus imposed and strives to assert and uphold values that are felt to be more permanent and more universal. The cruder and more violent is the socialized religion, the more will it encourage such reactions. Already in Nazi Germany such a reaction has taken place among certain elements of the Protestant churches, who feel that their principles embody something higher, more lasting, and more general than anything, however intense, which is at the basis of a nationalist and racialist conception of social aims.

This is the one domain in which traditional religion, with its universalist monotheism, will in the near future have a real advantage over socialized religion, which for some time will inevitably be bound up with nationalist states.

It is probable, however, that a universalist Humanism (and probably Communism too) will soon become a strong rival of the old theistic systems in this field. It is also probable that with the growth of intolerant socialized feeling, both in Communistic and Fascist societies, the pioneers of such a Humanism will be those most exposed to religious persecution, but also those who will be doing most for their form of socialized religion and for religious progress in general.

One final prophecy, and I have done. It seems evident that as the religious impulse comes to create these new outlets or expressions, whether by way of the Socialized State or by way of Humanism, it will be increasingly confronted by psychological problems—as indeed will the Socialized State itself. Men will realize that economic and social planning will not solve their problems so long as ignorance and absence of control obtain in regard to their own minds. Psychological science will then come into its own, with social psychology as its dominant branch. And this will mean a new understanding of religious phenomena, and new possibilities of integrating them with the life of the community.

To sum up, I would say first that the so-called 'conflict between science and religion' has been a conflict between one aspect of science and one aspect of religion. These aspects have both been concerned with man's relation to his *external* environment. The systems of religion which are in danger of collapse grew out of man's ignorance and help-lessness in face of external nature; the aspect of science which is endangering those religious systems is that which has provided knowledge and control in this same domain.

In the near future, the religious impulse will find its main outlet in relation to the internal environment of the human species—social, economic, and psychological—for it is the forces of this internal environment that are now causing distress and bewilderment and are being felt as Destiny to be propitiated or otherwise manipulated. Meanwhile science will find its main scope for new en-deavour in this same field, since it is here that our ignor-ance and our lack of control are now most glaring.

There will again be a race between the effects of ignorance and those of knowledge; but with several new features. For one thing, the growth of science in the new field will this time not lag by many centuries behind that of the new modes of religious expression; and for another, the facts concerning the religious impulse and its expres-sion will themselves fall within the scope of the new scien-tific drive. The probable result will be that in the Social-ized State the relation between religion and science will gradually cease to be one of conflict and will become one of co-operation. Science will be called on to advise what expressions of the religious impulse are intellectually per-missible and socially desirable, if that impulse is to be properly integrated with other human activities and har-nessed to take its share in pulling the chariot of man's destiny along the path of progress.

XV

LIFE CAN BE WORTH LIVING

I BELIEVE that life can be worth living. I believe this in spite of pain, squalor, cruelty, unhappiness, and death. I do not believe that it is necessarily worth living, but only that for most people it can be.

I also believe that man, as individual, as group, and collectively as mankind, can achieve a satisfying purpose in existence. I believe this in spite of frustration, aimlessness, frivolity, boredom, sloth, and failure. Again I do not believe that a purpose inevitably inheres in the universe or in our existence, or that mankind is bound to achieve a satisfying purpose, but only that such a purpose can be found.

I believe that there exists a scale or hierarchy of values, ranging from simple physical comforts up to the highest satisfactions of love, aesthetic enjoyment, intellect, creative achievement, virtue. I do not believe that these are absolute, or transcendental in the sense of being vouchsafed by some external power or divinity; they are the product of human nature interacting with the outer world. Nor do I suppose that we can grade every valuable experience into an accepted order, any more than I can say whether a beetle is a higher organism than a cuttlefish or a herring. But just as it can unhesitatingly be stated that there are general grades of biological organization, and that a beetle *is* a higher organism than a sponge, or a human being than a frog, so I can assert, with the general consensus of civilized human beings, that there is a higher value in Dante's *Divina Commedia* than in a popular hymn, in the scientific activity of Newton or Darwin than in solving a crossword puzzle, in the fulness of love than in sexual gratification, in selfless than in purely self-regarding activities—although each and all can have their value of a sort.

I do not believe that there is any absolute of truth, beauty, morality, or virtue, whether emanating from an external power or imposed by an internal standard. But this does not drive me to the curious conclusion, fashionable in certain quarters, that truth and beauty and goodness do not exist, or that there is no force or value in them.

I believe that there are a number of questions that it is no use our asking, because they can never be answered. Nothing but waste, worry, or unhappiness is caused by trying to solve insoluble problems. Yet some people seem determined to try. I recall the story of the philosopher and the theologian. The two were engaged in disputation and the theologian used the old quip about a philosopher being like a blind man, in a dark room, looking for a black cat—which wasn't there. 'That may be,' said the philosopher; 'but a theologian would have found it.'

Even in material matters of science we must learn to ask the right questions. It seemed an obvious question to ask how animals inherit the result of their parents' experience, and enormous amounts of time and energy have been spent on trying to give an answer to it. It is, however, no good asking the question, for the simple reason that no such inheritance of acquired characters exists. The chemists of the eighteenth century, because they asked themselves the question, 'What substance is involved in the process of burning?' became involved in the mazes of the phlogiston theory: they had to ask 'what sort of process is burning?' before they could see that it did not involve a special substance but was merely a particular case of chemical combination.

When we come to what are usually referred to as fundamentals, the difficulty of not asking the wrong kind of question is much increased. Among most African tribes, if a person dies, the only question asked is, 'Who caused his death, and by what form of magic?'; the idea of death from natural causes is unknown. Indeed, the life of the less-civilized half of mankind is largely based on trying to find an answer to a wrong question: 'What magical forces or powers are responsible for good or bad fortune, and how can they be circumvented or propitiated?'

I do not believe in the existence of a god or gods. The conception of divinity seems to me, though built up out of a number of real elements of experience, to be a false one, based on the quite unjustifiable postulate that there must be some more or less personal power in control of the world. We are confronted with forces beyond our control, with incomprehensible disasters, with death, and also with ecstasy, with a mystical sense of union with something greater than our ordinary selves, with sudden conversion to a new way of life, with the burden of guilt and sin. In theistic religions all these elements of actual experience have been woven into a unified body of belief and practice in relation to the fundamental postulate of the existence of a god or gods.

I believe this fundamental postulate to be nothing more than the result of asking a wrong question: 'Who or what rules the universe?' So far as we can see, it rules itself, and indeed the whole analogy with a country and its ruler is false. Even if a god does exist behind or above the universe as we experience it, we can have no knowledge of such a power; the actual gods of historical religions are only the personifications of impersonal facts of nature and of facts of our inner mental life.

Similarly with immortality. With our present faculties we have no means of giving a categorical answer to the question whether we survive death, much less the question of what any such life after death will be like. That being so, it is a waste of time and energy to devote ourselves to the problem of achieving salvation in the life to come. However, just as the idea of god is built out of bricks of real experience, so too is the idea of salvation. If we translate salvation into terms of this world, we find that it means achieving harmony between different parts of our nature, including its subconscious depths and its rarely touched heights, and also achieving some satisfactory adjustment between ourselves and the outer world, including not only the world of nature but the social world of man. I believe it to be possible to 'achieve salvation' in this sense, and right to aim at doing so, just as I believe it possible and valuable to achieve a sense of union with something bigger than our ordinary selves, even if that something be not a god but an extension of our narrow core to include in a single grasp ranges of outer experience and inner nature on which we do not ordinarily draw.

But if God and immortality be repudiated, what is left? That is the question usually thrown at the atheist's head. The orthodox believer likes to think that nothing is left. That, however, is because he has only been accustomed to think in terms of his orthodoxy.

In point of fact, a great deal is left.

That is immediately obvious from the fact that many men and women have led active, or self-sacrificing, or noble, or devoted lives without any belief in God or immortality. Buddhism in its uncorrupted form has no such belief; nor did the great nineteenth-century agnostics; nor do the orthodox Russian Communists; nor did the Stoics. Of course, the unbelievers have often been guilty of selfish or wicked actions; but so have the believers. And in any case that is not the fundamental point. The point is that without these beliefs men and women may yet possess the mainspring of full and purposive living, and just as strong a sense that existence can be worth while as is possible to the most devout believers.

I would say that this is much more readily possible to-day than in any previous age. The reason lies in the advances of science.

No longer are we forced to accept the external catastrophes and miseries of existence as inevitable or mysterious; no longer are we obliged to live in a world without history, where change is only meaningless. Our ancestors saw an epidemic as an act of divine punishment; to us it is a challenge to be overcome, since we know its causes and that it can be controlled or prevented. The understanding of infectious disease is entirely due to scientific advance. So, to take a very recent happening, is our understanding of the basis of nutrition, which holds out new possibilities of health and energy to the human race. So is our understanding of earthquakes and storms; if we cannot control them, we at least do not have to fear them as evidence of God's anger.

Some, at least, of our internal miseries can be lightened in the same way. Through knowledge derived from psychology children can be prevented from growing up with an abnormal sense of guilt and so making life a burden both to themselves and to those with whom they come into contact. We are beginning to understand the psychological roots of irrational fear and cruelty; some day we shall be able to make the world a brighter place by preventing their appearance.

The ancients had no history worth mentioning. Human existence in the present was regarded as a degradation from that of the original Golden Age. Down even to the nineteenth century what was known of human history was regarded by the nations of the West as an essentially meaningless series of episodes sandwiched into the brief space between the Creation and the Fall, a few thousand years ago, and the Second Coming and Last Judgment, which might be on us at any moment and in any case could not be pushed back for more than a few thousand years into the future. In this perspective a millennium was almost an eternity. With such an outlook no wonder life seemed, to the great mass of humanity, 'nasty, brutish, and short,' its miseries and shortcomings merely bewildering unless illuminated by the illusory light of religion.

To-day human history merges back into prehistory, and prehistory again into biological evolution. Our timescale is profoundly altered. A thousand years is a short time for prehistory, which thinks in terms of hundreds of thousands of years, and an insignificant time for evolution, which deals in ten-million-year periods. The future is extended equally with the past; if it took over a thousand million years for primeval life to generate man, man and his descendants have at least an equal allowance of time before them for further evolution.

Most of all, the new history has been a basis of hope. Biological evolution has been appallingly slow and appallingly wasteful. It has been cruel; it has generated the parasites and the pests as well as the more agreeable types. It has led life up innumerable blind alleys. But in spite of this it has achieved progress. In a few lines, whose number has steadily diminished with time, it has avoided the cul-de-sac of mere specialization and arrived at a new level of organization, more harmonious and more efficient, from which it could again launch out toward greater control, greater knowledge, and greater independence. Progress is, if you will, all-round specialization. Finally, but one line was left which was able to achieve further progress; all the others had led up blind alleys. This was the line leading to the evolution of the human brain.

This at one bound altered the perspective of evolution. Experience could now be handed down from generation to generation; deliberate purpose could be substituted for the blind sifting of selection; change could be speeded up ten-thousandfold. In man evolution could become conscious. Admittedly it is far from conscious yet, but the possibility is there, and it has at least been consciously envisaged.

Seen in this perspective, human history represents but the tiniest portion of the time man has before him; it is only the first ignorant and clumsy gropings of the new type, born heir to so much biological history. The constant setbacks, the lack of improvement in certain respects for over two thousand years, are seen to be phenomena as natural as the tumbles of a child learning to walk or the deflection of a sensitive boy's attention by the need of making a living.

The broad facts remain. Life had progressed even before man was first evolved. Life progressed in giving rise to man. Man has progressed during the half-million or so years from the first Hominidae, even during the ten thousand years since the final amelioration of climate after the Ice Age. And the potentialities of progress which are revealed, once his eyes have been opened to the evolutionary vista, are unlimited.

At last we have an optimistic instead of a pessimistic theory of this world and our life upon it. Admittedly the optimism cannot be facile, and must be tempered with reflection on the length of time involved, on the hard work that will be necessary, on the inevitable residuum of accident and unhappiness that will remain. Perhaps we had better call it a melioristic rather than an optimistic view; but at least it preaches hope and inspires to action.

I believe very definitely that it is among human personalities that there exist the highest and most valuable achievements of the universe—or at least the highest and most valuable achievements of which we know or, apparently, can have knowledge. That means that I believe that the State exists for the development of individual lives, not individuals for the development of the State.

But I also believe that the individual is not an isolated, separate thing. An individual is a transformer of matter and experience; it is a system of relations between its own basis and the universe, including other individuals. An individual may believe that he should devote himself entirely to a cause, even sacrifice himself to it—his country, truth, art, love. It is in the devotion of the sacrifice that he becomes most himself; it is because of the devotion or sacrifice of individuals that causes become of value. But of course the individual must in many ways subordinate himself to the community—only not to the extent of believing that in the community resides any virtue higher than that of the individuals which compose it.

The community provides the machinery for the existence and development of individuals. There are those who deny the importance of social machinery, who assert that the only important thing is a change of heart, and that the right machinery is merely a natural consequence of the right inner attitude. This appears to me mere solipsism. Different kinds of social machinery predispose to different inner attitudes. The most admirable machinery is useless if the inner life is unchanged; but social machinery *can* affect the fulness and quality of life. Social machinery can be devised to make war more difficult, to promote health, to add interest to life. Let us not despise machinery in our zeal for fulness of life, any more than we should dream that machinery can ever automatically grind out perfection of living.

I believe in diversity. Every biologist knows that human beings differ in their hereditary outfits, and therefore in the possibilities that they can realize. Psychology shows how inevitably different are the types that jostle each other on the world's streets. No amount of persuasion or education can make the extrovert really understand the introvert, the verbalist understand the lover of handicraft, the non-mathematical or non-musical person understand the passion of the mathematician or the musician. We can try to forbid certain attitudes of mind. We could theoretically breed out much of human variety. But this would be a sacrifice. Diversity is not only the salt of life but the basis of collective achievement. And the complement of diversity is tolerance and understanding. This does not mean rating all values alike. We must protect society against criminals; we must struggle against what we think wrong. But just as if we try to understand the criminal we shall try to reform rather than merely to punish, so we must try to understand why we judge others' actions as wrong, which implies trying to understand the workings of our own minds and discounting our own prejudices.

Finally, I believe that we can never reduce our principles to any few simple terms. Existence is always too various and too complicated. We must supplement principles with faith. And the only faith that is both concrete and comprehensive is in life, its abundance and its progress. My final belief is in life.